AGING & CULTURAL DIVERSITY:

New Directions
and
Annotated Bibliography

Heather Strange,
Michele Teitelbaum
& Contributors

BERGIN & GARVEY PUBLISHERS, INC.
MASSACHUSETTS

First published in 1987 by
Bergin & Garvey Publishers, Inc.
670 Amherst Road
South Hadley, Massachusetts 01075

789   987654321

Printed in the United States of America

Library of Congress Cataloging-in-Publication Data
Strange, Heather.
   Aging and cultural diversity.

   Includes index.
   1. Aged—Cross—cultural studies. 2. Aged—Cross-cultural
studies—Bibliography. I. Teitelbaum, Michele. II. Title.
GV485.S77   1986   305.2'6   86-3571
ISBN 0-89789-103-1

Dedicated to the memory of Vera Green—
teacher, colleague and friend.

Contents

II: Intra-Cultural Diversity

PART TWO:
ANNOTATED BIBLIOGRAPHY

ACKNOWLEDGMENTS

There are many at Rutgers University who have aided in the completion of this manuscript.

Work on the bibliography was started with the enthusiastic encouragement of Audrey O. Faulkner and financial support from the Institute on Aging, of which she was the director. Funds for the project were also provided by the Department of Anthropology. The completion of the manuscript was made possible by grants from the Research Council, the Institute for Research on Women and the Fellows of Douglass College. Tom Melchionne worked on the mechanical aspects of manuscript preparation.

Many people assisted the editors in the work on the bibliography. Research was carried out by Rita Srivastava and Shirley Sherman. Dorothy Gioia edited and typed many of the annotations. All three have been very generous with their time and efforts.

Edwina Segledi, secretary to the Department of Anthropology, capably provided typing and other clerical services.

To all of them, we extend our sincere appreciation.

PREFACE

A focus on aging and cultural diversity developed out of our belief in the importance of applying cross-cultural and intra-cultural perspectives to the study of aging. A culture-bound viewpoint inappropriately delimits study in the field. A cycle of ignorance begins with impoverished ethnography—when ethnographers ignore the aged in a society or represent old people solely in a particular role, such as that of grandparent. Generalizations are then made by others without adequate cross-cultural data to draw upon. Professionals involved in social planning and the provision of social services are then misguided by uninformed generalizations. The problem is clearly one that cross-cuts the concerns of professionals in several fields.

It seems reasonable to address these academic and applied concerns in one volume that (1) reflects some current directions in the study of aging, (2) suggests the scope and significance of a cross-cultural perspective, and (3) provides the reader with references to further work in the field. The book offers both original articles focusing on aging in inter- and intra-cultural contexts and an annotated bibliography. Most of the contributors are anthropologists; some are in social work or psychology. Some of the anthropologists have worked in health-care settings; most have been engaged in applied work. We intend the book to be useful to professionals in both scholarly and applied fields.

The approach combining articles and bibliography addresses the nature of current teaching on the subject of aging and the aged. Courses on aging are taught in several social science disciplines as well as in schools of nursing, public health, and social work. A basic reader is usually handy and appreciated by students, but instructors want to supplement the articles in a reader with work reflecting their own disciplinary outlook and specialized interests. A reader with a limited number of articles on a general theme permits this flexibility. At the same time, the bibliography can be used by students to pursue their own research; it greatly supplements the resources of the instructor.

The book may be used to introduce students in social science to the study of aging and its applications. It may also be used to introduce a cross-cultural perspective to preprofessional students in service-oriented fields. Ideally, it may be used in courses that attract students from both groups—facilitating a dialogue between them and interrupting the cycle of ignorance to which we have referred. More generally, for readers who do not plan further research on aging or work with the aged, we hope that the book suggests the relevance of its subject to the broader study of culture and society.

HEATHER STRANGE
MICHELE TEITELBAUM

PART I
New Directions

Aging and Cultural Diversity:
An Introduction

HEATHER STRANGE and MICHELE TEITELBAUM

In developing a volume on aging with contributing authors in anthropology and related fields, we were confronted with such diverse subjects as inner-city U S. blacks,
immigrant Mongols, modernization in Malaysia, and
gerontocracy in Africa. This diversity of material suggested not only that aging can be studied in different contexts,
but that cultural diversity itself is an important dimension
in the study of aging and the aged. We seek to demonstrate the relevance of that dimension to both scholarly and
applied concerns. We do so by offering a combination of
articles and annotated bibliography. The articles--all originally prepared for this volume--explore several aspects of
cultural diversity. The bibliography provides a starting
point for those interested in further study.

Those concerned with an "anthropology of age" (Keith
1980) know the pioneering cross-cultural work of Simmons
(1970). After a hiatus of more than two decades, the work
of Margaret Clark (1967) and Clark with Barbara Anderson
(1967) refocused anthropological concern on aging and the
aged. Among recent works, the collections of articles by
Fry (1980, 1981) and Sokolovsky (1983) have included studies emphasizing variation among the aged that caution
against simplistic assumptions. Bohannan, in his foreword
to Fry's book, states "old people are more different from
one another than are people at any younger ages"
(1980:vii). While that may prove to be an overstatement, it
is a firm stand against the popular view that old people

1

comprise a monolithic population, a view also found in some scientific writing on the subject. Writing about the United States, Pollak, for instance, points out that "society puts a premium on being young. To be old ... [in such a socie-ty] ... makes one a member of an undesired minority" (1980:1419).

The youth emphasis may not be characteristic of many subcultures, such as Native Americans, members of Spanish-speaking communities, southern blacks, and others. Among some groups both in the United States and elsewhere that emphasize ethnic identity, the aged persons who exem-plify and have knowledge about that identity are highly valued (Cool 1980; Williams 1980). Any generalization such as the aged as "an undesired minority" fails to enlighten us about the variety of life-styles, views, and experiences among the elderly of America and tells us nothing about how they are perceived by younger members of their socie-ty, community, ethnic, or other group. While having a youth-orientation may be characteristic of many middle-class white Americans, there is also a curious trend toward rejec-tion of the young by some middle-aged and older people. An article in the New York Times about adult communities points out that while there is a belief that the young reject the aged, a countertrend exists among middle-aged and old-er people. For example, a major selling point for housing in adult communities is a rule against live-in children and grandchildren who are under nineteen years of age (Costantinou 1983).

Successful research on aging as well as policy applica-tions of research must have as basic components the con-cepts of intra- and inter-unit diversity. Accepting this premise, we choose to highlight issues of diversity in this volume. Concerned scholars, administrators, and service-delivery personnel are becoming increasingly aware of the deficiencies in prior research. R.A. LeVine of the Harvard Laboratory of Human Development and a member of the SSRC Committee on Work and Personality in the Middle Years, indicated that the neglect of cross-cultural studies in adulthood and aging creates a problem in developing val-id universal generalizations regarding those subjects. LeVine suggests,

> policy and theory in these areas are often based on profoundly culture-bound conceptions of what is natural, necessary, normal or optimal for adult men and women...therefore...theories of psycho-social development during the adult years have consequently been formulated without adequate

evidence from the bulk of human societies.
(LeVine 1978:1)

A focus on diversity should be integral to anthropology, with its unique fondness for making sense of exotica. In most of the classic ethnographies, however, data on the aged or aging are virtually missing. Out of a convenience sample of seventeen recently published introductory anthropology texts, only one included significant information about the aged, while sixteen provided scant references, mostly about African age-set systems. Lack of regard for the subject of the aged in past anthropological research, we think, has reflected more general trends in anthropology. Pelto and Pelto (1975) drew our attention to a distressing former tendency in anthropology--although one perhaps less strongly felt in anthropology than in other social sciences--to characterize each culture in terms of a typical cultural patterning or a set of shared standards that are presumed to apply to all of its members. If most people in a society are young or middle-aged workers and are reasonably healthy, the relatively small subgroup of the aged, especially those who are old, not working, and infirm, deviate considerably from the stated ideals. Consequently, the ethnographer, in a generalized picture of that society, may allude to, but largely ignore, the latter phase of the life cycle of its members.

It is not only the small size of a subgroup within a culture that may lead to its lack of visibility to the scholarly community. Women were ignored for many years as cultural participants even though they are a numerical majority in most populations. When some women became politicized, when women's issues became prominent, when increasing numbers of women scholars expressed an interest, and when anthropology became more concerned with intra-cultural diversity, scholarship on the subject of women proliferated--although it tended to concentrate on young women during their reproductive years. While some anthropologists had often said before that cultural experience varied with respect to sex and age, we finally--as late as the 1970s--began to accumulate good documentation concerning the dimension of gender. In comparable terms, now that the population of the aged has grown, has become politically vocal and in some segments problematic, this group is no longer dismissed as a small, atypical, not terribly important part of our society. We are, at last, dealing in depth with age as a dimension of social organization.

Not surprisingly, behavioral science input is accelerated on certain topics in response to current social concerns. Our concern is that in the rush to remedy social problems, the most general formulations will be thought by some to have the broadest applications. In the long run, that approach may not be useful. For example, senior citizen resource centers and medical facilities for the elderly may be quickly erected in several locations, using the same general principles. However, the long-range success of each facility will depend on its successful articulation with the unique needs of each community. We believe that cultural variation, including elements of class and ethnicity, is an important determinant of local needs. Now that U.S. society has recognized cultural diversity by acknowledging our older members as worthy of analytical study, we must be attentive to dimensions of diversity that cross-cut the study of age.

Old people as a group have often been singled out for unflattering characterization, as some of the works in our bibliography demonstrate. In the 1950s, Golde and Kogan (1959) showed that attitudes toward old people differed from those associated with people in general. Ginzberg (1952) documented negative attitudes toward the elderly, and Barron (1953) dealt with the characterization of the elderly as similar to an ethnic minority. The prevalent attitudes these scholars demonstrated usually precluded much interest in investigation of variation among the aged, either generally or within and between communities with aged members. More recently, studies have appeared that show a growing concern for the significance of ethnic variation among the old. (See, for example, Gelfand (1979-80), Golden (1976), Koenig et al. (1977), Markides et al. (1977), and Wellin and Boyer (1979).)

There is continuing need for much more detailed information on the elderly. The SSRC study group pointed to a need "for anthropologists to educate themselves in the problems of aging as defined in other disciplines so that the data they collect will be of maximum theoretical and social significance" (LeVine 1978:5). Such understanding can also be enhanced by interdisciplinary programs in which anthropologists work with members of the other social and biological sciences and with workers in applied fields. A focus on gerontological questions requires us to be cognizant of contributions from many disciplines.

Aside from the relatively new academic awareness of the importance of cultural factors in the study of the aged, cultural and ethnic groups within contemporary nations are demanding that their values, life-ways and/or languages be considered worthy alternatives to the ones that are now dominant. In the United States, for example, the task-force panels of the President's Commission on Mental Health reflected this concern. Input by Native Americans

and Americans of Hispanic, black, Asian-Pacific, and European ancestry, was included.   Such recognition emphasizes
the importance of cross-cultural study and stresses the significance of intra-national studies in the present world context.

Members of some minority groups complain about the
lack of attention given to their needs, including the needs
of their elderly members.   One spokesman for the National
Indian Council on Aging indicated an opinion shared by
many Native Americans:

> I would only like to share with you the
> thoughts of the Indian elders ... which we all
> have in common ... the desire that we may be
> able to help our elders to end their years among
> their own people--not in some far-off nursing
> home--comforted by their loved ones and by the
> sound of their own familiar religious ceremonies.
> The motto of the United States of America is
> 'E pluribus unum'--'One out of many.'   Perhaps
> as Indian people, we are naive to think that this
> motto represents our right to remain Indian peo-
> ple, without assimilation into the melting pot!

The speaker's comments and some of the studies in
this volume serve to underscore dissatisfaction with the
concept of assimilation as an explanation for change.   There
is presently a greater awareness of other processes of culture change, including processes that draw upon traditional
cultural resources of groups.   As these views gain greater
acceptance, we think scholars and planners will increasingly
notice studies of inter- and intra-cultural variation of the
aged as well as others.   In preparing this volume, we were
struck with the extent to which general works on the aged
in the United States often start with the a priori assumption
that aging is problematic.   This may be a reasonable assumption in a society in which social services and medical
resources are being strained by the rapidly growing population of older Americans.   Proposed solutions usually entail
large expenditures of tax money and a strain on our bureaucratic resources.   In this context, we were impressed
by the many indigenous systems and ideologies supporting
the elderly in other cultures and in ethnic enclaves in the
United States.   Several of the articles will elaborate on this
point.

Aging and cultural diversity are addressed in this volume in two ways.   Part One, consisting of articles, is

further divided into two sections. Section I focuses on studies of the aged in other countries. Issues of both inter- and intra-cultural diversity are entertained. The editors also explore the relevance of these articles to some theoretical issues in the study of the aged. Section II highlights cultural diversity among the aged within and between subgroups in America. The material in this section, we believe, has particular relevance to those engaged in social planning and service delivery. Some may question our designation of differences among diverse subgroups in the United States as intra-cultural, rather than inter-cultural diversity. Insofar as these populations articulate to some extent--especially for the provision of services--with a more-or-less national culture, we think our designation is useful here.

Part Two consists of an annotated bibliography which shows the types of cultural diversity that can be found in works about aging and the aged. The bibliography draws attention to already published work and serves as well to suggest by omission the need for more ethnography of the aged and for more comparison. In addition to ethnic and other dimensions already mentioned, there are studies of contemporary industrialized societies such as Japan and the United States, of peasant populations, and of tribal societies. There are community studies in which the aged comprise the entire population and others in which the interaction between elders and people of other ages is the major focus.

The entries in the annotated bibliography are necessarily brief, but they do illustrate the concerns and foci in the growing literature of the anthropology of aging and in closely related disciplines. The case studies are examples of some of these concerns and viewpoints. Thus the complementarity of the two types of information serve to integrate what might otherwise be considered disparate segments into a functioning whole. It is hoped that this approach will serve to introduce and to interest members of both scholarly and applied fields to the concept of cultural diversity in aging as well as to point to the need for further research by academicians.

We view this book as an attempt to give the reader a general work with a variety of approaches to the aged and the aging as well as to broad anthropological concerns. For example, McCay analyzes social structure, Strange focuses on the effects of development, Teitelbaum analyzes political organization, and Green considers issues germane to any discussion of diversity among black Americans. We have also attempted to provide a complementary reference work. We think this approach makes the book doubly useful, providing a basis for understanding the breadth of theoretical, methodological, and practical problems involved in both research and the application of research findings. Toward that end, our introductions to the sections of articles also include cross-references to relevant sections of the bibliography.

Our rationale for the selections of the articles is similar to that offered by Van den Berghe when he attempted to cope with a subject as broad as aging. In support of his selection of materials to illustrate Human Family Systems (1979:129), Van den Berghe stated:

> Any non-random choice of case studies is justifiably suspect.... All I can do by way of justifying my choice, therefore, is to try to convince the reader that maximum cultural diversity and adequate information were my main criteria of selection.

In this book, neither the articles, in terms of the areas represented, nor the annotated bibliography, are exhaustive. Nevertheless, we believe that the selection and the combination are more than adequate for our goal: to underscore cultural diversity in the phenomena of aging.

REFERENCES

Barron, Milton
　　1953 Minority Group Characteristics of the Aged in
　　　　American Society. Journal of Gerontology
　　　　8 (4):447-82.

Bohannan, Paul
　ı 1980 Foreword. In Aging in Culture and Society. C.
　　　　Fry, ed. Brooklyn, N.Y.: Bergin.

Clark, Margaret M.
　　1967 The Anthropology of Aging, A New Area for
　　　　Studies of Culture and Personality.
　　　　Gerontologist 7:55-64.

Clark, Margaret and Barbara Anderson
　　1967 Culture and Aging, An Anthropological Study of
　　　　Older Americans. Springfield, Ill.: C.C.
　　　　Thomas.

Cool, Linda
1980 Ethnicity and Aging: Continuity Through Change
for Elderly Corsicans.   In Aging in Culture and
Society.   C. Fry, ed.   Brooklyn, N.Y.:   Bergin.

Constantinou, Marianne
1983 For Empty-Nesters, The Adult Village.   The New
York Times, Section 8:2, 14 (May 15).

Fry, Christine
1980 Toward and Anthropology of Aging.   In Aging in
Culture and Society.   C. Fry, ed. Brooklyn,
N.Y.:   Bergin.

1981 Dimensions: Aging, Culture, and Health.   South
Hadley, Mass.:   Bergin and Garvey.

Gelfand, Donald E.
1979-80 Ethnicity, Aging and Mental Health.   Aging
and Human Development 10 (3):289-98.

Ginzberg, Raphael
1952 The Negative Attitude toward the Elderly.
Geriatrics 7 (5):297-302.

Golde, Peggy and Nathan Kogan
1959 A Sentence Completion Procedure for Assessing
Attitudes about Old People.   Journal of
Gerontology 14 (3):353-63.

Golden, H.M.
1976 Black Ageism. Social Policy 7 (3):40-2.

Gordon, Milton
1964 Assimilation in American Life: The Role of Race,
Religion and National Origin.   New York: Oxford
University Press.

Keith, Jennie
1980 The Best Is Yet to Be: Toward an Anthropology
of Age.   Annual Review of Anthropology.   Palo
Alto, Calif.:   Annual Reviews 9:339-64.

Koenig, R., et al.
1977 Ideas about Illnesses of Elderly Blacks and Whites
in an Urban Hospital.   Aging and Human
Development 2 (3):217-25.

LeVine, R.
1978 Adulthood and Aging in Cross-Cultural
Perspectives. Items. Pp. 33:1-5. N.Y.: Social
Science Research Council.

Markides, Kyriakos S., et al.
1977 Psychological Distress among Elderly Mexican-
Americans and Anglos. Paper presented at the
conference of The Gerontological Society of New
York.

Pelto, Pertti J. and Gretel H. Pelto
1975 Intra-Cultural Diversity: Some Theoretical
Issues. American Ethnologist 2 (1):1-18.

Pollak, Otto
1980 Shadow of Death over Aging. Science 20:1419
(March 28).

Simmons, Leo
1970 (orig. 1945) The Role of the Aged in Primitive
Society. Hamden, Conn.: Archon.

Sokolovsky, Jay, ed.
1983 Growing Old in Different Societies:
Cross-Cultural Perspectives. Belmont, Calif.:
Wadsworth.

Van den Berghe, Pierre
1979 Human Family Systems. San Francisco, Calif.:
Chandler.

Wellin, E. and Eunice Boyer
1979 Adjustments of Black and White Elderly to
the Same Adaptive Niche. Anthropological
Quarterly 52 (1):39-48.

Williams, Gerry C.
1980 Warriors No More: A Study of the American
Indian Elderly. In Aging in Culture and Society.
C. Fry, ed. Brooklyn, N.Y.: Bergin.

I: INTER-CULTURAL DIVERSITY

Introduction

Our exploration of aging and cultural diversity begins with studies of the aged in countries other than the United States. Toward an exploration of inter-cultural diversity, each of the studies in this section can be viewed in comparison with the others. Each study entertains issues in intra-cultural diversity by exploring factors that cross-cut the dimension of aging in the society under discussion.

In chapter 1, Strange contrasts two villages in rural Malaysia--one that has been exposed to many modernizing influences and one that has not. Her data contradict the stereotypic assumption that older people are resistant to change. Strange also explores the impact of gender roles on aging, demonstrating that important differences in life experience do not merge into an undifferentiated mass among the aged. Teitelbaum (ch. 2) explores the relationship between power and the attributes associated with old age in a Liberian gerontocracy. She describes the ways in which old people may gain power in a tribal society. However, perhaps more importantly for this volume, she contrasts the plight of the powerful elderly with that of the more numerous nonpowerful elderly in the same society. McCay's (ch. 3) study was conducted in a rural fishing village in Newfoundland. It offers an unusual contrasting view of a peripheral, impoverished sector of an industrialized nation. The old people are studied not in isolation, but within the context of the developmental cycles of the rural family and family fishing firms. Wilson (ch. 4) considers the study of aging cross-culturally with respect to

10

nutrition, a subject that includes both biological and cultural considerations.

Some general themes and important contrasts emerge from a comparison of the three societies discussed by Strange, Teitelbaum, and McCay. Foremost among the themes discussed is dependency. The elderly in the Newfoundland community are dependent upon younger people for the provision of many services, including transportation and miscellaneous errands. The situation is far from one-sided, however, since old people in the community receive pensions and often compensate the young people in cash. The elders can also patronize the church and other institutions in need of support. Thus, the situation McCay describes is really one of interdependence, in which old people give to the community as much as they receive from it. Thus, their experience with old age is, as Amoss and Harrell (1981) might predict, a fairly comfortable one in comparison with other stages of their lives. Some--especially men who have been skippers of fishing crews--may experience a loss of status in old age, but they are scarcely disengaged from the social life of the community. They are a vital part of it.

The Liberian situation is one in which gerontocratic politics and ritual activities provide opportunities for a small percentage of old people to accumulate a great deal of power and prestige. These prestigious elders also give much to the community. Money is irrelevant in this situation, but the distribution of land, the accumulation of esoteric knowledge, and the employment of leadership skills are the prerogatives of the prestigious elders. Once again, for those who can give, the need to receive presents no problem. The high status elderly in this society expect to receive food and shelter from their juniors, and they consider their debts to be more than repaid. Teitelbaum also shows that a different situation exists for those old people who have not achieved positions of power and prestige and who are not perceived as providing vital services to the community. These old people are treated with varying degrees of tolerance and/or kindness, but not with respect. They are cared for, but they are regarded as dependent upon their juniors who provide them with the necessities of life. Their behavior is severely constrained, and they can make few decisions for themselves.

Contrast the above with the Malaysian situation. Here, again, not all old people earn a great deal of respect. Some can be said to be given only what Strange calls "formal consideration," and elders may be economically dependent upon their juniors. However, all but the mentally incompetent have more privileges associated with age per se and retain more autonomy than the nonprestigious elderly in the Liberian situation. What accounts for the contrast? In attempting to develop a hypothesis, we found that we had to consider the entire life cycle in each society and the ways in which these are discussed by the Malays and the Liberians. For example, in Malay society children enjoy a prolonged period of privileged dependency similar to that enjoyed by most American middle-class children. Young adults then speak of caring for their elders as a sort of re-payment for care provided in childhood. This is not direct repayment as in the Newfoundland situation. Rather, this is an indirect, delayed repayment, the expectation of which contributes to a favorable attitude toward the elderly.

In the Liberian village, children cease to be truly de-pendent as soon as they pass the toddler stage. Children work at tasks related to farming and food processing as soon as they are able. Often, they are not brought up in the homes of their natural parents, but they live with foster parents, individuals who are more in need of their services. Not surprisingly, care of the elderly is not spo-ken of as repayment for care provided in early life. In this society, care of the elderly can only be seen as repay-ment for currently rendered services in the case of the very few powerful and prestigious elderly. Other old peo-ple suffer from a drastically imposed dependency.

By suggesting a relationship between care of children and care of the elderly, we have scarcely proved or dis-proved a general hypothesis in our exploration of the de-pendency issue in these societies. However, what we think most significant in this investigation is the manner in which we have had to consider (1) the elderly in the context of the important institutions of each society, and (2) old age in the context of the entire life cycle. We started this project by deploring a myopic view that would draw so-called universal generalizations from a limited universe of data. We emphasize in this section that by broadening our data-base we also raise questions about the manner in which we define relevant variables.

One of the problems in defining such variables in the study of aging is that biological universals interact with culturally defined variables. Therefore, this section ends with Wilson's article which explores both physiological and social factors relevant to the study of nutrition among the aged. Diet varies from culture to culture, and Wilson points out: "Some cultures set people apart or define their status by assigning them different types of foods or diets according to the age they have attained." If we are study-ing, for example, the effect of diet on longevity, both inter- and intra-cultural diversity must be considered. The importance of diversity extends beyond our present concern with the sociocultural study of aging and the aged.

Further resources on these topics can be found in the following sections of the Annotated Bibliography. For those interested in aging in other countries, Section II.B. includes studies in Asia, Africa, Canada, and other areas. Section III.B. offers comparisons between two or more ethnic, national, or racial groups in countries other than the United States. Additionally, several aspects of social organization--including marriage and the family, work and retirement--are represented in Section I.C., Social Roles and Attitudes.

REFERENCE

Amoss, P.T. and S. Harrell, eds.
    1981 Other Ways of Growing Old: Anthropological
        Perspectives. Stanford, Calif.: Stanford
        University Press.

1

Rural Malay Aged in Contrasting Developmental Contexts

HEATHER STRANGE

Socioeconomic development taking place at different rates in different places and the effects on rural Malay aged was the subject of the pilot study on which this article is mainly based.[1] Cowgill and Holmes (1972) had made the point that modernization has adverse effects upon the aged. One of their general propositions is, "The status of the aged is inversely proportional to the rate of social change" (ibid.:9), and the generalization is reiterated in their conclusion (ibid.:322) along with others pertaining to the status of the aged.

My own field research suggested that rural Malay aged did not constitute a category with a particular status but rather that there was a good deal of variation in the treatment of elders by their own family members and by members of the community at large. My earlier research had not focused specifically on the aged, and the literature about Malays provided little information regarding them. There are a few references to economic activities and assistance from children and other kin (Firth 1966; Fraser 1960; Djamour 1965), and Wilson (1967:130) points out that within the household "respect status correlated with generation." One change for the elderly between 1940 and 1963, the two research periods Firth (1966) spent in Kelantan, was the availability of some welfare support at the later time. Now, in the 1980s, welfare services to the needy elderly have expanded. It is, however, an elder's children and grandchildren who are the first line of support.

14

Given two contrasting areas--one changing at the pro-
verbial snail's pace and the other extremely rapidly--would
family support of the elders be strongest in the more stable
area?   Would elders in a slowly changing area have high
status while those in a rapidly changing area were experiencing reduced status?   Is status within the community an
important component of an elder's life or is position within
the extended kinship network the main concern?   Does high
status imply respect, esteem, or other honoring attitudes
about elders that are realized in behavior toward them?   Is
it respect or other factors that are most important in allow-
ing an elder to feel content with his or her life?

Discussion of the situation of the aged in society often
includes attention to the prestige, deference, respect, esteem and/or politeness they receive.   In his early examination of age categories, Linton (1942) noted that even where
formal prestige was associated with old age it seemed doubtful that it benefited the aged in daily living.   Simmons
(1945) provided many examples that age alone is not equat-
ed with respect and high status.   Palmore (1975:18-9) suggests that "politeness and deference" toward aged Japanese
may be "criticized on the grounds that modern Japanese do
not really respect the aged as much as the forms of respect
would indicate."   He finds no conclusive evidence that this
is the case and points out that "The Japanese express their
respect for the aged through maintaining their integration
in the society."

Cross-cultural surveys drawn from the Human Relations Area files by Maxwell and Silverman (1970,1978) indicate that esteem for the elderly and deference to them are
related to their control of useful knowledge.   In a rapidly
developing society or area, what was useful knowledge for
an elder can be judged obsolete by younger persons.

Working to establish valid cross-cultural categories for
analyzing prestige of the elderly, Press and McKool (1972)
isolated four related components: advisory (shown by both
the seeking and heeding of advice from the aged); contributory (based on contributions of the aged to social activities); control (by the aged of resources or specific functions); and residual (residues from prior abilities and functions).   They also found that status decline was associated
with early passing of resources from older to younger family members, fewer economic activities outside the home, and
increasing heterogeneity in the economic sector.   Increasing
heterogeneity means more specialization, one of the characteristics of socioeconomic development.

Thus the first references raise the issue of whether
formal prestige of the aged or the forms of respect to them
have consequences extending beyond formality, while the

latter studies point to other statuses and roles (rather than age alone) as sources of prestige or esteem and seek to explain why elders may lose prestige and experience reduced status in rapidly changing societies.

RESEARCH DESIGN

The pilot study was carried out between January and July, 1979, in three villages in the east coast state of Trengganu, Malaysia: Rusila--a large coastal village (192 households) in an area that has been developing more and more rapidly during the past two decades and where I have worked for several periods since 1965; and two small inland villages (87 households in the combined sample) that have undergone far less change.   The purposes of the pilot study were to gain an overview of the effects of developmental change on the status of older men and women and to determine the adequacy of a 133-question interview schedule for use in a larger, future study.

The interview schedule includes a number of questions that have a direct bearing on development--about housing and home ownership, amenities, and water source; attitudes about change and conveniences (i.e., paved road, electricity, piped water, and general clinic--all except the clinic are present in Rusila but none of them are in the inland villages); mobility, how people travel and where, for what purposes, outside of the village and in it (to the mosque, shops, other homes).   There are general questions about birthplace (and if other than village of residence why the person relocated) and attitudes about the village.   There are questions relevant to status generally as well as the kinship network: children and grandchildren--sex, occupation, residence, and other questions; similar questions about siblings, great-grandchildren, other kin, and neighbors; income sources of the elderly, including productive land (by type) and capital equipment, and money and goods received from or given to children and other kin; questions about mosque attendance, the pilgrimage to Mecca (haj) and financing of it; illness--most importantly, who are the caretakers, but also type, length, and forms of treatment including hospitalization; a question stated as "some people worry about the future..." with discussion about why or why not and the elder's perceptions of the future and his or her worries; services elders provide for children, grandchildren, and others; and services provided to them by kin and nonkin.

Participant observation, open-ended interviews, and photography, as well as the interview schedule were the research techniques used. During the summer of 1982, I had the opportunity to computerize these data. Information had not been collected with that procedure in mind and, because of the small sample, some response categories had to be combined. Nevertheless, interesting correlations emerged as well as ideas for revision of the questionnaire for use in a larger study. During July 1983, I returned to Trengganu and visited many of the elders in the sample.

VILLAGE AND SAMPLE SELECTION

The coastal village of Rusila, located in Marang District, eight to nine miles south of Kuala Trengganu, the state capital, was picked because I had worked there during 1965-66 and 1975, have a large amount of background data and, most importantly, have rapport with the people. I am known to them and they to me. The selection of inland villages was limited to the same district on the assumption that administrative and bureaucratic features affecting the villages would be more uniform than for villages in different districts. The villages of Gong Beris and Kampung Kubu were chosen in consultation with the district officer, Encik Zahid bin Muda. The project was outlined, and his advice as to which villages in the district had the smallest number of modernization features was requested. These features had been selected from literature on the subject, including Gamst (1974), Hunter (1969), and Smelser (1967), and from Cowgill and Holmes's cross-cultural work, Aging and Modernization (1972). The indices considered included mechanization of agriculture, access to mass transportation, distance to educational and health facilities, percentages of children enrolled in primary and secondary schools, differentiation of economic activities, and the availability of mass media. On the basis of these criteria, Gong Beris and Kampung Kubu seemed to stand in almost total contrast to Rusila.

Two different methods of sample selection were used. In Rusila, as part of an ongoing, diachronic research project, a complete survey of the 192 households in the village was carried out during March 1979. Identity cards (IC) were not examined at that time. However, IC ages for more than 50 percent of all village adults and most of the elders were already in my 1966 records so a check of official age (however accurate or inaccurate relative to chronological age) against a person's self-perceived age could be made.

Identity cards were introduced during the emergency period following World War II. Many people were not listed in official records, and other records had been destroyed. Rural Malays do not celebrate birthdays and, with primary schools not yet established in this area, exact age was something most adults ignored. Individuals had always assumed a place in the village work force and filled other statuses as they were able to do so and, in later life, relinquished them in similar fashion. Exact chronological age was irrelevant; functional age was an individual's reality. Confronted with the need to provide a birth date to an authority for IC purposes, everyone did so or perhaps had one assigned--with greater or lesser accuracy.

The comparison that I made between any individual's stated age and the IC age revealed that the older a person becomes, the greater his or her tendency to add years to the official (IC) age. Nevertheless, all persons who stated an age of seventy years or more--an arbitrary point based on prior data showing the age-exaggeration tendency--were scheduled for interviews, the premise being that a person's self-perception about age is more important than actual chronological or official age. If an individual says, "I am seventy years old" and believes it, then behavior can be expected to accord with local views about what is appropriate for that age. The final sample of elders included nine women and eleven men, with one married couple among them.

In Gong Beris, the ketua kampung (village headman) was asked for the names of people in his village whom he believed to be seventy years of age or older. The village is small, with 58 households and approximately 300 residents, so it seemed unlikely that the headman would overlook anyone. Interviewees were asked about other elders living nearby,and the same question was posed at random to other village adults. All of the names received by these means had already been obtained from the headman.

Ten people, five men and five women--including one married couple--were interviewed. No complete survey of households was made in Gong Beris, but a long discussion about local economy, out-migration, education, and other topics, as well as the situation of local elders was held with the ketua kampung. Informal visits were made to a few homes in which there were no elders in residence, just to chat about life in the village.

In Kampung Kubu the same procedure was followed. Later, the Kampung Kubu interviews were removed from the sample. While there are six elders (in twenty-nine households), for reasons such as physical impairment, only two of them could be interviewed. Also, because there are some economic and ecological differences between Gong Beris and Kampung Kubu I decided not to include even those two interviewees.

QUALITATIVE AND QUANTITATIVE DATA

Certain types of data can be obtained during a brief field research period; others cannot. Some information sought by an interviewer has been forgotten by the informant--whatever his or her age--or is thought to be insignificant and hence not worth mentioning. In the short term, behavior contradictory to interview responses might not be observed. For instance, one section of my interview schedule concerns the forms of assistance that elders get from their children, grandchildren, and/or others--both distant kin and nonkin. One series of questions addresses whether the elder receives food from children et al., with each person previously established as close kin, neighbor, and so on, named individually. The type of food, the circumstances under which it is given, and related questions are raised. Only those elders living with a child acknowledged receipt of food from anyone.

Yet I know from living in Rusila that food is exchanged among close kin frequently if not regularly. To illustrate: during one day, I observed an elderly widow in the sample receiving six mangoes from a son, and, later, two fish from a daughter-in-law. Another son had told me that he gives his mother a monthly gift of husked rice, enough to meet her needs for an entire month. But the woman answered "no" to the questions about receiving food from each of these children. When asked specifically about the rice, mangoes, and fish, she grinned, tapped her head and said, mock-seriously, "nyanyuk" (senile). I know this elder very well. She functions perfectly normally, although she is sometimes forgetful. The particular section of the formal interview under consideration was administered several days after she received the fish and mangoes and about two weeks after the monthly rice gift had been given. Had the questions been posed on the day the gifts were received, she might have mentioned them without any memory nudges. There is another aspect to her not mentioning them: such exchanges between close kin are part of a generalized reciprocity system that tends to be taken for granted. The elders have given to their children and may continue to do so according to their resources and abilities. That the children now give to them balances the system.

One does not see everything no matter how long one lives in a particular village. Familiarity with patterns of behavior and interrelationships among villagers offer insights that cannot be duplicated through interviews alone. Interview schedules are an excellent supplement to participant-observation but they are not a substitute. As other researchers have noted (e.g., Fry 1980; Keith 1980b; Kerns 1980) quantitative and qualitative techniques are most effective when used to complement one another.

AGE AND STATUS IN RURAL MALAY SOCIETY

Malaysia's population is young, with an estimated 41 percent under fifteen years of age, only 3 percent over age sixty-four, and a general life expectancy of sixty-one years (Haub and Heisler 1980). Chan (1980:4, 16), using the most recent Malaysian census data reports that between 1970 and 1980 the sixty-five-and-older cohort grew 1.68 times faster than the rest of the population, and the estimated life expectancy at birth of Peninsular Malaysian males and females is 66.2 and 71.4 respectively. Nevertheless, a person can be defined as old at fifty. I have a number of newspaper clippings using the phrase "an elderly man" (or woman) whose age is then given as anything from the middle fifties and up. Not only are people initially defined as old in their fifties but, in rural areas at least, they tend to add years to their official ages thus placing themselves solidly in the orang tua or "elders" category.

Only two persons (one man and one woman in the Rusila sample) stated ages that accorded with the ones on their Identity Cards. No one whose age could be checked against an IC claimed an age younger than the official one. The pattern suggests that being classified as an old person is positive and that the status is not only accepted but sought. Thus as a rural Malay ages, he or she is likely to "think older," i.e., develop a self-perception that adds a few years—from two to twenty in my sample. What benefits are gained from age-exaggeraton?

The conventional idea, expressed by young and middle-aged, urban and rural, Malays is that old age is venerated. Villagers of various ages express awe at the idea of extreme age—100 seems to be the magic number—but I find no evidence that the attitude automatically translates into respect for old people as a category. Even the elders who are thought to be centenarians (but whose Identity Cards indicate younger ages) are not visited by those expressing their amazement unless there is a close kinship tie between them.

In a draft of this article I contrasted "respect" (admiration for achievement) with "politeness" (formal consideration) and was questioned about the dichotomy. There is, more accurately, a continuum between behavior toward elders who are respected and those who are treated with only formal politeness, although the contrast between the poles emphasizes the extremes. There can be notable differences between the treatment an elder receives from children and grandchildren and from members of the community at large. If we follow Palmore (1975) and equate respect for the aged with maintenance of their integration in society, we are left with the question of whether or not integration within the extended family network equates with integration in society. A number of field observations suggest that the two are not the same, but one example will make the point.

An elderly widow, who is assisted by her children and visited regularly by grandchildren, came into a home where some other villagers and I were visiting. It was the holiday week following Ramadan, 1983, and coffee, tea, and a variety of cakes had been served. The old lady was greeted by the hostess and invited to sit on the floor (although several chairs were occupied by teenagers who, if their grandmother had arrived would have offered her a place to sit). The old woman helped herself to a cake but she was not served a beverage. The conversation flowed around her but no attempt was made to include her in it. She left after about ten minutes. On a later occasion I asked the hostess whether young people usually gave seats on buses or chairs in their homes to older people, especially old people. I was told, "Of course! If not, they'd feel ashamed." I mentioned the visit of the old lady to her home a few days earlier and the hostess seemed surprised. "Oh, (name of old lady)"; she then shrugged and changed the topic of conversation. Other villagers, when asked about the old woman, knew who she was and that she lived in a small house near a son's home with a grandchild for company. More than that, even members of her age cohort did not know. They saw her in the village, exchanged greetings, and that was all. This old woman is integrated into her extended family but appears to be only peripheral to village society.

Age is a less important social status than others, e.g., family or religious status in the Malay example; it is the others (such as Maxwell and Silverman's [1970, 1978] "knowledge-controller" or ones suggested by Press and McKool's [1972] prestige components) that determine how an old person—indeed any adult—is treated by other members of the community.

Based on his research in three Malay villages, S. Husin Ali (1975) points out that elders might be learned in Islam, wealthy, or fill other statuses (such as headman) that merit respect. They are considered more knowledgeable about family and customary matters (adat) than younger persons and therefore may be considered wise in the family context.

Only one man in the Rusila sample is considered learned in religion; no one in either sample is said to have village-wide influence nor can any be considered wealthy. The respected statuses most common among Rusila elders are haji and hajjah, the titles of a man and woman who have performed the haj. But these statuses are not limited to elders and are (in Rusila) shared by many younger villagers. In Gong Beris, none of the elders had made the pilgrimage nor did they anticipate being able to do so. In neither sample is there an imam or a village headman. These statuses are filled by younger men. Turning to the "wise about family matters and customs" as a source of respect, it can be noted that of thirty elders in the two samples, only one claimed to be consulted by his children about family matters. Three noted that they were consulted about agricultural questions. The others said their children did not consult them about anything. Are consultations few or have the informants forgotten about being consulted? If so, does this suggest that they perceive the consultations as unimportant, i.e., not an example of respect?

Observations drawn from field notes made in Rusila illustrate the point. Consultation of elders who fill no respected statuses by younger family members is often pro forma, carried out to make the elder feel good and to provide him or her with information. The elder's advice is not necessarily followed unless it happens to accord with a decision already reached by other family members. Or, when a difference of opinion exists, between husband and wife for example, one or both may seek to bolster a viewpoint by calling upon an elder (usually a parent or grandparent) for advice--when the consulter believes that the consultee will support his or her argument. In contrast to this pattern, the former imam (who was in his seventies when he died a few years ago) was consulted about a wide range of personal problems as well as religious questions. His advice was usually followed.

The average Malay elder is treated with more politeness than respect by members of the community at large. Traditionally, younger persons are expected to act politely toward those older than themselves--and the older the person the greater the politeness should be. A person who has gained the status "elder" ideally can expect polite consideration from a great many people--younger family members, friends and acquaintances, and even strangers. But even politeness may be mere form--a greeting and an invitation to sit. Elders who have achieved other statuses such as imam or headman (both possible only for males), who are learned in religion or have made the pilgrimage to Mecca, or who are wealthy (but not miserly), receive respect for their accomplishments as well as politeness.

If an older person does not gain respect simply on the basis of age, the question about age-exaggeration remains. The status "elder" allows a person to avoid--without being subject to sanctions--many activities, commitments, and responsibilities that a younger person would either have to assume or bear the social penalty for avoidance. I am referring to healthy elders because no one expects very much from a person who is ill or frail. One incident will illustrate this.

In response to a series of interview questions about types of assistance given to various kin and neighbors, several elders said they help their children with feast preparations. In one situation, women were preparing batter and baking cakes--300 small ones and a number of large ones--over outdoor fires. The women and girls were working at a hectic pace, and additional assistance would have been welcomed. An elder who said she helped with feast preparations arrived, sat in the shade chewing betel, and watched the other women. When asked by her daughter to beat some batter, she said she was tired. That ended the discussion. A younger women would have been expected to work whether she was tired or not or else she would have been the subject of negative comments or gossip. I am sure the elder had beaten a lot of batter in her younger days. Now, as an elder, she can refuse and yet be socially involved in the event. She has more freedom to do what she feels like doing.

Another advantage of the status "orang tua" for a woman is the relaxation of many modesty rules imposed before menarche. The newly postmenopausal woman, in her early or middle fifties, is not to be confused with an elder in regard to such relaxation. The former is sometimes described as (sexually) "useless" (tidak ada guna), although some postmenopausal women do remarry after being divorced or widowed, and those who are married continue to be sexually active into their sixties.

Only old women, those labeled by themselves and others as orang tua, are free from the restraints of modesty they have lived with during most of their lives. Their double entendre banter with young men is acceptable, even amusing and clever; similar behavior by a younger woman would elicit comments about brazenness. An old woman can relax on her porch, in full view of anyone and everyone, dressed only in a sarong cinched under the armpits, leaving shoulders, calves, and even knees exposed, without criticism.   A younger woman can bathe at a well or engage in work near her house in such attire; but she cannot relax clad only in a sarong except in the privacy of her home.

Elders may continue working according to their abilities, but there is no shame involved in giving up work, especially strenuous tasks such as land preparation (for men) or the transplanting of seedlings (for women), as stamina decreases--assuming one can afford to give up these tasks. The elder who tries to perform the same hard work as a younger person may be regarded as foolish, or if he or she must do such work in order to survive, pitied.   If one has children and grandchildren, onerous work should not be necessary.

Support of destitute parents is required both by custom (adat) and Muslim law and is characteristic of Malay society from southern Thailand (Fraser 1960:214) to Singapore (Djamour 1965:44).   Ideally, adult children are expected to give money, food, clothing, or other gifts to parents of any age if they have the financial wherewithal, irrespective of parental need.   The more generous the child, the greater the prestige is said to be for the parent among his or her peers.   Some parents brag about a child's generosity when a major gift such as a television set is given; others are more subtle in their dissemination of information.   The child who is generous is referred to by parents and other kin as "good," while excuses tend to be made for the child who is not generous.   That small gifts, particularly food, are taken for granted and the giving defined as normative is a partial explanation of why people do not readily recall them. Responses to the interview in both Rusila and Gong Beris indicated that several elders received money on a regular basis from either children or grandchildren and others mentioned cloth or "help as needed."   Many provide "help as needed" according to their abilities.

There is no implication of parental dependence, no suggestion that accepting gifts and assistance has detracted from their autonomy as people.   Interdependence, as defined by Johnson (1983) in her discussion of Italian American aged, "as a style of interpersonal relations where primacy is given to cohesiveness and mutual support within the primary group" appears apt, particularly between the generations and among siblings.   Malays also place a high value on individual satisfaction in interpersonal relations so that, for example, divorce is preferable to an unhappy marriage.

Most people who are now young adults enjoyed a relatively carefree childhood and youth, far different from that of their parents.   Few demands aside from school lessons and occasional chores were made of them.   Many are appreciative. They accept the local view that giving to parents represents a balance, and they appear to take pleasure in being able to help or provide luxuries for parents and elderly grandparents. The "ethic of interdependence" (Ikels 1980:85) spans the generations.

In many traditional societies, "children are viewed not merely as emotional extensions of their parents but also as investments in social security and future old age support" (Hareven 1976:202-3). Despite rapid development in Malaysia, that view has not changed. Three relatively young persons (forty-to-fifty years of age) in Rusila have mentioned looking forward to a financially carefree old age because they have lots of children. Reversing the statement, one rural Malay argument for having a large family is: an old person can expect adequate assistance. A married couple in their fifties made the pilgrimage to Mecca in 1982 because their older, wage-earning children paid for it, and several widowed grandmothers received similar assistance from grandchildren during recent years. Such help reflects the new prosperity; twenty years ago there were few wage-earners or salaried professionals with local roots who had the wherewithal for such generosity, even if there were several contributors.

Health differences among older people are acknowledged by themselves and by other members of the community and have a direct effect on the types of work performed. Women engaged in pandanus weaving, for example, can continue to produce goods for sale or home use well into their later years, but they may have to shift from making intricately patterned, multicolored mats to weaving twill-patterned, one-color mats if their sight deteriorates. There is no positive value placed on disengagement. There is a high degree of variation among elders with regard to the number and types of activities pursued and to their attitudes about work and other activities.

Asked about health and illnesses, eight people in the combined sample, six men and two women, stated that they enjoyed good health; nine acknowledged "old age"--a general health decline but no specific ailment; several others referred to particular illnesses. Commonly, people try a range of treatments beginning with self- or family-administered local remedies and then have recourse to a bomoh (Malay medical-magical practitioner) or a clinic doctor or both. In both villages, the person with a health problem is cared for at home by a spouse (usually male patient and female caretaker) and/or children and grandchildren. When the problem is recognized as serious, hospitalization is an option. In Rusila, there has been a decided attitudinal shift since 1965 when hospitalization was inextricably associated with death. Now it is generally accepted that often a person can recover, even from a serious illness, and return to family and village.

Senility (nyanyuk) was likened to infancy by one informant: the person is not responsible for behavior, has no control over bodily functions, and forgets the accumulated knowledge of a lifetime. The condition is said to be rare. The recent example remembered in Rusila was a woman, now deceased, who became nyanyuk in her early seventies. There was no one to stay with her constantly because her only child, a widowed daughter, had to work outside the home at least part of each day to support the two of them. When the elder's behavior became completely unpredictable, a small room that could be locked from the outside was built for her in the main section of the house. It was feared that outdoors, alone, she might wander onto the road or drown in the sea. It had become impossible for the daughter to make her mother wear clothes or to keep her clean, so the little room was also a means of protecting the modesty of the old woman and the self-respect of her daughter.

After talking about the situation of that elder, it is inevitable for the speaker to refer to the oldest person in the village. She was officially ninety-four when I visited her in 1983 and as witty and bright-eyed as ever, although she complained of feeling tired much of the time. The contrast between the two women is not only striking but the normalcy of the latter is the model of advanced old age that all hope for.

CONTRASTS IN DEVELOPMENT

It has been widely accepted that modernization in the West led to a gradually worsening situation for old people. But it now appears that the decline in status experienced by elders "bottoms out" (Cowgill 1974) and reverses in "the most modern societies" due in part to pension programs and national support systems of various kinds (Keith 1980a). In developing nations, status decline experienced by elders may occur in some sectors and not in others. The social position of old people where development is occurring may look rather different depending on whether it is the nation or smaller units that are the focus of study. The villages in my study were selected for their differential rate of development: Rusila was rapidly undergoing numerous changes in educational, economic and other sectors, while Gong Beris had been far less affected.

Gong Beris, the less developed of the two villages, has the most discontented elders and the fewest with children and grandchildren nearby. Their situation is not unlike that of the Sherpa elderly in Nepal whose extended family networks were weakened through out-migration of the young to India (Goldstein and Beall 1981:54). Rusila, the most developed village, has the fewest discontented elders and the most--in percentage as well as numbers--with children and grandchildren living nearby. Many traditional values in Rusila are comfortably coexisting with better educational and occupational opportunities, higher literacy rates, modern transportation and communication systems, improved health care, and so on. The contrast suggests that the development features found in Rusila not only make life easier for the elders but make it more likely that younger people, the children and grandchildren so important in an elder's life, will want and be able to live in such a village.

Rusila lies south of Kuala Trengganu, the state capital, and three miles north of the district office at Marang. It is located along the coastal highway that links Kuala Trengganu and environs with Kota Baru to the north and Kuantan and other points south. Buses and service taxis pass through the village frequently making it easy for villagers to get transportation to other areas for a variety of purposes. Electricity and piped water are available to those in the main section of the village who can afford them. Neither service has been introduced to Rusila's two inland hamlets because they are so far from the main lines along the highway as to make the costs prohibitive to the average family. There are 192 occupied homes--a majority occupied by nuclear families, although there are some extended, polygynous, single-person, and other types present in the village; 120 houses have electricity and 26 have piped water. Television arrived in Rusila during the early 1970s, and by 1979 there were 48 homes (25 percent) with television sets. There is one telephone in a booth centrally located in the village. Twenty-five cars and vans are owned by local people, and there are almost twice that number of motor scooters.

The economic base was already multifaceted in 1965, and many new occupations, particularly wage-paying jobs in Marang and Kuala Trengganu, could be added to the list by 1979. Agricultural production, both of rice and cash crops such as tobacco, still engages more adults of both sexes than any other single occupational category. There are several types of shops in the village--general stores, coffee and snack shops, and those selling items such as pandanus mats and batik fabric to tourists. A government agency,

Lembaga Kraftangan, has a training facility for pandanus- and brocade-weavers combined with a big shop in a very modernistic building next to the modest clinic run by the government-trained midwife. There are an electric padi mill and four two-story tobacco-drying kilns.

The primary school was built in 1952 and, at this point in time, the literacy rate for older children and adults under forty is very impressive--almost 100 percent. The nearest secondary school is three miles from the village, near the bus route. In 1979, 62 percent of both males and females in the twelve/thirteen-to-eighteen-years cohort were attending secondary schools; several persons had earned B.A. degrees or were enrolled in universities or other post-secondary programs.

The old village mosque is an important identity feature for Rusila residents, symbolizing their devotion to Islam and the value of community cooperation (gotong royong): they built the structure and they have maintained it without government assistance. Local men also built two prayer houses from materials purchased with money raised in the village. The imam accepts no honorarium from the government, nor did his father before him, although his status as religious leader entitles him to it. Further emphasis on the religious aspect of life is shown by the claim that there are more hajis and hajjahs than in any other village in the area. More than fifty men and women have performed haj and, as of July 1979, eight had made the pilgrimage to Mecca twice.

Gong Beris is reached by an unpaved and very rocky road, two-to-three miles from the coastal highway. Monsoon rains sometimes isolate the village for days at a time. The nearest bus service is along the highway; no one owns an automobile or van, but several young men have motor scooters. Neither electricity nor piped water has been introduced, and there is no telephone. Transistor radios are commonplace but television has not yet arrived. There are two general shops, the only type of shop in the village.

There are fifty-eight households in Gong Beris, less than a third of the number in Rusila. The predominant family type is supplemented nuclear. Economic specialization is far less than in Rusila. Almost everyone is involved with agricultural production: rice, vegetables, and rubber, with tobacco becoming important during the past few years. There are five people from Gong Beris working in Singapore and others in some Malaysian towns. As the headman stated the situation, "People like to work outside now."

Children must walk two miles to another village to attend primary school, in which one local man teaches, and travel considerably further to reach a secondary school.

One young man currently attends a university, the first person from the village to do so.   There is a midwife's clinic near the primary school and a multipurpose clinic in Marang, eight miles north and east of Gong Beris.   The village mosque was financed by the government and built a few years ago.   The imam receives an annual honorarium of M$120.00 from the government.   There is only one haji in the village, and according to the headman, most people lack the financial means to ever perform the pilgrimage to Mecca.

Two examples highlight the differences between the villages: access to transportation and development of tobacco as a cash crop.   In Rusila, no one lives more than one-half mile from the coastal highway, and a majority of residents are much nearer to that major transportation route.   Cars and vans are available for emergencies, for example, to take an ailing person to the Kuala Trengganu hospital.   Both public and private transportation enable children to reach secondary schools easily;   and adults have ready access to jobs, markets, and other facilities in the state capital and in Marang.

For Gong Beris residents, the situation is far different.   The highway is two-to-three miles from village houses and the access road is difficult for those on foot or for vehicular traffic and becomes unusable after heavy rains.   In an emergency, a man on a motor scooter must be sent to another village to get the midwife, telephone for aid, or to look for someone with a car.   Children must walk farther to reach the primary school--which leads to low attendance during the monsoon--or to get a bus to reach the secondary school.   Adults also must make the trek to the coastal highway to get transportation.   Mobility of older persons is highly circumscribed as a result of the distance and poor conditions of the access road.

Another example of the differences can be seen in the way that tobacco as a cash crop has been developed in the two villages.   Tobacco was introduced into both areas at approximately the same time because the district officer was actively committed to promoting this new source of income for agriculturalists.

By 1979, in Rusila, there was a tobacco grower's cooperative run by local people.   The organization was responsible for building four kilns in the village during 1975, and now organizes the drying, grading, weighing, and sale of tobacco.   Growers who are not members can sell through the cooperative.   Seasonally, the organization employs local persons as laborers and clerks, expanding the economic spectrum and encouraging the development of some new job skills.   In Gong Beris, the tobacco seeds and fertilizer are provided by a Kelantanese Malay entrepreneur who owns

kilns two miles from the village.   Having accepted seeds
and fertilizer, a villager grows the tobacco crop for the entrepreneur.   He or she is involved only as a farmer.

Contentment with the kampung of residence as a place
to live is strongly conditioned by personal situation.   However, it is notable that four of ten respondents in Gong
Beris and only two in Rusila (of twenty) would rather be
living elsewhere, most naming towns in which a child or
children are living.   Gong Beris has a narrower economic
base and a large number of young people seeking job opportunities outside the area.   As a kampung, Rusila has a
higher degree of economic diversity and specialization.   It
is easier to live in Rusila and work in the city of Kuala
Trengganu or Marang town because of good transportation
facilities close at hand.   This is not to suggest that no one
leaves the village seeking better job opportunities.   Many
do.   And some return: for example, three male teachers
who were working elsewhere in Malaysia a few years ago
have managed transfers that allow them to live locally and
commute to their respective schools nearby.   Rusila is their
natal village and the place where their parents are living.

All of the respondents in both samples favor a range
of conveniences--whether or not they see them as possible
for either their kampung or themselves.   Conveniences
(electricity, piped water, a clinic, a paved road, a telephone) are more real to the people of Rusila because all of
the ones named, except a general clinic, are present in the
village.   Two bits of folk wisdom are again challenged: the
idea that villagers are conservative and do not want change
and the idea that old people are doubly conservative and
even less likely to embrace change.   Village elders, like a
large number of their younger coresidents, would be de-
lighted to have electricity and piped water in their homes,
have their padi fields plowed with a disk plow, have better
transportation facilities and other conveniences.

Despite the great difference in the availability of
transportation between the two villages, none of the women
in either makes regular trips to Kuala Trengganu or
Marang.   Some men in both samples do so, usually in conjunction with economic pursuits.   For the active males, this
represents continuity; for some of the women, in Rusila at
least, it represents decreased mobility.   A few years ago
those women were actively selling produce in the Kuala
Trengganu market.   The women have shifted their activity,
most frequently leaving the kampung now in order to visit
kin--especially children--and friends in other villages, a
pleasure for which there was less time when they were more
active economically.

There are several indicators that women in the sample are more family-oriented in their behavior than the men. This is not to imply that Malay men do not value family bonds and relationships very highly. They do, but women in the sample are more active in maintaining the bonds through regular visiting and providing assistance such as child care.

All of the men in the sample are married (although one had been deserted), but there are only two married women. The others are widows or divorcees. This highlights the age difference that is usual between spouses, the husband being senior to the wife by three or more years. The men are in the sample of elders, but most of the wives are not eligible. By the time the women reach "seventy," many of them will be widows. Also, given widows and widowers who are elders, the widower will likely marry a younger woman within a year or so of his wife's death while the widow will either not have the opportunity or she might not choose to take advantage of it. Widows as a group tend to be disadvantaged. Few of them own productive land, and more of them live in houses owned by someone else, usually a child (a reflection of Muslim inheritance laws). Compared with other elders, they are the most dependent upon the generosity of children and grandchildren.

One can be highly religious without going to a mosque or prayer house. The five daily prayer periods can be observed at home and the Quran can be read there. Nevertheless, within the sample villages, the mosques (and the two prayer houses in Rusila) are the only public places drawing most elders, at least those who are healthy, on a regular basis. Even those in Rusila who are infirm, except one very elderly lady, make a weekly effort, supported (literally) by friends or kin.

A contrast is obvious in terms of the number of hajis and hajjahs: zero in Gong Beris and sixteen (80 percent of the sample) in Rusila. This probably indicates the greater affluence of those in the Rusila sample at some point during the past two decades. There is also a strong social emphasis to save or use wealth for this purpose rather than another, and some children and grandchildren also contribute. Rusila villagers express admiration for those making the pilgrimage, regardless of age, and performing haj a second time has been possible for a few people (including several in the sample) who describe that experience as even more meaningful than the first.

The worries about the future expressed by elders in both villages are shared by many old people in other parts of the world: concern about health and finances are foremost. Equally interesting are those few who feel they have no worries about the future: four persons, two women and one man in Rusila and one woman in Gong Beris. The women feel content because their children are comfortably settled. The male informant felt comfortable himself. (An interesting difference but hardly more than suggestive due to the small sample.)

The question of worries—or the lack of them—about the future was among the data analyzed by computer. Here, I focus only on that variable and what correlates with it, i.e., where contingency coefficients were close to .7 and thus probably meaningful. It must be emphasized that the number of informants ($\underline{N}$=30) is too few to be more than suggestive. The computerized data indicate that those who say they they have no or few worries about the future:

* Have one or more child living in the village, especially when at least one child is female.
* Have one or more grandchildren of either sex living with them or nearby.
* State that they give assistance (anything from money to help with feast preparations) to children and grandchildren.
* Receive regular visits from children and grandchildren; receive help from them.
* Characterize neighbors as helpful and self as helpful to neighbors.
* Own his or her home; (ownership of productive property was not significant).
* Had no recent, major illnesses.
* Depict the village as a good place to live.
* Think developmental features such as good roads, schools, clinics, piped water, and electricity are desirable for self and village.

Several of the responses emphasize the values of interdependence and reciprocity. Elders define themselves as "giving" as much as they acknowledge "getting" in relations with close kin and neighbors. Elders who assess change as positive are more content with their lives.

While the two villages are experiencing very different rates of developmental change, even the slowly changing area is not isolated from the effects of change occurring in the larger society and beyond. Young people leave both villages, but particularly Gong Beris, to seek work in other parts of the Federation and Singapore.

Family support for the elders is found in both areas but all of the aged in Rusila have children and/or grandchildren living in the village—a factor related to having few or no worries about the future and to contentment with their lives. Status of elders in both villages varied. No one has village-wide influence. A few years ago both the imam and the village headman in Rusila were elders, but today younger men fill those positions as is the case in Gong Beris. Most of the Rusila elders are hajjahs or hajis as are many younger persons. All are addressed by these titles before their names and are admired by others who place emphasis on religion for using their money for such a worthy purpose. No elders in Gong Beris have made the haj and none expect to do so, but there is less public emphasis on religion there and fewer effects of the Islamic revitalization movement.

Prosperity differences, not only among the elders in the two villages but among their children and grandchildren, are another part of the explanation. Gong Beris elders do not have the means to make the pilgrimage. Greater prosperity in Rusila is related to the earlier availability of schools and to the easier access to them for young people. Certainly more of the children and grandchildren of Rusila elders have regular incomes from wages and salaries.

The six elders who want to live elsewhere named places where children are living. The emphasis on children and grandchildren in response to many questions suggests that position within the extended kinship network is more important to elders than status in the village generally. Prestige among one's peers is gained by having children and grandchildren who meet the ideal of generous treatment of old parents and grandparents.

EPILOGUE--1983

Trengganu's off-shore oil revenues have brought wealth into the state at a fast rate. One result has been expanded transportation and communication systems: the major highways are said to be among the best in the nation; the telephone system has been developed and television is taken for granted in many parts of the state. In 1979, there was one public telephone in Rusila. Now it is possible to have them in the home, and a few people, including two elders in my sample, do have telephones. Color television is replacing black-and-white, and portable sets now vie with large consoles. There are more homes with refrigerators and stoves, piped water, and indoor toilets. There are also more cars.

The appliances and amenities are appreciated. Almost everyone complains about the increased traffic--the dirt and noise and, particularly, the dangers to young children and old people. One of the elders, a widow, had her house moved across the highway to the same side as the homes of a son and a daughter, on land between the two. The children insisted on the move because it had become more and more difficult and dangerous for their old mother to get across the road, and she is in the habit of making daily visits to their homes.

There has been a notable political shift in Rusila since 1965 when most of the villagers were affiliated at least nominally with UMNO, a Malay party that is a leading member of the National Front coalition that holds a large majority of seats in parliament and runs the federal government. UMNO is also the dominant party in Trengganu politics today although no longer so in Rusila where approximately two-thirds of the adults support PAS, the Islamic party in which the local imam is a leader. The political shift has had social concequences: in 1965 and as late as 1975, social interactions and politics were two separate spheres and no one was vehemently political. Political polarization had reached the point by 1979 where some villagers would not attend feasts sponsored by supporters of the other party; by 1983 social invitations across party lines were rarely made.

The old Rusila mosque has been expanded to twice its previous size to meet the needs of a growing community and the demands of people who come by the bus load to hear the dynamic imam speak every Friday morning before the midday prayers. No government money was accepted to pay for the project. Women and girls have not donned the veil but many have adopted knit caps as well as a garment that covers the head and reaches to the waist. None of the women elders in the sample have done so, feeling free from such new norms of modesty. Two of the women elders and one man have made a second pilgrimage to Mecca since I interviewed them in 1979. Many younger people have made a first pilgrimage.

The physical changes in and around Rusila are almost overwhelming. On the hill west of the village a multimillion dollar telecommunications center is almost completed. The road passing the primary school was widened and paved to facilitate construction equipment reaching the building site. Near the site, approximately 60 bungalows, of a planned 200, are complete--neat rows of them standing on a treeless tract. A Malay entrepreneur from Kuala Trengganu has purchased land in Rusila for an additional 200 housing units. As there are just over 200 homes in the village at the present, soon there will be almost twice as many "outsiders" as there are locals.

To say that the elders are worried about these changes is accurate; but they are not alone. People of all ages express concern about the amount of building, the number of new houses, and the number of "outsiders" that can be expected to flow into the area during the next few years. Rusila people fear that the character of their village will be irretrievably lost. Rusila is not the only village facing the problem. Coconut groves and open areas near the beaches along the nine miles of highway between Rusila and Kuala Trengganu are disappearing as blocks of houses—30 units here, 50 there—are built. Within a few years, there will be one vast suburb sprawling out from the city.

Despite their concerns, elders continue to express contentment with their daily lives because they have children and grandchildren nearby. Local prosperity in the form of wage-paying jobs is continuing to keep many of the young in the area as well as enabling them to be generous to parents and grandparents.

Gong Beris is little changed so far. However, brush and trees along the dirt road from the highway to the village have been cut and cleared. The road is due to be paved soon.

NOTES

[1]My deep appreciation is extended to the elders, headmen, and the many other residents of Rusila, Gong Beris, and Kampung Kubu who gave their cooperation and time so generously, and to colleagues at Universiti Malaya who attended my seminar about rural Malay aged and gave me the benefit of their knowledge and insights. Very special thanks are due to Abdullah Baginda, Mano Maniam and the staff at MACEE, Mohd. Taib Osman, Michele Teitelbaum, Lillian Troll, Chaim I. Waxman, and Zahid bin Muda for assistance in the field, or their thoughtful comments about the study, or both. Linda Petty and Ellen Rosen patiently tried to teach me Basic and transform my total ignorance about computers into a recognition of basics; they took time from their own research to help me examine mine from a different point of view and provided insights in the process.

REFERENCES

Chan Kok Eng
　　1981 The Elderly in Peninsular Malaysia--A Neglected
　　　　　Group? Some Socio-Economic Implica-
　　　　　tions. Occasional Paper No. 5, Unit Penga-
　　　　　jian Kependudukan, Faculti Ekonomi Dan
　　　　　Pentadbiran. Kuala Lumpur: Universiti
　　　　　Malaya.

Cowgill, Donald O.
　　1974 Aging and Modernization: A Revision of the
　　　　　Theory. In Late Life: Communities and
　　　　　Environmental Policy. J.F. Gubrium, ed.
　　　　　Springfield, Ill: Charles C. Thomas.

Cowgill, Donald O., and Lowell D. Holmes, eds.
　　1972 Aging and Modernization. New York:
　　　　　Appleton-Century Crofts.

Djamour, Judith
　　1965 Malay Kinship and Marriage in Singapore.
　　　　　London: Athlone Press.

Firth, Rosemary
　　1966 Housekeeping Among Malay Peasants. New York:
　　　　　Humanities Press.

Fraser, Thomas M.
　　1960 Rusembilan: A Malay Fishing Village.
　　　　　Ithaca: Cornell University Press.

Fry Christine L.
　　1980 Toward an Anthropology of Aging. In Aging in
　　　　　Culture and Society: Comparative Viewpoints and
　　　　　Strategies. Christine L. Fry, ed. Brooklyn,
　　　　　N.Y.: Bergin.

Gamst, Frederick C.
　　1974 Peasants in Complex Society. New York: Holt,
　　　　　Rinehart and Winston.

Goldstein, Melvyn C. and Cynthia M. Beall
　　1981 Modernization and Aging in the Third and Fourth
　　　　　World: Views from the Rural Hinterland in Nepal.
　　　　　Human Organization 40:48-50.

Hareven, Tamara
    1976 Modernization and Family History: Perspectives
        on Social Change. Signs 2:190-206.

Haub, Carl, and Douglas W. Heisler
    1980 1980 World Population Data Sheet of the Population
        Reference Bureau. Washington, D.C.:
        Population Reference Bureau.

Hunter, Guy
    1969 Modernizing Peasant Societies. London: Oxford
        University Press.

Ikels, Charlotte
    1980 The Coming of Age in Chinese Society:
        Traditional Patterns and Contemporary Hong
        Kong. In Aging in Culture and Society.
        Christine L. Fry, ed. Brooklyn, N.Y.: Bergin.

Johnson Colleen L.
    1983 Interdependence and Aging in Italian Families. In
        Growing Old in Different Societies: Cross-
        Cultural Perspectives. Jay Sokolovsky, ed.
        Belmont, Calif.: Wadsworth.

Keith, Jennie
    1980a The Best Is Yet To Be: Toward an
        Anthropology of Age. In Annual Review of
        Anthropology. Bernard J. Siegel, ed. Palo
        Alto, Calif.: Annual Reviews.

    1980b Old Age and Community Creation. In Aging in
        Culture and Society. Christine L. Fry, ed.
        Brooklyn, N.Y.: Bergin.

Kerns, Virginia
    1980 Aging and Mutual Support Relations among the
        Black Carib. In Aging in Culture and Society.
        Christine L. Fry, ed. Brooklyn, N.Y.: Bergin.

Linton, Ralph
    1942 Age and Sex Categories. American Sociological
        Review 7:589-603.

Maxwell, Robert J. and P. Silverman
    1970 Information and Esteem. Aging and Human
        Development 1:361-92.

Maxwell, Robert J. and P. Silverman
    1978 The Nature of Deference. Current Anthropolgy
        19:151.

Palmore, Erdman
    1975 The Honorable Elders. Durham, N.C.: Duke
        University Press.

Press, I. and M. McKool
    1972 Social Structure and Status of the Aged: Toward
        Some Valid Cross-Cultural Generalizations. Aging
        and Human Development 3:297-306.

S. Husin Ali
    1975 Malay Peasant Society and Leadership. Kuala
        Lumpur: Oxford University Press.

Simmons, Leo
    1970 (orig. 1945) The Role of the Aged in Primitive
        Society. Hamden, Conn.: Archon.

Smelser, Neil J.
    1967 Toward a Theory of Modernization. In Tribal
        and Peasant Economies. George Dalton, ed.
        Garden City, N.Y.: Natural History Press.

Wilson, Peter J.
    1967 A Malay Village and Malaysia. New Haven,
        Conn.: HRAF.

2

Old Age, Midwifery and Good Talk: Paths to Power in a West African Gerontocracy

MICHELE TEITELBAUM

In the cross-cultural study of power, few designations have been used more ambiguously than that of gerontocracy --rule by the elders of a society. Radcliffe-Brown (1940:xix) told us that among Australian aborigines "order is maintained by the authority of the old men." Gluckman (1965:146) told us the same for hunting and gathering bands in general. However, power at the band level of organization has generally not been considered worthy of extensive study. Concerning more complex levels of political organization, Radcliffe-Brown (1940:xxii) noted that gerontocracy is found in some parts of Africa in conjunction with systems of age sets and age grades; but studies of such organizations (reviewed by Gulliver, 1968) have often focused on the more physically active age sets, not on the elderly. Some authors have focused on specialized areas of control by the elderly. For example, Spencer (1965) defined gerontocracy in terms of the control of wives by old men in some societies. Hamer (1972) dealt with a situation in which old men control land and cattle.

Simmons (1970:105ff) summarized anthropological references to the aged--especially aged men--as holders of positions of power. He pointed to the ways in which specialized knowledge can be used by the old to gain power in the context of secret society organizations. Rosow (1962) alluded to this theme as well, and some, such as Little (1965) and Murphy (1980, 1981), have described this phenomenon for the Kpelle and other West African societies. In spite of these and other examples, the relationship of power to a multiplicity of attributes associated with old age

39

has generally been treated as a given: a relatively unin-
teresting one, noted in passing but not considered worthy
of detailed explication. Other related assumptions often
made are (1) that gerontocracies, where they exist, involve
only the participation of old men, not of old women; and
(2) that in societies characterized as gerontocratic, all old
people hold positions of power. Some, such as Murphy
(1980), have already criticized the latter idea.

THE RESEARCH PROBLEM

My field research with the Jokwele Kpelle, a population
of sedentary swidden cultivators, was conducted from July
1974 through December 1975 in what was considered, by
outsiders to be a modern Kpelle town in central Liberia.[1] I
was interested in studying the political cognition of a tribal
people whose leadership, since the early part of this century, had been officially integrated into the national political
system of Liberia. My investigations revealed a Kpelle
theory of leadership based on complex relationships between
the notions of age, gender, fertility, and power. In theory
and in practice, old men and old women in this society have
authority in several important areas. In this chapter, I
seek to (1) explicate the Kpelle theory according to which
old people may gain access to power and (2) suggest the
relevance of this material to generalizations that have been
made about the aged in nonindustrial societies.

In my work with the Kpelle, I did not initially intend
to study the aged per se or the aging process. In my
investigation of the political domain in this culture, my
informants repeatedly drew my attention to this segment of
the population. Indeed, in the early days of my field
research, my own biases led me to believe that the initial
suggestions of townspeople that I interview several of the
elderly indicated only a formality that I must perform before
gaining access to the really powerful individuals in the
contemporary community. I subsequently learned otherwise.
My study suggests the possible significance of the aged to
anthropological studies of conventional domains, particularly
in studies of nonwestern populations conducted from a
cognitive, or emic, point of view.

Since I was interested in the contemporary Kpelle
political situation, my approach and my results differed
from those of some other researchers. Fulton, for example,
offered an interpretation of the relationship of Kpelle politics to ritual with the proviso, "No Kpelle area now operates in the manner herein described" (Fulton 1972:1231).
The system I describe here and elsewhere (Teitelbaum 1977,

n.d.) was definitely in operation at the time of my research. I have learned from Fulton's work as I have from
the work of others who have studied various aspects[2] of
politics, ritual, or law in Liberia and Sierra Leone. I
share Fulton's view that local variation in political organization is significant in this part of West Africa, and I believe
that some differences in our interpretations reflect the
occurrence of the same important elements in different
configurations.

I conducted my research before the Liberian coup of
1980; the national government was still dominated by
Americo-Liberians, the reputed descendants of the black
American settlers who founded the Republic of Liberia in
1847. For most of the time since the founding of the country, barriers--geographical, technological, social, and
linguistic--obtained between the several thousand
Americo-Liberians, who live primarily in the developed
coastal areas, and the more than one million members of the
indigenous societies, who live in the undeveloped areas.
The Kpelle speakers are the largest of the indigenous populations, but, while they may number about 250,000 in
Liberia, they have never been known to act as a unified
political body. Many different local political organizations
have existed for some time. Since the early twentieth
century, the country of Liberia has attempted to articulate
with local Kpelle leadership through a system of
chieftaincies and a hierarchy of chiefs that are responsible
to representatives of the national government. The Jokwele
area, previously a dialect area, was proclaimed a
chieftaincy, presided over by a paramount chief, during the
early efforts toward centralization. The chieftaincy is
divided into eight districts called clans. The term clan
does not connote any traditional anthropological usage when
used in this manner in Liberia. The clan is presided over
by a clan chief, and each town within the clan has its own
town chief. Each chief has a court. The national government prescribes the jurisdiction of the courts of the paramount chief and clan chiefs. It assigns additional duties of
the chiefs--such as tax collection--and sets limitations of
their powers.

I have written elsewhere (1977, n.d.) of the extent to
which modern leadership in the Jokwele area is actually
incorporated into a more traditional system of government.
The Jokwele chieftaincy has little local significance as a
political unit. The salient units of Kpelle political activity
are the ritual lodges, the many local organizations of poro
and sande ritual[3] into which the area is subdivided. The
ritual lodge in which I lived happened to include nearly the
same territory as the modern political unit of the clan. The

political activities of the clan and all the towns within it (about twenty towns, with a total population of several thousand) are subordinate to the activities of the ritual organizations.

JOKWELE KPELLE RITUAL LEADERSHIP

In Jokwele Kpelle society, the loi namu,[4] or 'owners of the land,' are holders of the highest ritual office. They are the old people who are in charge of running the societal initiation schools: poro for males, sande for females. These are popularly known in Liberia as 'bush schools.' Loi is a form of the word land, and namu expresses the ability to manipulate and use something. The loi namu are closely associated with the history and sanctity of the land and are particularly venerated for having the knowledge to choose an appropriate place in the forest in which to conduct the 'bush school.' In the actual poro and sande rites, initiates are ritually killed and reborn as knowledgeable adults. Success of the ritual is important not only for the individual initiates, but it is said to be associated with the continued fertility of the farmland and of the people in the ritual lodge.

In the Kpelle area in which Murphy worked, the loi namu title is apparently reserved for members of an important landowning lineage (Murphy 1980, 1981). In the town in which I lived--the seat of the clanship and ritual lodge organization for the area--a landowning lineage is not yet clearly established. The town was founded in 1919, when a local Kpelle leader obtained the backing of the national government and used soldiers of the Frontier Force to end warfare in the Jokwele area. The soldiers forced the resettlement of many people from old, nearby towns to a new, more accessible site that was located on an old trading route. The old route was developed into a main road, and subsequent settlers came to the area voluntarily. Fifty-five years later a "founding lineage" was still in the process of being formed by real and fictive affiliation with the founder of the town, who had no surviving direct descendants in the immediate area (I intend for this to be the subject of another paper on Jokwele politics). Suffice it to say that at the time of my research, lineage manipulation was within the means of people who otherwise fulfilled criteria for high ritual office.[5] Once they achieved such office, the elders could then attempt to control the genealogical manipulations of their ambitious juniors.

The Kpelle ritual cycle, being associated with fertility, requires both male and female participation. This is effected by dividing the ritual cycle into periods of four and three years, four being the number associated with[6] males, three being the number associated with females.[6] During the four years of the boys' bush school and four years of ritual inactivity immediately following it, the male loi namu are said to be in control of the land. During the three years of the girls' bush school and three years of ritual inactivity immediately following it, the female loi namu are said to be in control. When I arrived in the area, there were four male and four female loi namu. One of the men died shortly thereafter and was not succeeded during my stay in Liberia. The eight loi namu were estimated to be in their early sixties to early seventies. Most elderly Kpelle people do not know their birth dates. My estimates were made by correlating the life histories of the loi namu with remembered historical events and with the life histories of the few older individuals whose birth dates could be documented.

RITUAL AND SECULAR INTERACTION

As a result of their ritual relationship with the land and association with fertility, the loi namu exercise considerable authority in secular matters. First, loi namu have ultimate authority over actual land use. Second, they have responsibility for all affairs that may result in unnatural deaths, whether these involve bloodshed or the use of traditional medicine.[7] All these matters are referred to as 'land business' (noi meni). The Kpelle use 'land' as a metaphor to express a dimension of seriousness. These most serious matters can only be adjudicated by the loi namu, who outrank all other leaders as decision makers. Third, the loi namu are presumed to be responsible for successful childbirth, the female loi namu being in control of all local midwives. Fourth, the ritual leaders select the secular leaders. No leaders can exercise authority within the ritual lodge without the approval of the loi namu who are presently in control of the land. During the male part of the cycle, the male loi namu have the final say concerning leadership. During the female part of the cycle, the female loi namu prevail. None of the chiefs can act without the advice and consent of the reigning loi namu. Nor can the chiefs even appear to act autocratically. The Kpelle term galong, used for 'chief,' designates a person who exercises authority in public. In the Jokwele area, these are usually vigorous middle-aged men. However, they are merely the public administrators of the power which is vested in the elderly loi namu. A corollary of this principle is that while the loi namu hold power, they cannot appear to exercise authority in public. Their position comes close to what Westerners may think of as "the power behind the throne." Chiefs may issue most of the commands in town, but they are constrained in their leadership behavior by elderly ritual leaders whose authority is hardly apparent in town on a day-to-day basis.

There is linguistic evidence that Jokwele Kpelle differentiate between the type of leadership represented by the chiefs and other modern leaders and that associated with traditional leadership roles. The former are described as being modern, or kwii. The traditional leaders such as the loi namu and the 'town elders' on the other hand are not described as kwii, but as noi.[8] Noi means 'land,' and the term connotes the traditional value placed on land. Additionally, the chiefs, their modern superiors, their messengers, and under-officers may be referred to collectively as officers (ofisers), a modern designation taken from English and never applied to traditional leaders. The loi namu and 'town elders' may together be designated 'elders' (nuu polo) in a general sense.

To understand the separate contexts in which the leaders perform, it is necessary to appreciate the differentiation made by Kpelle between public and private contexts. The term taa, literally 'village' or 'town,' may be used in the phrase 'town business' to signify a public context when contrasted with noi, literally 'land,' or loo, literally 'forest' or 'bush.' These last two terms, when used in the phrases 'land business' or 'in the bush,' are used to describe contexts that are private, whether they actually occur in the forest or in the privacy of one's home. Being 'in town' thus does not necessarily refer to being inside one of the houses. A private, serious conference is said to have taken place 'in the bush' whether it was held in a house or in the forest. By contrast, being 'in town,' refers to being out of doors in town, in public view. Of the two contexts, the private one is said to be the more serious, and it includes all poro and sande business. The term polong, which refers to all ritual activity in general, and men's ritual activity in particular, also is used to designate a private and serious context.

The leaders originally designated to me as noi, including the loi namu, are associated with authority in private contexts, whereas the chiefs, or kwii leaders, are associated with public contexts. For example, visibility is always emphasized in discussing the role of a chief. He is expected to spend time in town performing diplomatic and social functions even when he has no official business. By contrast, traditional leaders are rarely expected to be seen or heard in public. These public/private and modern/traditional dichotomies in the modern Jokwele Kpelle system parallel those of many traditional African political systems that are based on an interaction of secular and sacred leadership categories (see, for example, Fortes 1945).

One incident illustrated these principles particularly well. Shortly before the clan chief was to stand for reelection according to national law, a meeting of all leaders in the clan was called to discuss his candidacy. At the time, the female loi namu were in control, and they were critical of some of the actions of the clan chief. Since Jokwele women do not customarily assume a public forum, the female loi namu first met privately, and their objections were conveyed by male loi namu who attended the meeting. The objections were: (1) When the women conducted the last bush school, they were not paid the money that the clan chief had collected for them from the families of the initiates. (2) Money collected in the marketplace (a five cent fee is collected by the chief's officer every market day from each of the vendors) was missing. This money, too, was intended for the female loi namu, who control the local market. They had previously delegated some duties to the clan chief, who gained a great deal of prestige from his association with one of the largest markets in central Liberia.

At the meeting, the matter was discussed to the satisfaction of all who were present. The men present thought that the clan chief had generally been a good leader. They agreed that if he would return the missing money and promise to be more careful in the future, the embarrassing indiscretions would be forgotten. The meeting ended amid a flurry of congratulatory back slapping. The results of the meeting were then presented privately to the reigning female loi namu. They disagreed with the view that had prevailed. They saw the clan chief's transgressions as overstepping the appropriate boundaries of the powers that were delegated to him: "He took himself to have power that a chief cannot take for himself." The female loi namu did want the reelection of the clan chief, as they acknowledged that his general performance in office had been good. However, they said that he ought to be punished for his transgressions, lest he forget his position relative to theirs. The women made their point by relieving the chief of his prestigious authority over the market. A 'market chief' (lo galong), was appointed by the women. This was a previously nonexistent office, and the particular selection was a man to whom one of the female ritual leaders was known to be indebted. The man, in an effort to advance himself politically, had provided a house for a female loi namu to live in.   Subsequently, when he was announced as the new market chief, it was apparent to all that the choice had been made by the loi namu who was repaying a debt. There was no doubt as to who made decisions in town and who had reminded the clan chief of the proper order of things.   Two male loi namu who were discussing this incident claimed that the women would rather have as clan chief a man who had been publicly humiliated by them in this fashion.   It was one of the better ways in which the women could publicly demonstrate their power, and they were now confident that the clan chief would not overstep his authority in the future.

In the questioning of a general sample following this incident, informants were adamant that they could not comply with the leadership of a chief in town if he were not supported by the ritual hierarchy.   Rationalizations for this view included, "If we had a chief that the loi namu did not want, then the crops would be bad and the children would be born dead."   Also, "It is the bush schools that make us what we are.   Where would we be if we did not respect the old people who run them for us?"   The same informants also stated that they would be willing to have as clan chief a person who was not given approval by the national administrators in the nearby county seat.   The main concern was that the loi namu approve.

I believe that Jokwele Kpelle have had this type of private/public and sacred/secular division of political powers for some time.[10]   In the modern context of indirect rule, national governments tend to articulate only with public, secular political leaders.   These are not only more visible, but, as in the case of the Kpelle chiefs, they are more akin to what modern national rulers expect of leaders in terms of age, gender, and public behavior.   It does not follow that the public local leaders will then acquire more power from this new source of legitimacy.   On the contrary, central governments often constrain severely the local leaders that they recognize.   All the while, more obscure, ostensibly religious leaders may retain their original powers.   Consequently, if traditional leadership roles in the private domain are fulfilled by the elderly and by women--contrary to the expectations of modern centralized governments--these roles may be officially ignored by the national government, while they remain locally important. This phenomenon became apparent as I investigated the sanctions associated with the different types of Jokwele Kpelle leaders.

LEADERSHIP AND FORCE

Informants often observed that the modern officers were obeyed because "when you are kwii and part of the government, you can use fosi." The word fosi is derived from the English word "force": Jokwele Kpelle claim that there is no proper equivalent of the term in Kpelle. Force is often mentioned as the most notable characteristic that distinguishes the modern government from the old form of organization: "The kwii government is obeyed because it uses force. Some of us remember being beaten by the soldiers when we were made to build this town. Our own people--the town elders and the loi namu--are obeyed because they are good." The chiefs can impose fines, and in some instances they can use physical force to obtain compliance. In the middle 1970s, under the rule of the government of President Tolbert, they were empowered to employ these sanctions in relatively trivial cases involving possible fines in amounts up to ten dollars and possible imprisonment up to terms of three months. All more serious matters were required by law to be directed by the chiefs to the magistrates of the national courts. The chiefs were not empowered by the national government to administer capital punishment. Nor were the powers of the chiefs embellished locally by the expectations of the populace.

When informants are asked about sanctions applied by the loi namu, a different pattern emerges. Some people first state that, "If I disobeyed, they would not like me." This simplistic response expresses concern about such serious matters as not having the support of the loi namu in disputes, particularly in matters concerning land. A few informants suggested that the loi namu could fine people using the concept of tong. A tong is a breach of an old Kpelle law that must be restituted by monetary or other compensation. Additionally, female loi namu are particularly feared. They control sande midwives who might be ordered to abort the pregnancies of noncompliant women or of the wives of men with whom the ritual leaders have some griev-ance. They are also associated with medicines that induce convulsions. These are thought of in connection with both abortions and ritualistic executions. Most importantly, informants acknowledge that the loi namu collectively have a right to kill in retaliation for offenses concerning land, bloodshed, and the revelation of ritual knowledge to noninitiates.

We might then ask, why are the loi namu considered not to be characterized by the use of fosi when informants believe that they have the right to administer capital pun-ishment? This apparent contradiction needs to be dealt with. As Swartz, Turner, and Tuden (1966:10) noted, force itself has to be based on something other than force as a source of legitimacy. The use of capital punishment by the loi namu is not considered fosi because the loi namu derive their authority from a ritual association with the land. They are, in particular, associated with ritual activity in the forest.

Jokwele Kpelle fear the power of the forest. This might be compared with the fear of God that leads a religious American to pursue an upstanding life in lieu of exposing oneself to the wrath and punishments of God in the afterlife. The loi namu thus become the arbiters of what is right and proper behavior both in and out of the forest. To displease the loi namu would taint the bush school ritual and jeopardize the relationship of Jokwele Kpelle to the land from which they earn their living. While the power of the loi namu is derived directly from his or her association with the land and the ability to ritually manipulate the forest, the kwii use of force was introduced to Kpelle speakers by people who were not associated with the land or with ritual sanctions. Kpelle people see no similarity between force derived from ritual control of the land and force derived from the power of modern weaponry. The former is legitimate; the latter is not.

The Jokwele Kpelle theory of leadership can be summarized as follows: First, the source of legitimacy must be separate from the performance of official public duties. The ritual leaders must thus approve the leadership behavior of the chiefs, but they cannot perform the public roles themselves. Second, private activities are associated with traditional values, in particular with the ritual relationship to land; whereas public activities are associated with modern values, in particular with the performance of decision-making duties carried out in the name of a central power that is associated with force. Third, noi contexts and ritual leadership are regarded as superior to kwii contexts and secular leadership. Traditional leaders, modern leaders in town, as well as laymen, all regard the secular leadership roles as possible paths to ritual leadership.

ATTAINMENT OF RITUAL OFFICE

The title of loi namu is first used when a person participates in the choosing of a site for the bush school. The bestowal of the title automatically connotes both admission to the highest ritual rank and shared authority with other loi namu over the several domains I have discussed.

The many powers over life and land make the loi namu also
sought after for blessings to ensure success in various
endeavors, in particular in farming. All the female loi
namu and most male loi namu are also <u>sale namu</u>, 'medicine
owners,' who are asked to employ their medicines for various purposes. Small payments or services to the loi namu
are made for the blessings and medicines. Gifts may also
be made to them by individuals who wish to secure consideration for future leadership roles. While a loi namu will
customarily own a farm, he or she will only work on that
farm occasionally as a form of recreation. Family, neighbors, initiates in the bush schools, and others seeking
favors will work on a loi namu's farm. In the event of a
crop failure or shortage, some of these same individuals will
feed the loi namu at their own expense.

For the old people who have become loi namu, we can
make two generalizations that are consistent with Amoss and
Harrell's (1981) suggestions regarding the achievement of
high status by the elderly: (1) the high status of the loi
namu is associated with their control of land, a strategic
resource that is needed by all members of the farming
community; and (2) there appears to be a reasonable balance between the costs to the community in maintaining the
elderly ritual leaders and the contributions that they are
able to make in turn. Indeed, if all Jokwele people became
loi namu, life for the old in that society would be ideal.
Nevertheless, this status can only be achieved by a select
few who follow a specialized path to ritual leadership.

The attainment of the position of loi namu is reached
partly by participation in ritual activity. One advances in
the ritual hierarchy by playing a larger role in each suc-
cessive bush school. It is believed that the coreigning loi
namu of each sex should have all attended bush school at
the same time, and that this should be the oldest bush
school in the memory of anyone alive. However, elevation
in the ritual hierarchy toward loi namu status is only
possible for those who also meet a number of other criteria.
A loi namu must have gained an association with the land
by having been born within the ritual lodge and having
lived and worked on its land long and hard enough to know
its history and its 'secrets.' In Kpelle theory, ritual and
secular leadership should come from different parts of the
ritual lodge, ideally from two towns that are paired for this
purpose. The older town should yield ritual leaders; the
more recently founded town should yield secular leaders.
In actuality, this is impossible in the Jokwele area because
successful secular leaders eventually become ritual leaders.
Therefore, an old person who has attained or is close to loi
namu status will "find" a farm near an old town, usually in

an area associated with his or her mother's or father's family, and subsequently claim that as a place of birth.

To become a loi namu one must also earn a reputation for speaking well and advising. Speaking skills are greatly respected in this population, which admires good oratory and provides frequent forums for its use. Advisement is regarded as crucial to everyone's well being. A loi namu should be able to give advice that helps to keep peace in town; in particular, he or she should be able to resolve conflicts that might lead to unnatural deaths. A loi namu also needs to have served for several years in a position involving nurturant activity, a job that is said to prove one is capable of caring for people. This can be accomplished by serving either as a midwife (fahlenei) or as a chief. In the town in which I lived, aspiring female loi namu are invariably midwives; in some other Kpelle areas they may be midwives or chiefs. Aspiring male loi namu, in any Jokwele town, can only be chiefs. Elsewhere (Teitelbaum n.d.) I have written extensively about how the chiefs conduct themselves in office in a manner that will gain favor and attain advancement to ritual leadership. Those who succeed and fulfill the other criteria, will become loi namu when they retire from public office; those who do not succeed are said to become merely "old chiefs" when they cease to be active public leaders. Each of the current male loi namu[11] served as town chief or quarter chief in the early days of the town. Two of the men and two of the women also served as farming group leaders (kuu laa nuu), a service which is further cited to document their ability to care for people.

In some instances, ill health may interfere with the attainment of the office of loi namu if it impedes one's ritual and secular activities. Once the position is earned, however, most infirmities will not decrease the prestige or activities of a loi namu. An exception is an impairment of speech or hearing which would interfere with the duties of speaking and advising.

Once the status of loi namu is achieved, these individuals are accorded several indicators of high prestige in Kpelle society. One is being addressed and referred to respectfully; that is, being called ma, 'mother,' or nang, 'father,' by people who are not one's children and being addressed and referred to more formally as nenii-polo, 'old woman,' or shia-polo, 'old man.' These latter terms may be used as terms of address or reference for all individuals who command respect, regardless of chronological age. On the other hand, the terms may only be applied as descriptive adjectives for old people who do not command respect. A second indicator of prestige is being able to make requests of people to do things for you and give things to you without the expectation of direct payment. This is evident in the gifts, food, and farm labor given to the ritual leaders. A third indicator has to do with speaking prerogatives--for example, being the first to speak in a situation or the last one to have a say in a matter. Loi namu outrank all others in their use of speaking prerogatives. There is also the expectation of a display of generosity. The generosity of a high status person in general is expressed either with expenditures of money or goods or by making oneself available for advising and assisting people in nonmonetary matters. There is a difference in the way modern and traditional leaders fulfill these expectations. Chiefs display generosity with goods and money; loi namu help people by advising and speaking for them in a number of contexts. Even if a loi namu has become wealthy in the course of his or her life, it would be inappropriate for a traditional leader to display wealth conspicuously.

Clearly, the loi namu do not attain their positions simply by becoming old. Their ritual rank is dependent upon the attainment of a number of skills and statuses that may appropriately accompany old age, but which must be demonstrated. The components related to loi namu status in Kpelle society are those that Press and McKool (1972) suggest generally shape the acquisition of prestige by older adults. They entail: advisement, contributions to social activities, control--in this instance of land and serious sanctions--as well as some residual prestige associated with their former statuses. These factors are ideally associated with old people, but they may be attributed as well to exceptional younger people. There are a few young, educated people in town who are presumed to share some attributes with the more accomplished old people. These young people may be permitted to function as 'town elders' in the settlement of disputes, and they may at times be accorded speaking prerogatives generally associated with prestigious older people.

ELDERS AND THE ELDERLY

Characteristics associated with the aging loi namu represent high standards against which all old Jokwele people are judged. Old people who cannot measure up to these standards are treated with varying degrees of tolerance and/or kindness, but not necessarily with respect. An extreme example was provided by an old man in the town who might be diagnosed by Western physicians as suffering from senile dementia. Kpelle people said that he was 'not right in the head.' He lived by himself in a house provided by kinsmen and frequently walked around town nearly naked, muttering to himself. Relatives and neighbors literally dumped food on his doorstep once or twice a day. I never saw a town resident attempt to converse with this old man, and most people ignored him to the point of avoiding eye contact.

Other old people, who had all of their faculties intact, varied with respect to their attainment of prestige. Old people who had not the outstanding qualifications of a loi namu, but who were known for speaking well and giving good advice, could achieve the status of 'town elder' (taa nuu polo). Also, an individual qualified to be a loi namu, but whose age set had not yet succeeded to ritual office, might serve in this capacity for several years. At the time of my research, nine individuals in a town of 757 people were clearly considered to be 'town elders.' They were active primarily in the settlement of disputes in private hearings held in the home. At these hearings, which were used more often to settle disputes than were official court procedures, disputants would call nearby 'town elders' to serve as advocates and as mediators. 'Town elders' are also considered to be appropriate advisors to chiefs, although they are outranked in this capacity by loi namu. For the duties they perform, 'town elders' are given frequent gifts. The gifts and the generosity of relatives and friends can provide all the material needs of a 'town elder.'

By contrast, those elderly individuals whose abilities and achievements have not earned a position as either loi namu or 'town elder,' find their behavior severely constrained by younger people, usually younger kinsmen upon whom they are dependent for food and shelter. In these instances, the necessities of life are provided out of a sense of duty, not generosity. I recall one old man who possessed all of his faculties, but who, for lack of talent and/or ambition, had not achieved one of the prestigious positions that may be accorded the elderly in Kpelle society. This old man wanted a photograph of himself, and after a long while he asked me to take one of him--but not before he had asked permission of five people, all younger kinsmen upon whom he felt dependent. This fellow would not initiate even a stroll around town for himself without permission. A higher status old person such as a loi namu or 'town elder' would take such freedom for granted.

The experience of the average Jokwele old person is far from that of the idyllic picture sometimes presented of old people in West African societies (see, for example, Shelton 1965, 1972). Some observers of traditional African societies seem to confuse economic security with high status. Note Fuller's (1972:51) comment: "So long as traditional Bantu culture persists the elderly have maximum security, but social and cultural change threaten this favored status." While the elderly in many parts of the world might appreciate the security of being fed and cared for in an African society, being dependent is rarely considered to be a "favored status." It is simply a way of staying alive, and it is the lot of many Kpelle old people. Using my census data, life histories, and general observation, I estimate that about 10 percent of the population of the town I lived in might be fifty years of age or older, which is old in Africa. Nevertheless only about 2.3 percent of the population have achieved the status of either loi namu or 'town elder.' The remaining old people can no longer expect to achieve high status in their lifetime if they have not thus far demonstrated appropriate abilities.

CONCLUSIONS

These data are indirectly supportive of some of Goody's (1976) ideas regarding the aged in nonindustrial societies. Goody suggests that, in general, in agricultural societies, because of their position in the domestic group and the need to pass on resources to heirs, old people should fare better than in industrial societies. This formulation assumes that land is passed down within family, or domestic, groupings. Goody acknowledges that in subsistence economies based on hoe cultivation, given no shortage of land, parental control is less likely to apply (ibid.:118). This is the case for the Jokwele Kpelle, among whom an elite group of old people holds land in common for all members of their ritual lodge. Most old Jokwele people cannot share the same powers or prerogatives. The Jokwele data emphasize that it is difficult to generalize about all old people in any one traditional society, even one in which some old people are powerful. Intracultural, as well as intercultural, diversity must be considered. It is true that nonindustrial societies are more likely to provide ways--such as gerontocratically organized politics and ritual activity--in which old people can repay the services of those who provide for them economically. However, even when old people have the means to achieve power and prestige, those who do not measure up in achievement may well end their days in a situation similar to that of many economically dependent old people in the United States.

The nonindustrial nature of Kpelle society is important in this framework. Rosow (1962:184) pointed out the extent to which low production might be associated with the availability of positions of prestige and power for the elderly. Note that Kpelle cultivation requires intensive labor and demands hard work of almost all members of the population, especially women. Even children must work in the home and on the farm. Even with every able-bodied person at work, it is difficult for an individual or a household to produce a surplus and accumulate wealth. Some secular male leaders are able to do this through polygyny--more wives can farm more land--and the use of fees that they earn from their official duties; some clever women are able to parlay a small surplus into a large profit through enterprising market activity. These achievements are relatively rare. Most people farm only to subsist. It is no wonder that religious and political leadership is drawn largely from the ranks of old people who are no longer physically able to make a significant contribution to farming. Jokwele Kpelle justify these arrangements by a complex set of symbolic values. From an observer's point of view, it is a sensible system for the use of people as economic resources; the pool of able-bodied farmers is not depleted. I believe it is a system that will persist for some time insofar as Jokwele land is not considered useful for development by any outside parties. Nor are there many economic opportunities for Kpelle people other than traditional farming. As long as the land remains in the control of the ritual leaders, it should continue to provide a source of legitimacy upon which the present political system is based. For similar reasons, political systems based on sacred/secular or private/public dichotomies of leadership, systems in which old people may have prominent roles, may persist elsewhere. When these are dismissed as gerontocracies without explication, we are deprived of detail about the relationship of power to attributes associated with old age. We are also left without an understanding of the ways in which unexceptional old people may fare in these systems.

I have already alluded to the biases of colonial or other centralized governments which may overlook the sacred or private components of traditional political systems. There is, as well, a bias among some ethnographers and interpreters of ethnographic data. Consider, for example, a well-known theory concerning public and private domains (Rosaldo 1974), which suggests that power is in the public domain and therefore inaccessible to those in the private domain. This formulation would be nonsensical to Jokwele Kpelle who regard all traditional sources of power as originating in the private domain. Women are in the private domain, where they may gain power through their two unique associations with fertility: midwifery and predominance in Kpelle farming activities. Old people in general are in the private domain, and they may gain power through their association with land and the bush schools as well as through their demonstration of superior ability in speaking, advisement, and leadership.

In summary, I have sought to (1) explicate the Kpelle theory of leadership according to which old people may gain access to power; (2) discuss the implications for all the Kpelle elderly, including those who never achieve leadership status; and (3) suggest the general implications for the study of the elderly in nonindustrial societies. Not the least of my goals has been to suggest that lack of sufficient data on how old people attain positions and function as traditional leaders has left wanting our knowledge of political systems in general.

NOTES

[1]Cuttington University College and the Liberian Research Association cosponsored the research in Liberia. The National Institute of Mental Health, The National Science Foundation, and the Institute for International Education all provided funding for various phases of the project. Many Kpelle people contributed to my understanding of Kpelle elders and elderly; in particular, I owe much to the two Jokwele elders known as Fama and Kellemu. I thank Heather Strange for encouraging me to consider these data in light of recent work on aging.

[2]These include: Bellman 1983; Bledsoe 1980; Fulton 1968, 1972; Gibbs 1962, 1963, 1968, 1969; Harley 1941; Jedrej 1976a, 1976b; Little 1949, 1965, 1966; Murphy 1980, 1981; Watkins 1943; Welmers 1949.

[3]Local terms are polong for the male ritual organization, sanang for the female ritual organization. I am using here the terms that are more familiar in West African ethnography.

[4]Kpelle nouns are not modified to form a conventional plural.

[5]Elsewhere (Teitelbaum 1980), I have attributed cognatic descent to the Jokwele Kpelle in general. Patterns of lineage affiliation for families associated with high office

differ somewhat and shall be the subject of a separate exposition.

[6]When a male is born, his mother remains confined for four days and the midwife's fee is calculated in multiples of four; when a female is born, her mother remains confined for three days, and the midwife's fee is calculated in multiples of three. The numbers appear again, associated with males and females respectively, in association with funeral rites and other life cycle events as well as in poro and sande ritual.

[7]Bellman (1974) has written extensively on the subject of traditional Kpelle medicine.

[8]Kwii and noi are not used as opposites in ordinary Kpelle conversation. Noi was suggested by several informants as an opposite of kwii in response to my queries, and subsequent informants were able to use this framework without difficulty in structured inquiries. Throughout this article, the designation of any persons or concepts as "traditional" indicates a current categorization by Jokwele Kpelle, not historical reconstruction.

[9]The women were so circumspect in their exercise of power, that I lived in the ritual lodge and studied its organization for several months before I was convinced that the female loi namu were in control in more than a ceremonial manner.

[10]There is a leadership role, that of the 'land chief' (loi galong), which mediates between sacred and secular leadership, between private and public domains. This role is critical to a complete understanding of the Jokwele Kpelle political system. I have described it elsewhere (Teitelbaum 1977), and I shall deal with it in future works. Since the loi galong role is not germane to a discussion of old people and leadership, I do not discuss it here.

[11]A quarter is a segment of a town.

REFERENCES

Amoss, P.T. and S. Harrell, eds.
    1981 Other Ways of Growing Old: Anthropological
        Perspectives. Stanford, Calif.: Stanford
        University Press.

Bellman, B.L
    1975 Village of Curers and Assassins: On the
        Production of Fala Kpelle Cosmological Categories.
        The Hague: Mouton.

    1983 The Language of Secrecy: Symbols and
        Metaphors in Poro Ritual. New Brunswick, N.J.:
        Rutgers University Press.

Bledsoe, C.H.
    1980 Women and Marriage in Kpelle Society. Stanford,
        Calif.: Stanford University Press.

Fortes, M.
    1945 The Dynamics of Clanship Among the Tallensi.
        London: Oxford University Press.

Fuller, C.E.
    1972 Aging Among Southern African Bantu. In Aging
        and Modernization. D.O. Cowgill and L.D.
        Holmes, eds. Pp. 51-72. New York:
        Appleton-Century-Crofts.

Fulton, R.M.
    1968 The Kpelle Traditional Political System. Liberian
        Studies Journal 6:1-19.

    1972 The Political Structures and Functions of Poro in
        Kpelle Society. American Anthropologist
        74:1218-1233.

Gibbs, J.L., Jr.
    1962 Poro Values and Courtroom Procedures in a Kpelle
        Chiefdom. Southwestern Journal of Anthropology
        18:341-350.

    1963 The Kpelle Moot: A Therapeutic Model for the
        Informal Settlment of Disputes. Africa 33:1-11.

    1965 The Kpelle of Liberia. In Peoples of Africa.
        J.L. Gibbs, Jr., ed. pp. 197-240. New York:
        Holt, Rinehart and Winston.

1969 Law and Personality: Signposts for a New
Direction. In Law in Culture and Society.
L.Nader, ed. Pp. 176-207. Chicago: Aldine
Publishing.

Gluckman, M.
1965 Politics, Law and Ritual in Tribal Society.
Chicago: Aldine Publishing.

Goody, J.
1976 Aging in Nonindustrial Societies. In Handbook
of Aging and the Social Sciences. R.H. Binstock
and E. Shanas, eds. Pp. 117-129. New York:
Van Nostrand Reinhold.

Gulliver, P.H.
1968 Age Differentiation. In International Encyclopedia
of the Social Sciences, Volume I. New York:
Collier-Macmillan.

Hamer, J.
1972 Aging in a Gerontocratic Society: The Sidamo of
Southwest Ethiopia. In Aging and
Modernization.D.O. Cowgill and L.D. Holmes,
eds. Pp. 15-30. New York: Appleton-Century-
Crofts.

Harley, G.W.
1941 Notes on the Poro in Liberia. Cambridge, Mass.:
Papers of the Peabody Museum of American
Archaeology and Ethnology 19.

Jedrej, M.C.
1976a Medicine, Fetish and Secret Society in a West
African Culture. Africa 46:47-57.

1976b Structural Aspects of a West African Secret
Society. Journal of Anthropological Research
32:234-245.

Little, K.
1949 The Role of the Secret Society in Cultural
Specialization. American Anthropologist
51:199-212.

1965 The Political Function of Poro, I.
Africa 35:349-365.

1966 The Political Function of Poro, II.   Africa
36:62-72.

Murphy, W.P.
1980 Secret Knowledge in Kpelle Society.   Africa
50:193-207.

1981 The Rhetorical Management of Dangerous
Knowledge in Kpelle Brokerage.   American
Ethnologist 8:667-668

Press, I. and M. McKool, Jr.
1972 Social Structures and Status of the Aged.
International Journal of Aging and Human
Development 3:297-306.

Radcliffe-Brown, A.R.
1940 Preface.   In African Political Systems.   M. Fortes
and E.E. Evans-Pritchard, eds. Pp. xi-xxiii.
London: Oxford University Press.

Rosaldo, M.Z.
1974 Woman, Culture and Society: A Theoretical
Overview.   In Woman, Culture and Society.   M.Z.
Rosaldo and L. Lamphere, eds.   Pp. 17-42.
Stanford, Calif.: Stanford University Press.

Rosow, I.
1962 Old Age: One Moral Dilemma of an Affluent
Society.   The Gerontologist 2:182-191.

Shelton, A.J.
1965 Ibo Aging and Eldership: Notes for
Gerontologists and Others.   The Gerontologist
5:20-23, 48.

1972 The Aged and Eldership Among the Igbo.   In D.
Cowgill and L. Holmes, eds.   Pp. 31-49.   Aging
and Modernization.   New York: Appleton-Century-
Crofts.

Simmons, L.W.
1970 The Role of the Aged in Primitive Society.
Hamden, Conn.: Archon Books.

Spencer, P.
1965 The Samburu: A Study of Gerontocracy in a
Nomadic Tribe.   London: Routledge and Kegan
Paul.

Swartz, M.J.; V. Turner and A. Tuden, eds. 1966 Political
Anthropology. Chicago: Aldine Publishing.

Teitelbaum, M.
1977 Officers and Elders: A Study of Contemporary
Kpelle Political Cognition. Doctoral dissertation,
Rutgers University.

1980 Designation of Preferential Affinity in the Jokwele
Kpelle Omaha-type Relationship Terminology.
Journal of Anthropological Research 36:31-48.

n.d. Selecting a Forum for Dispute Settlement:
Decision-Making Strategies and Political Choice.
Unpublished manuscript.

Watkins, M.H.
1943 The West African "Bush" School. American
Journal of Sociology 48:666-675.

Welmers, W.E.
1949 Secret Medicines, Magic and Rites of the Kpelle
Tribe in Liberia. Southwestern Journal of
Anthropology 5:208-243.

3

Old People and Social Relations in a Newfoundland "Outport"

BONNIE J. McCAY

I carried out anthropological field research on Fogo Island, Newfoundland, from October 1972 to August 1974. While in the field, I focused on topics in rural development and ecology rather than social organization and gerontology (see McCay 1978, 1979). When asked to write a chapter for this volume by Dr. Vera Green, I used a household survey that I had conducted in 1974 and other data that I had collected plus my memory, interpretive skills, and brief returns to the research site to produce this ethnography of the old people of a small "outport" fishing community of rural Newfoundland. Although I have returned to the island almost every year since 1974, the ethnographic present of this analysis is the early 1970s.

This analysis places the elderly of Grey Rock (a pseudonym), Fogo Island, within the context of the developmental cycle of the rural Newfoundland family. It locates and depicts demographic factors and cultural rules that account for the observed distribution of household types of the elderly of Grey Rock. It describes how old people there cope with the practical and social problems of old age and reveals some reasons they also anticipate and celebrate its coming. It suggests that transactions of dependency and interdependency entered into by old people in Grey Rock reflect a cultural form--patronage--that symbolizes and reproduces one mode of survival in a peripheral, impoverished sector of the world economic system.

GREY ROCK: HISTORIC, ECONOMIC, AND DEMOGRAPHIC SETTING

Grey Rock is one of nine coastal settlements, or "outports," that fringe the shores of Fogo Island, about 10 miles off the coast of northeastern Newfoundland.[1] In 1971 the island's population was 4,257, and Grey Rock's population was 406. Virtually everyone on the island is descended from eighteenth- and nineteenth-century settlers. They came from West Country, England, and southern Ireland to work in what was the northern frontier of the British Newfoundland fishery. They stayed to live and reproduce within a peripheral, fish-exporting sector of the world economic system. The monocrop determined by the place of Newfoundland in the international division of labor was, first and foremost, Atlantic cod (Gadus morhua). With the ascendancy of industrial production in North America, the center of economic activity to which Newfoundland is a peripheral outport shifted away from Europe. The transition was formalized in 1949 when Newfoundland became a province of Canada. Concomitantly, the second major export of Newfoundland and places like Grey Rock became labor; the principal imports became both manufactured goods and "transfer payments" from Canada. On Fogo Island there are few alternatives to fishing, shopkeeping, labor migration, and government transfer payments--including the old-age pension. Most people are poor by North American standards and thus the old-age pension takes on a special meaning.

The age and sex composition of the Fogo Island population (Figure 1) reflects the demography of a population with high rates of birth and outmigration and low rates of death. The skewed sex ratio (123 males per 100 females) reflects high female outmigration. Skewedness continues into old age: more of the old people are men than women, the reverse of the general North American pattern. The age composition of Fogo Island's population varies greatly among the communities (Table 1). While Grey Rock stands out as the community with the highest proportion of persons aged sixty-five years and older, its dependency ratio is lower than that of four other communities on the island because of its smaller proportion of persons aged fourteen years and younger. This in turn reflects Grey Rock's unusually high rate of bachelorhood.

Demographically, Grey Rock is both representative of Fogo Island and a special case. It is also special in being an Irish Catholic community on an island and in a region (northeastern Newfoundland) in which the majority are of English background and Protestant religious affiliation and

FIGURE ONE

Age and Sex Composition, Fogo Island Communities, 1966*

Age	Male		Female	Total
65+	158		117	275
55-64	119		91	210
45-54	162		159	321
35-44	178		119	297
25-34	155		125	280
15-24	325		242	567
5-14	503		425	928
0-4	212		195	407
		500 250 0 250 500		3285

*Excluding the Town of Fogo

where other Catholics live in mixed communities. Grey Rock residents can trace their ancestry to emigrants from the Irish counties of Limerick, Tipperary, and Waterford, plus one or two from the English county of Dorset. They are all active members of the Catholic parish of the island; the priest's residence is in Grey Rock. Grey Rock's settlement pattern, however, is typical of the region: houses are tightly clustered around a sheltered harbor, the focus of the fishery. Landward, the houses are backed by infield kitchen-gardens and, in scattered pockets of arable land, fenced outfield meadows and potato gardens. The interior of the island is a vast, uninhabited commons used for livestock grazing, trout-fishing, small-mammal and bird hunting, and cutting firewood and lumber. Roads, only partly paved in 1974, connect Grey Rock with the other outports on the island, including the town of Fogo where most services, especially medical care, are concentrated. The island is connected to the Newfoundland mainland by a car-ferry. When ice swept from the Arctic on the Labrador current in the late winter prevents boat travel, government subsidized airplane service is available.

SOCIAL ORGANIZATION

The settlement pattern of Grey Rock and many elements of its social organization reflect the Atlantic fringe heritage of the early settlers. Grey Rock's settlement pattern bears a strong resemblance to the open-field systems of parts of West Country, England (Finberg 1969), and to the clachan/rundale complex of Ireland (Evans 1973). The latter remained strong in some areas of the southeast and east coast of Ireland well into the early nineteenth century (Evans 1973:55). The similarity may only be a simple coincidence produced by the geographical constraints of an economy based on fishing. It may also be the result of historical British Newfoundland policies militating against the development of agriculture and landed property (Sider 1980).

The households of Grey Rock are tightly clustered around the harbor. Their gardens and outfields are carved out of the commons of the island by community-sanctioned rules of usufruct and inheritance (as were, for much of Grey Rock's history, important fishing sites). Yet the households are in some ways the social equivalents of the dispersed family farmsteads of much of the Atlantic fringe (Arensberg 1963; Kenny 1963). The goal of each married couple in Grey Rock is household self-sufficiency--a goal that continues into old age, even for unmarried persons. When a couple marry, they move immediately or by the birth of their first child into their own house. The decision to marry often hinges on their ability to do so. The small or nuclear family household is the ideal and norm; stem families are rare, and joint families rarer still. Kinship is essentially bilateral albeit patrifocal (a widespread European principle [Hammel 1972]). To this extent Grey Rock social organization is similar to that of North America in general.

Some differences reflect a long history during which families have[2] been principal units of production as well as consumption. Clusters of households in Grey Rock are united not only by kinship but also by coparticipation in certain kinds of fishing, notably the Labrador schooner fishery which was important in Grey Rock around the turn of the twentieth century, and the cod trap industry, important from about 1870 to the present. The high labor and capital requirements of schooner and trap fishing are managed by cooperating groups of agnatic kin. These family firms (or "effective crowds" [Faris 1972]) may be three generations deep. They are comprised of fathers, sons, brothers, paternal uncles, and/or patrilateral parallel cousins plus wives and unmarried daughters and sisters who work together in the fishery but who may live in separate households. Upholding this economic system is a strong rule of postmarital virilocal residence and the custom of patrilineal,[3] partible inheritance of house-sites and fishery capital. Households that work together are also close neighbors, within a culturally-defined space called a "gar-

TABLE 1

Population by Age, Unincorporated Fogo Island Communities, 1966

Community	Age Group 0-14 Years	15-64 Years	65 Years & Up	Total	"D"*
A (Grey Rock)	170	21	57 (12.8%)	444	104.6
B	73	167	34 (12.4%)	274	64.1
C	390	525	7 (7.8%)	992	88.9
D	36	38	5 (6.3%)	79	107.9
E	208	266	35 (6.9%)	509	91.3
F	49	52	8 (7.3%)	109	109.6
G	160	193	26 (6.7%)	379	96.4
H	187	160	19 (5.2%)	366	128.7
I	86	89	14 (7.4%)	189	112.3
Total	1359	1707	275 (8.2%)	3341	95.7

* "D" is the dependency ratio: the number of persons Aged 0-14 years And 65 years and up per 100 persons aged 15-64 years.

Data obtained from Canada Department of Regional and Economic Expansion, Ottawa, 1971. Comparable data for the town of Fogo was not available.

den," "premise," or "room,"[4] that includes the houses, barns, storage sheds, and fishery buildings of one or more family firms. The fishery firms fission as old people retire or die and young ones grow to maturity. Married couples usually spend ten to twenty years cooperating as production units with the husbands' agnatic kin and their wives, before their own sons are old enough and numerous enough to allow the creation of new family firms. The process is encoded as: "I fished with my father and then I went off by myself." Although attenuated for fishermen who use less capital- and labor-intensive technologies such as handlines and gill-nets, the system described applies generally to Grey Rock as well as to other Newfoundland fishing communities heavily dependent on trap and schooner fishing (Firestone 1967; Faris 1972; Britan 1974; Breton 1973).

SOCIAL STATUS OF OLD PEOPLE

Through the developmental cycle of the family fishing firm, a man with sons can look forward to attaining a position of power and prestige: "skipper." Although "skipper" is a term of reference and address applied to all adult males in outport Newfoundland, its use denotes the respect accorded to one who actually has the role of skipper on a fishing crew. A man rarely becomes a skipper until his forties. Becoming a skipper is usually tied to the retirement of a man's own father and the coming to maturity of his own sons. A woman can also look forward to attaining the power and prestige of being a skipper's wife, with authority over the work of the "shore crew" of women and children involved in the work of "making" dried salt-cod, just as her husband has authority over the entire fishery. Correspondingly, the skippers in the community (plus the priest and local male schoolteachers and shopkeepers) are most actively involved in matters such as obtaining government assistance for building new facilities and providing employment during the long winter off-season (November through May).

The skippers' position is comparable to that of the rural Irish "old men" in discussing and managing community affairs (Arensberg and Kimball 1968). They too meet often in each other's kitchens, telling stories and singing songs, discussing the news of the outside world and deciding the fate of their own world; they also meet in groups at the parish club and in the small shops. Younger men listen and occasionally join in, but are careful to defer to "the skippers" on matters of importance. The younger men are more likely, particularly if they are unmarried, to be "out on the path with the boys" carousing and drinking heavily. Women in general have little public power and prestige, except within certain spheres of the church.

The general status of "skipper," and especially the hard-won status of "big fish-killer," remain with a man until his death. However, the power associated with the status disappears rapidly after a man gives up his active role as skipper of a fishing crew. He and his wife become disengaged from much that is important in economic and political life. One sign of this is when a skipper appears with his wife at the weekly bingo game rather than spending the evening drinking beer at the parish club with other skippers. Another is his failure to appear at a special meeting held by government fisheries officers at the community hall.

Spheres of activity of retired skippers are restricted more and more to the household and the households of their children. On a fair day groups of two or three retired skippers form on the grassy knolls overlooking the harbor, where they exchange news, watch the goings-on in the harbor, and recall old times. Decisions about where and whether to set cod traps, about the relative merits of the new fishing vessels or the new cooperative, and about community politics are taking place elsewhere. An old man may help his son build a punt or skiff or he may put in long hours mending fishing gear, but his son, if now a skipper, will decide how to use the technology. The power and prestige of old age is that of being an active skipper; the prestige that remains with retirement devolves into diffuse respect.

RETIREMENT AND THE OLD-AGE PENSION

Retirement from fishing takes place usually between the ages of sixty-five and seventy years, when people become eligible for government old-age pensions. Although a man has the option of continuing to fish through and after these ages, declining physical strength and health and an egalitarian ethos encourage him to retire as soon as he is eligible for the old-age pension. Jobs, including shares in a fishing firm, are believed by members of Grey Rock to "belong" first and foremost to those who need them the most, i.e., people without other sources of support.[5] Moreover, although a man's sons' marriages do not hinge upon his retirement, their attainment of full adult status, as "skippers" rather than "boys," does, and they may pressure him to retire. As in Ireland (Arensberg and Kimball 1968), men are often called "boys" if they are not skippers or full partners in fishing crews (see Moreton 1863:9 for an early account of this practice in northeastern Newfoundland).[6]

Retirement is positively valued in Grey Rock because it provides relative financial security. Canadian government assistance programs for the elderly include an old-age pension, guaranteed to all citizens at the age of sixty-five years of age; a pension plan into which workers contribute and which includes workers' disability and survivors' benefits; and a guaranteed income supplement, granted to pensioners who have no income other than the old-age pension. Very few of the aged of Grey Rock receive anything from the workers' pension plan because they have not been in the labor force (as opposed to working as self-employed fishermen and casual laborers) long enough to qualify. All receive the old-age pension, a guaranteed income supplement and, where appropriate, the spouse allowance. The amounts they receive keep them below the official Canadian poverty lines--in 1974 they received from about $2,000 to $4,000 per pensioner household--but within the local context, the amount is substantial and secure.

Old people of Grey Rock remember a not very distant past of scarce cash and stringent poverty, the past prior to Newfoundland's federation with Canada in 1949. They recall the "truck" system, when their household expenses were met by running up debts at the store of the fish merchant. If all went well, the debts were paid off by their deliveries of salted, dried cod fish to the merchant at the yearly "squaring up time" in the fall. If all did not go well,as often happened, the fishermen had to count on the patronage of the merchants to carry the debts over into the next fishing season. The old-age pension is wealth in this remembered context.

The pensions also compare well with alternative incomes on the island. During the early 1970s the household incomes of fishermen rarely exceeded $4,000. Incomes for households in which at least one person engaged in semi-skilled labor, commerce, or service occupations ranged between $4,000 and $5,000, but mostly in the low end of the range and, during periods of unemployment, considerably lower. The old-age pension compares well here, too. It is also more predictable. Other incomes represent patchworks of many sources of money, periods of windfall income followed by long periods of none, moderated by social assistance ("welfare") and unemployment compensation. Only about 10 percent of the able-bodied adults of Grey Rock held regular jobs throughout the year (e.g., teachers, clergy, postal employees, workers on the highway crews). The rest were dependent on government transfer payments and irregular incomes from wage-labor and fishing, plus some remittances from emigrated sons and daughters. In this setting, the amount and predictability of the old-age pension represent financial security, a sharp contrast to the situation for many of the lower-class elderly in urban-industrial North America and Europe.

The old-age pension comes as a relief and blessing to many people who had not been able to attain the goals of household self-sufficiency in their younger lives. Although times are often hard, and jobs and fish often scarce (the latter increasingly so since the early 1960s), the people of Grey Rock try to avoid "going on the dole," reflecting a work ethic they share with the majority of North Americans (cf. Wadel 1973). Welfare assistance comes with negative social connotations and calls for ingenious and personally costly coping strategies (ibid.); in Grey Rock most households try to avoid it as much as possible. Between January 1971 and December 1974 there was no month when more than fourteen of the approximately one hundred households were dependent on "able-bodied" welfare assistance. The old-age pension comes with no negative social valuations.

The strains of making a living in Grey Rock are intense, particularly for two groups: alcoholics and the semi-disabled or subclinically ill. Alcoholism and heavy drinking are common among Grey Rock men. Male social life is mediated by alcohol. Today both cash and liquor are more readily available than in the recent past. Alcoholics and heavy drinkers who cannot work or hold a job comprise the bulk of the relief rolls and suffer the social stigma of being on welfare—not of being alcoholics or drunks. The stigma is lifted when they switch to the old-age pension. A more poignant social problem is posed for those whose illnesses and disabilites are not deemed serious enough by the physicians at the hospital in the town of Fogo to make them qualified for what is colloquially called "disable-bodied assistance" (ibid.) The population of Grey Rock and Fogo Island is epidemiologically civilized: major causes of death are cancers, heart disease, diabetes, and stroke. Hypertension is particularly rampant. For the middle-aged and the old, these problems are combined with the residual effects of early lives spent within a less civilized epidemiological regime: undernutrition, severe infectious disease (especially tuberculosis and rheumatic fever) and other stresses. They are intensified by the hard physical labor, often in cold, damp conditions required for most work available to rural Newfoundlanders. Consequently, by middle age many suffer from "bad back," "a poor heart," high blood pressure, and vaguer symptoms of "dis-ease," difficult to diagnose and treat. For the majority, dis-ease is not legitimized as "disease" by the local physicians because of diagnostic ambiguities or because the resident physicians often believe that their patients are shirkers. It is thus extremely difficult for Grey Rock men to obtain the certificate of true, enduring, disabling illness that is required for long-term social assistance. Many of the people between the ages of forty and sixty-four are forced either to apply for regular welfare assistance (and the derogatory social status that goes with it) or to continue working, despite their ailments. They can only hope to live long enough to qualify for the old-age pension.

The loss of economic and political power occurring when a man who was once a skipper retires and becomes a "shore skipper" is counterbalanced by the relative financial security of the old-age pension. The old-age pension also makes possible the attainment of respectability in old age for those unable or unwilling to do so earlier.

Independence of the elderly in Grey Rock is reflected in the household composition of pensioner households. Relative self-sufficiency is highly valued. It is possible because being elderly and even living alone are not very difficult. First, the old-age pension provides an unusual amount of financial security. Second, the elderly can reduce their living expenses by modifying their houses. Third, most are living in close proximity to their kin and the many friends and associates of their lifetimes. The phenomenon of elderly people living alone is common to urban-industrial North America and Europe. But the place of the elderly in Grey Rock contrasts markedly in other ways from urban-industrial societies: in the latter, reliance on government old-age pensions often means extreme poverty; cutting down on expenses may require migration; and kin and old friends are dispersed.

In 1974 there were ninety-eight households in Grey Rock, of which twenty-eight included one or more persons receiving old-age assistance. Table 2 gives the distribution of pensioner households by marital status and by living arrangement. The predominance of two types of living arrangement is striking: living alone and living with unmarried offspring. Together these account for 78.6 percent of the cases. Also noteworthy is the high proportion of bachelor households: 28.6 percent. Comparisons with data on living arrangement of the elderly in the United States (Treas 1975) suggest that Grey Rock has an unusually high proportion sharing households with offspring, but is similar to the United States in having a very small proportion of households encompassing elderly parents, their children, and their grandchildren. Stem-family households are rare.

THE RULE OF INDEPENDENT RESIDENCE

The rarity of stem-family households in Grey Rock would require no further comment were it not for the existence of two special factors that might be expected to encourage the formation of more stem-family, as well as joint-family, households. The first is the close economic cooperation of extended family units in the fishery. The second is the rule of ultimogeniture: inheritance of the old peoples' house and their savings goes to the youngest son, who is in turn expected to live with his parents and, when married, to continue responsibility for their welfare (see Firestone 1967:54). Cases are recalled of joint-family households: brothers and their wives and children. But the only acceptable and stable version constituted two households in one house, that is, a house literally divided in two. The same device had been used for stem-family households. The following instance was reported in another community on Fogo Island. When the only son married, he and his father attached part of another old house to his parents' house. At first the two couples lived together in the enlarged house, "using the same kitchen." But within a few years they had created two kitchens, two living rooms, two sets of bedrooms, and two separate entrance doors and porches. When the old woman died, the widower and his son remodeled the house back into one household.

The rarity of such arrangements reflects more widespread and enduring sentiments against extended family households in Europe and North America, neatly expressed in Fox's summary of the position of the Tory Islanders of Ireland:

> The "extended household"...is not popular with the islanders. They tend to regard it as somewhat overextended, and so do not favor "two women in the kitchen"--at least if those two women are affines and not mother and daughter or two sisters. (Fox 1978:156)

In Grey Rock the stem-family, in which two couples (or their remnants) linked by a parent-child kinship relationship live together, is for the most part a transient arrangement early in the married lives of the young or late in the lives of the old. A newly married couple may move in with the parents of the husband or wife until they acquire their own house. There were four cases of this in 1974, all begun during that year and disbanded by 1975. Also, old people may move in with married offspring because of severely declining health. In 1974 there was one case, an el-

TABLE 2

Pensioner Households
By Marital Status and Living Arrangements

Grey Rock, 1974

Status	Widow/Widower	Married Couple	Bachelors	Total
Alone	4	3	6	13
With Married Offspring	1	0	0	1
With Unmarried Offspring	4	5	0	9
With Unmarried Siblings	1	0	2[a]	2
With Widowed Offspring	1	0	0	1
Other[b]	1	0	1	2
Total	12	8	9	28

(a) One household is not included in the total because it is counted under widow/widowers column: it includes a widow and her bachelor brother.

(b) "Other" includes a widow and her widowed brother-in-law, viewed locally as a morally questionable arrangement, and a bachelor who lives with a couple not closely related to him.

derly widow who moved in with her son and his family. (Elderly women do move in for a few months to help their daughters and daughters-in-law when, for example, they give birth.)

The transience and rarity of stem-family living arrangements hold sway despite the rule of ultimogeniture. Stem-family households created by the rule of ultimogeniture occurred in the past, but women in particular recall them as situations of friction and conflict among in-laws.   When it is economically feasible, the youngest son and his family will instead live close by, providing the old people with firewood, water, house maintenance, and transportation. The meaning of the rule is less inheritance than it is to assign responsibility for the welfare of the old people. The latter may not require living together.

The lack of stem-family households is mirrored by a high proportion of the elderly living alone, as married couples, widows, widowers, and bachelors. None of this need be interpreted as the outcome of modernization. While the pattern is found in the contemporary United States (Treas 1975), it was also found in the preindustrial English family (Laslett 1977). The "rule of continued independent residence by the old" (Laslett 1977:207) in Grey Rock is stronger than pressures to form joint- and stem-family households. In Grey Rock, as in contemporary and historical North America and Western Europe, most older people choose to live apart, alone or with their spouse, loathe to intrude on their children's lives and to sacrifice their own privacy.

THE INTEGRITY OF THE NUCLEAR FAMILY

Grey Rock has a high proportion of elderly persons sharing households with offspring--but not with married offspring. Fifteen (53.6 percent) of the twenty-eight pensioner households were composed of one or more pensioners living with other people (Table 2). In two cases the elderly lived with unmarried siblings (a widow with her bachelor brother and a bachelor pensioner with three bachelor brothers). Four cases were exceptional, as explained in the footnotes to Table 2. Nine households were composed of pensioners living with unmarried offspring, primarily bachelors. The composition of pensioner households in which the elderly bachelors do not live alone, plus those of elderly bachelors who do live by themselves is generated by a strong cultural value on the integrity and persistence of the nuclear family.

In Grey Rock, as in parts of Ireland (Fox 1978), the parent-child bond is sacred. The ideal is to grow old without severing entirely the "Holy Family." The Irish studied by Fox developed an unusual solution: natolocal residence (married couples residing in their respective natal homes). In Grey Rock this solution is inconceivable because marriage is predicated upon the ability to establish a new household, albeit close to the man's agnates. The Grey Rock solution is instead to keep one or more children from marrying and at home. It depends on having children who have neither died, nor emigrated, nor married.

TABLE 3

Distribution of Family Size By Age Group

Grey Rock Women, March 1974

Number of Children[a]

Age	0	1	2	3	4	5	6	7	8	9	10	11
20-45 (N=30)	7	2	10	1	2	1	1	2	0	2	0	1
46+[b] (N=46)	4	0	5	4	5	6	5	6	2	6	2	1

[a]Excluding miscarriages, still-births, and infants who died soon after birth.

[b]Excluding women who were deceased or who had emigrated by the time of the survey.

The solution depends on two very Irish (post-famine) demographic strategies: high rates of marital fertility and high rates of nonmarriage (Kennedy 1973). As in Ireland, high marital fertility helps compensate for celibacy and out-migration. The average completed family size for Grey Rock women aged forty-five years and older in 1974 was 7.32 children (Table 3.)[8] Although the chances are great that some children will leave the community, the chances are fairly good that some will remain, including one or more as bachelors or spinsters. Unmarried adults whose parents are alive reside with their parent almost universally; when the old people die, they are left to fill the ranks of the elderly living alone. The rule of maintaining the integrity of the nuclear family leads, through the developmental cycle, to the rule of the independent residence of (bachelor) old people.

Spinsters living with elderly parents are less common than bachelors. Only four women over thirty years of age were spinsters in 1974 (approximately 6 percent). The rate is lower than in the past. The difference is that now it is easier for young Grey Rock women to emigrate, which they do in large numbers. The only acceptable social role for an adult woman in Grey Rock is to be married. On the other hand, 29 percent of Grey Rock men over thirty years of age in 1974 were bachelors, a proportion that differs little from the past. The social dynamics of bachelorhood in northeastern Newfoundland involves individual decision-making about marriage, emigration, and bachelorhood within the context of the family fishery and fluctuations of fortune (Britan 1974). A family fishing firm with bachelors is better able to survive periods of economic distress because it has a higher ratio of workers to consumers: once marriage is postponed for this reason, it becomes more difficult for a man to "leave the continuing agnatic enterprise" (Britan 1974:161). Although bachelors are unlikely to attain the valued social status of "skipper," the status of "boy" is by no means entirely negative. "The boys" of Grey Rock--bachelors and young married men--enjoy a life of minimal responsibility, peppered by a high level of sociality framed around drinking, camping in the woods, and hunting. Accordingly, while young men also emigrate in large numbers, they are more likely to return to the island and remain bachelors for most or all of their lives. Their choices help make possible the persistence of the nuclear family throughout the lives of their parents.

THE NETWORK OF FAMILY AND FRIENDS

Old people who live alone and those who have managed to keep unmarried offspring with them into old age are rarely isolated in Grey Rock. The term "lonely" is foreign. "Lonesome" is common, but indicates a fearful, anxious, nostalgic state of mind rather than the condition of isolation: "I was some lonesome yester evening. Harold's son brought to mind poor deceased Phonse." Independence is valued. Cutting down on expenses in old age does not require moving away from one's kin and friends. Village endogamy promotes a high degree of interconnectedness within and across generations.

The value of independence can be illustrated by the extent to which the elderly, including bachelors, try to maintain their own households until the are physically incapable or until they die. In 1974 four old men, aged between sixty-seven and eighty-four, kept their own houses despite episodes of severe illness and offers from kin to take them in. One even lived by himself in a nearby cove, the residents of which had long since moved through the government's resettlement program. He stayed there until he died, surrounded by cats and having refused help from his married sister. Some are forced to accept dependent status, especially when the priest intervenes for the sake of the community and the person's soul. One old man was thus forced to move in with a middle-aged couple in exchange for loss of control over his old-age pension, because of his disheveled and unwashed state, heavy drinking, and habit of wandering aimlessly around the harbor. (He had no close kin in the community.)

Instead of being passive recipients of help, older people in Grey Rock as in the United States (Treas 1975), often help their relatives, especially their siblings and children. The relative financial security and size of the old-age pension, combined with the egalitarian ethos of the community makes this possible. Younger people show signs of resenting the old for having substantial and predictable incomes and say, "it is only right" that the old give some of their money to the young: "What else will they do with all that money?" Old people help their sons build and remodel houses with gifts of cash and provide financial assistance for investment in the fishery. Bachelors also help their married siblings, even pensioners. Old Mr. Lambert, aged eighty-two in 1974, gives much of his pension to his seventy-four-year-old brother who used the money, together with his own pension, to build a modern house for himself and his wife. It is by no means certain that Mr. Lambert will move in with his brother if and when he must stop living alone. It is as likely that he will remain alone until he dies: "People do get set in their ways."

The old who live alone continue to live within the extended-kin neighborhood of their youth. Getting old in Grey Rock does not require moving to cheaper accommodations. Instead, cheaper and more labor- and energy-efficient accommodations are created upon or moved to the ancestral property. Most of the elderly have switched from wood or coal fuel to oil in order to reduce the labor required to keep warm and to cook and not become dependent on others for help. Some consolidate all activities, including sleeping, into the kitchen and board up the rest of the house. A more radical tactic is to reduce the size of the house. In Grey Rock, houses are both malleable and movable property while house-sites are fixed and embedded within the virilocal group. Many of the pensioners live in "cut-down" houses: former two-story houses from which the top story has been removed. Sometimes the new "bungalow" is a remnant of the original home; sometimes the original, larger home is given to a married son or daughter and an already "cut-down" house is purchased. Unless there are special provisions, buying a house does not include the land the house is on; land, unlike housing, is an imperfect commodity. During the early spring when the harbor is solid with ice, all of the able-bodied men of Grey Rock will drag the purchased house across the ice and place it among the houses and outbuildings on the pensioner's "premise."

The houses of the elderly remain, then, on the extended family "premises," together with the houses of their male children and other members of the virilocal extended family. In rural Newfoundland the door is always, figuratively, open: kin, friends, and neighbors walk in and out without prior announcement and without knocking. Therefore even the immobile elderly who live alone may not be isolated from social life. Whether they receive visitors depends more on their personalities than on their age. The network of kin and friends is typically wide and deep within the community. While inheritance is patrilineal, fishing firm recruitment agnatic, and postmarital residence virilocal, kinship is reckoned bilaterally.

Interaction with kin as kin is limited. For the most part bilateral kinship is an intellectual construct. Late in the evening old people may sit in a kitchen and "trace links" among themselves and others, living and dead. They will take pains to point out that people related only through great-great-grandparents or through marriage are "not really related." Marriages between third cousins are considered the same as marriages between strangers. Although true kin are defined narrowly and although the rule of virilocality sends daughters off to live with their husbands' "people," the network of kin and friends is typically extensive. Virilocality makes little difference if the daughters marry within the settlement, and having few kin left in the community may be compensated for by the vast number of friends and associates engendered by a lifetime spent in the same place. Both are facilitated by village endogamy.

Of the eighty-two never-married women in Grey Rock in 1974, only seventeen (21 percent) were born elsewhere. Only five of the husbands of the eighty-two women (including men deceased in 1974) were born elsewhere. Half of the in-marrying women came from other communities on Fogo Island; in the older generation they all did. Village endogamy is not general in rural Newfoundland. Faris (1972) found the opposite in Cat Harbour, not far from Grey Rock. Nor is it as complete elsewhere on Fogo Island. The insularity of Grey Rock is special. It is related to the maintenance of a unique, although very Irish, dialect of Newfoundland English; to the old practice of Grey Rock men driving out "strangers" who courted Grey Rock girls; to Grey Rock's existence as a completely Roman Catholic community in a region characterized by Protestant or mixed communities; and to a denominational and fragmented school system that kept young people from interacting with people from other communities at critical stages of courtship.[9]   For the old people, Grey Rock's insularity and the endogamy that reflects and sustains it mean that they are likely to live close to married daughters as well as sons and to live in the community of their birth.   No wonder "lonely" is a foreign word.

TRANSACTIONS OF DEPENDENCY

The services for which the old people of Grey Rock are often dependent on the young include drawing water from wells and pumps; hewing, transporting, and splitting firewood, running errands to local shops, the post-office, etc.; and specialized services such as home-remodeling. Because only one of the pensioners in Grey Rock owned an automobile in 1974, they are also dependent on the young for transportation outside the community.   (There are no buses or taxis).   The aging process increases one's dependency on others for these and other services.   The old-age pension provides one means--money--of ensuring that necessary services will be available.   Filial obligations help, too.   But transactions of dependency also involve subtle negotiations over power.   The old people have the power of surplus cash and of the general respect due to them.   The younger people have, in their turn, the power of being unavailable to help out when needed, recognized by the old people as "their right to live their own lives."   The strong cultural value of independence that keeps the elderly in their own households also makes it difficult for them to obtain necessary services.

The old people of Grey Rock rely more on giving money than on respect.   They give money for all services, even those provided by their youngest sons, who have the most responsibility for their welfare.   When a son or grandson arrives to pick up the water buckets, he is given a small amount of money, which is shoved into his pocket if he refuses to accept it.   He is likely to refuse to accept the money at first: accepting money from someone for services that one should provide anyway turns a diffuse responsibility into a specific obligation.   The latter is what the elderly want.   Giving money for services places people under obligation and thereby helps ensure continued availability of services.   However, Newfoundland outporters in general try to keep from being obligated to others (see Chiaramonte 1970).   This may be interpreted as an outcome of the political economy of Newfoundland's old mercantile system within which the merchant maintained his power by transforming debts into obligations (Faris 1972:114-125). It is also expressed in the practice of asking for less money than a service or job is worth (Chiaramonte 1970). Old people often try to offer more money than the service is worth, but this carries the risk of losing control entirely. The helper or worker may refuse to take any money and hence be free from all obligation in the future. Prepared for this eventuality, the old person will be sure to have several bottles of beer on hand; a small obligation is better than nothing.

Not surprisingly, must of the "surplus" pension money goes instead to an impersonal entity that provides diffuse benefits to the donors and to the entire community now and hereafter: the church. Through their participation in bingo games and lotteries and their outright gifts of money to the priest, the elderly play a major role in sustaining the parish church. In exchange they receive pastoral care, such as visits from the priest on Sundays when they cannot attend Mass. They are also confident that the money they offer will not be rejected and that the priest cannot easily deny his obligations to them. In this one case, a gift is not also "poison" (Mauss 1967) to the donor as well as the recipient.

The church does not provide transportation for the elderly. Apart from the old-age pension itself, there are no formal services for old people on Fogo Island (apart from a yearly dance held by the Lion's Club since 1973). To a large extent this is appropriate because, as already suggested, being old is not a glaring social problem. But transportation is a problem for most people in Grey Rock, especially for the elderly, the majority of whom do not have resident offspring who own automobiles. The style of transaction between elderly persons and those with automobiles takes the form of the patron-client relationship that has, for centuries, patterned economic exchange.

In the winter and spring, walking around the harbor to visit friends and kin and to the church, the parish club, and the shops is difficult for the old people. Roads are treacherous with snow and ice (and, since about 1972, careening snowmobiles). Crossing the harbor on the ice that forms in the winter is also difficult and dangerous, especially in the spring when the ice begins to break up. For trips to the cottage hospital clinic, the bank, and the larger shops in the town of Fogo, more than twenty miles away, an automobile is definitely needed. Few automobiles and drivers are available to the elderly. Most are being used by workers, including labor migrants. Owners of the rest are reluctant to make the trip to Fogo.   In 1974 only six miles of the distance was paved.   A trip to Fogo is a special occasion, a "time" (cf. Faris 1968), in more ways than one.   Because the clinic is busy and no appointments taken, the driver must wait around for two to six hours with nothing to do (there were no restaurants or taverns in the town in 1974).   The trip is extended further because passengers expect that they will be allowed to stop off at one or more of the small dry goods and grocery shops on the way.   For the driver, it means a full day and hours of sitting in the car.

The transportation problem is less severe for old people whose children have automobiles, but "you can't get anywhere without your own [kin] having a car."   For the many (more than half) of the elderly whose "own" did not have automobiles in 1974, the only recourse was hiring one of the three drivers occasionally willing to serve as a taxi to town.   Because any of these drivers might have excuses ("they all have excuses," people complain), negotiations are subtle and complicated.   They begin with a cautious question: "You wouldn't be going to Fogo this week?"   This is a typical way of opening transactions of dependency without forcing the recipient of the request to refuse outright (see Wadel 1973; Chairamonte 1970).   If the car owner shows some indecision or even a positive response, "Well, I don't know...I might be going," then the supplicant gives the reason for making the trip and waits for an offer to provide the ride.   The request is neither direct nor made with an explicit offer of money.   Understood is that the elderly are not likely to be niggardly about how much they will pay for the service.   It is up to the car owner to weigh silently the financial benefits of the trip (which, once negotiated, might involve four or five people, each contributing between $5 and $15) against the time lost, the wear and tear on the car, and opportunity costs.

The car owner will also consider the alternatives that are probably available to the supplicant versus the extent to which the person is dependent on him or her for a ride. In turn, over a longer period of time, elderly persons will try to use just one one driver for all of their trips in order to emphasize their dependence, creating in effect a relationship of client to reluctant patron.   The strength of this tactic was revealed when my next-door neighbor, an elderly woman without any close kin left in the community, consistently refused my offers to give her a ride around the harbor for Sunday Mass (although she gladly accepted my reluctantly offered trips to Fogo).   Instead she waited for a man and his family to drive all the way around the harbor to pick her up.   She paid him a few dollars each time.   She finally explained her behavior to me. If she stopped using him, he would start making excuses for not coming around. Since I would eventually leave the community, she would have no reliable transportation (even though there were six other cars in the immediate neighborhood). In 1975 she died of a stroke while walking around the harbor on a stormy night to play bingo at the church hall. She had not wanted to overuse her driver.

The style of this and other transactions reflects the exploitative relationships between fishing firms and fish merchants, an imperfect patron-client system framed by the morality of the community (cf. Faris 1972). While fish merchants usually needed the fish produced by the people of Grey Rock, the car owners willing to make trips around the harbor and to Fogo find the money given to them by their passengers small payment for the trips. Only the morality of the community keeps the diffuse paternalism of patronage effective for the elderly today. Emphasizing dependency is one way to activate that paternalism. Giving money is an attempt to convert it to an obligation. Dying rather than risking the overuse of paternalism reveals the fragility of the system.

CONCLUSION

It is customary to view high dependency ratios and a high proportion of the elderly as evidence of economic distress. In a marginal rural part of a welfare state the opposite is possible. From the perspective of Grey Rock, a high dependency ratio means not only that there are relatively few persons engaged in wage-earning and fishing, but also that many people are bringing social welfare money into the community—without the stigma of "being on the dole." The transfer payments that accrue to the very young and the very old include "family allowances," paid monthly to families for each dependent under the age of nineteen, and the old-age pensions. The state has taken much of the burden of supporting dependents that, in the past, resided in the producers themselves, alleviated only somewhat by the patronage of the fish merchants who controlled and profited from the outward flow of salt fish and the inward flow of foodstuffs and manufactured goods. In so doing, the state supports a system of production and reproduction that continues to generate cheap fish and labor for the larger system. Inadvertently, it also makes the economic status of the elderly pensioners in Grey Rock relatively high and sustains a cultural heritage that emphasizes household independence into old age.

The economics of the old-age pension in Grey Rock is only part of the picture. This exploration of the position and household types of the aged suggests the importance of cultural rules and patterns derived from an Irish and Atlantic fringe heritage and molded within the exigencies of the Newfoundland experience. Grey Rock's high valuation on the primacy and integrity of the nuclear family and its negative views toward joint- and stem-family households reflect a historically deep (Laslett 1977) and geographically widespread (Arensberg 1963; Treas 1975) cultural pattern, given special intensity by an Irish Catholic heritage. Emphasized also have been the distinct features of culture and social organization that affect the quality of life for the elderly of Grey Rock: virilocality, the family fishing firm, village endogamy, ultimogeniture, patrilineal inheritance, the treatment of houses as movable and malleable commodities, and the style of transactions of dependency.

One small matter that this ethnography explains is why the celebration of one's sixty-fifth birthday in Grey Rock is an occasion for joy, not for anxiety about the unknowns of retirement. Birthdays are memorized widely: almost everyone can tell whose birthday is on a given day. A sixty-fifth birthday is anticipated by one and all in the community and is celebrated widely. Friends and relatives come to visit and to imbibe home-brewed beer, commercial beer, moonshine, and rum. They bring no gifts, but bear witness to the coming of age, which is very special in Grey Rock. People come and go and stay into the night, sharing and reproducing the culture of the community through their gossip, songs, dances, recitations. A sixty-fifth birthday is almost as good as a wake.

Chronological age is not, by itself, "a particularly salient variable...in explaining interesting behavior" (Maddox 1972:294). Nor should we expect that a focus on old people in a society will yield explanations of the organization and culture of that society, except as our elderly informants help us in that quest and through their lives intensify and reveal the subject matter of anthropology.

NOTES

[1]The data from which this essay derives were obtained during predoctoral field research on Fogo Island between 1971 and 1974 and many postdoctoral visits since then. Predoctoral research was supported by a traineeship of the

National Institute of General Medical Sciences under the auspices of Columbia University's program in ecological anthropology, by a dissertation fellowship from the Woodrow Wilson Foundation, and by a research fellowship from the Institute of Social and Economic Research of Memorial University, Newfoundland. I am indebted to my elderly friends in Grey Rock and other Fogo Island communities and to Rutgers University's Program in Gerontology for wakening my interest in old people as old people. I am also indebted to George Morren, Michael Moffatt, and Miriam Kaprow for their criticisms and suggestions and to Vera Green for pushing me to the task.

[2]On Fogo Island merchants had switched from hiring labor, owning their own vessels and gear, and managing their own stages for fish processing to a reliance on family-based work groups by the beginning of the nineteenth century.

[3]The strength of virilocality is showed by the fact that in Grey Rock only three men live near their wives' agnates rather than their own. One lost his father when young and had no brothers. One moved into Grey Rock sixty years ago as a fisherman and stayed. The third recently agreed very reluctantly to live in Grey Rock because his wife teaches school there. Sometimes derisively, sometimes absentmindedly, these men are often called by their wives' surnames.

[4]The extended family property goes from the edge of the harbor to a more or less defined point inland and includes the outbuildings of the fishery, houses, barns, and space for kitchen gardens. Where the last is extensive, the property is referred to as a "garden"; where it is small and if the extended family has had a long history as relatively large-scale fishermen the terms "rooms" or "premise" are used instead. "Room" is an ancient term applied to fishery-related property in Newfoundland.

[5]Grey Rock's "image of limited good" in relation to jobs is expressed in many ways, including the difficulty of women obtaining work because, as residents say, "she doesn't need it as much as a man; after all, he has a family to support."

[6]In Newfoundland the term of address "boy" is more highly generalized than in Ireland: "my b'ye" is a casual term of address for any male, just as "skipper" is a normal

way of showing respect to a man, no matter what his relative age.

[7]Conflict is described as most intense between sis-
ters-in-law and mothers- and daughters-in-law.   It may
occur between father- and daughter-in-law and between
father- and son-in-law (cf. Firestone 1967:54).   Strained
relations among affines are for the most part limited to
intrahousehold and fishing crew associations.

[8]It is still expected that a woman should bear her first
child as soon as possible after marriage and that subsequent children will come in two- or three-year intervals.
Birth control was not available until very recently, but few
Grey Rock women use accepted means of contraception even
now.

[9]Newfoundland's school system is mostly run by the
churches.   On the island each church had its own school
system from kindergarten or first grade through eleventh
grade.   Each community had its own schools for each of its
major denominations.   In 1969 a regional, multidenomina-
tional high school was built and lower grades were
consolidated within Protestant and Catholic groupings.

REFERENCES

Arensberg, C.M.
    1963 The Old World Peoples: The Place of European
        Cultures in World Ethnography.   Anthropological
        Quarterly 36:75-99.

Arensberg, C.M. and S.T. Kimball
    1968 Family and Community in Ireland (second edition).
        Cambridge: Harvard University Press.

Breton, Y.
    1973 A Comparative Study of Work Groups in an
        Eastern Canadian Peasant Fishing Community:
        Bilateral Kinship and Adaptive Processes.
        Ethnology
        12:393-418.

Britan, G.M.
1974 Fishermen and Workers: The Processes of
Stability and Change in a Rural Newfoundland
Community. Ph.D. dissertation, Columbia
University.

Chiaramonte, L.J.
1970 Craftsman-client Contracts; Interpersonal
Relations in a Newfoundland Fishing Community.
St. John's: Institute of Social and Economic
Research.

Evans, E.E.
1973 The Personality of Ireland: Habitat, Heritage,
and History. Cambridge: Cambridge University
Press.

Faris, J.C.
1968 Validation in Ethnographic Description: The
Lexicon of "Occasions" in Cat Harbour. Man
(n.s.) 3:112-124.

1972 Cat Harbour: A Newfoundland Fishing Settlement.
St. John's: Institute of Social and Economic
Research.

Finberg, H.P.R.
1969 West-Country Historical Studies. New York:
A.M. Kelley.

Firestone, M.M.
1967 Brothers and Rivals: Patrilocality in Savage
Cove. St. John's: Institute of Social and
Economic Research.

Fox, R.
1978 The Tory Islanders: A People of the Celtic
Fringe. Cambridge: Cambridge University
Press.

Hammel, E.A.
1972 The Zadruga as Process. In Household and Family
in Past Time. P. Laslett, ed. Pp. 335-373.
Cambridge: Cambridge University Press.

Kennedy, R.E., Jr.
    1973 The Irish: Emigration, Marriage, and Fertility.
         Berkeley: University of California Press.

Kenny, M.
    1963 Europe: The Atlantic Fringe.   Anthropological
         Quarterly 36:100-119.

Laslett, P.
    1977 The History of Aging and the Aged.   In Family
         Life and Illicit Love in Earlier Generations.   P.
         Laslett, ed., Pp. 174-213.   Cambridge:
         Cambridge University Press.

Maddox, G.L.
    1972 Age As Explanation.   Science 178:294-295.

Mauss, M.
    1967 The Gift.   New York: W.W. Norton.

McCay, B.J.
    1978 Systems Ecology, People Ecology, and the
         Anthropology of Fishing Communities.   Human
         Ecology 6(4):397-422.

    1979 "Fish is Scarce:" Fisheries Modernization on Fogo
         Island, Newfoundland.   In North Atlantic Maritime
         Cultures.   R. Anderson, ed. Pp. 155-189.   The
         Hague: Mouton.

Moreton, J.
    1863 Life and Work in Newfoundland.   London:
         Rivingtons.

Sider, G.
    1980 The Ties that Bind: Culture and Agriculture,
         Property, and Propriety in the Newfoundland
         Village Fishery.   Social History 5 (1):1-39.

Treas, J.
    1975 Aging and the Family.   In Aging: Scientific
         Perspectives and Social Issues.   D. Woodruff and
         J. Birren, eds. Pp. 92-108.   New York: Van
         Nostrand.

Wadel, C.
    1973 Now, Whose Fault is That? The Struggle for
          Self- Esteem in the Face of Chronic
          Unemployment. St. John's: Institute of Social
          and Economic Research.

4

Nutrition and Aging
Considered Cross-Culturally

CHRISTINE S. WILSON

Nutrition research has contributed to knowledge of at least three aspects of aging, or the conditions of aged members of population groups. With respect to the first--the role of nutrients and their interactions in senescence (the aging process)--a good deal has been published. On the second--nutritional needs of aging and the aged--some published works are also available. Concerning comparisons of dietary and related treatment of elderly people across cultures (of perhaps greater import to social scientists) far less information is available in the literature.

One of the difficulties both in studying and in writing about nutrition and aging arises from the fact that the aged or elderly are not homogeneous in the sense that ethnic groups may be considered to belong to the same subculture. Not only do older people in technically developed countries belong to varied economic and educational strata on which ethnic group differences may be superimposed; they also vary widely in degree and extent of the biological aging process--senescence. This heterogeneity should be kept in mind in considering statements referring to a hypothetical need that are made about nutritional needs or the effects of nutrients on a particular bodily function in older or elderly people. The range for any nutrient need or the function to which it applies is necessarily large.

Nutritional needs are also altered or affected by degenerative diseases, such as diabetes, cancer, hypertension, cardiac disorders, kidney failure, arthritis, and rheumatism, which are frequent concomitants of growing older and more prevalent among older age groups. Whether dietary treatment can prevent most of these conditions has not yet been proven. Diet alterations may alleviate some symptoms or effects, dietary cures are moot. Because there is a vast literature on nutrition for many of these illnesses, its role in disease among the elderly will not be treated here, except for an occasional brief mention. Instead it is assumed that the populations discussed are as normally healthy as can reasonably be expected in the latter part of life.

INTERRELATIONS OF NUTRITION AND AGING

The effect of diet on longevity has been studied primarily in experimental animals under controlled, laboratory conditions. Natural experiments on human beings are rare; they would need to be retrospective, with all the uncertainties attending after-the-fact data determination. Deliberate experiments are difficult to do, if not unthinkable; nor can they be expected to be carried out for long enough periods to determine the effects of particular regimens on the lifespan and health of the eater.

About fifty years ago Clive McCay, a nutrition scientist at Cornell University, conducted a series of experiments on rats showing that restriction of food or caloric intake over a lifetime markedly increased lifespan compared with that of rats of the same biologic makeup that were allowed to eat the same laboratory food at will (McCay, Crowell and Maynard 1935). Other researchers have noted that early underfeeding can lead to the stunting of growth, delay in attainment of maturity (fertility) and in the rate of other biological processes in animals (Kahn 1972). A severe degree of undernourishment also deprives the young animal of other nutrients in amounts needed for growth during development, since standard laboratory chow provides vitamins and minerals required by growing animals in addition to sources of energy and protein. Ross (1977), who has more recently studied the timing of maximum effectiveness of a reduced diet in relation to longevity in rats, found that a short-term restriction immediately after weaning was almost as effective as a life-time reduction in food intake in its effect on lifespan. Intermittent fasting throughout life has similar results. If underfeeding was begun while the animals were still suckling, however, lifespan was shortened (Widdowson and Kennedy 1962). Rats restricted through the postweaning period and then fed ad libitum were longer lived than those in which restriction was instituted at maturity.

The caloric intact of McCay's food-restricted, longevous rats was reduced almost two-thirds from that of a normal rat. Felstein in a (British) study of old age (1973) pointed also to the work of McCarrison, comparing rats fed the diets of tribal people (Pathans) and Sikhs in India (whole grain and fresh vegetable foods) with other rats fed a Madras or Bengal diet of much rice and few, less fresh vegetables, or those given a typical British working-class diet of boiled potatoes and vegetables, white bread, margarine, and tinned meats. The animals fed the fresh, relatively unprocessed foods had, over time, better survival rates due to better health and resistance to disease, with minimal infant and maternal mortality.

A rat is not biologically or in other ways like a human; nor is it like a mouse. Some strains of mice demonstrate responses similar to those of McCay's or McCarrison's rats when placed on similar regimens; others do not. It is generally held that for most species, including human beings, overfeeding in early life hastens maturity and shortens lifespan, whereas overfeeding after the organism has reached the adult state increases the incidence of degenerative diseases, either metabolic or structural-functional ones.

NUTRITIONAL NEEDS OF AGING AND THE AGED

The need for specific nutrients does not change greatly upon aging, although decrease in digestive, particularly absorptive, functions may be expected. As with other physiologic systems, great individual differences in slowing of these processes may be encountered. A British study (Corless 1973) suggested daily nutrient needs of the elderly to be as follows: vitamin A 5000 International Units (1500 micrograms [ug.], expressed as retinol equivalents), thiamine 0.8 mg., riboflavin 1.3 mg., folic acid 250 ug. This researcher found folic acid deficiency common in the elderly. A dietary and biochemical study of 100 free-living healthy older people sixty-three to ninety-six years of age in Oregon found calcium, vitamin A, and thiamine to be the nutrients most likely to be deficient, especially in women (Yearick, Wang and Pisias 1980). Although 41 percent of these people had low serum protein levels, 90 percent had acceptable values for most other nutrients measured biochemically, except folic acid. Twenty people had low levels of this vitamin in their diets. This intake was reflected in low serum blood levels of folic acid.

The 1980 Recommended Dietary Allowances of the U.S. Food and Nutrition Board for persons over fifty years are presented separately by sex, and assume an average body weight of 70 kg. (154 lbs.) for males, 55 kg. (120 lbs.) for females. Recommended intakes of vitamin A by these criteria are 1000 ug. for males, 800 ug. for females. Thiamine intake of older males should be 1.2 mg. daily; for older females 1.0 mg. is suggested. The amount of riboflavin recommended for males is 1.4 mg. per day, that for females, 1.2 mg. Intakes of folic acid for both sexes at all ages beyond childhood should be 400 ug. per day, according to these standards. The Food and Nutrition Board does not recommend reductions in intake of other essential nutrients after age fifty, with the exception of iron for postmenopausal women. Allowance for this mineral is lowered from 18 to 10 mg. per day at that time, since bodily losses are reduced upon cessation of the menstrual flow.

The Recommended Dietary Allowances do suggest adjustments in caloric intake with advancing age, from 2700 ($\pm$ 400) for males at age fifty to 2400 ($\pm$ 400) between the ages of fifty-one and seventy-five and 2050 ($\pm$ 400) for those seventy-six and older. Figures for women in these age groups are 2000 ($\pm$ 400), 1800 ($\pm$ 400), and 1600 ($\pm$ 400), respectively. The reasons for these recommended reductions are that nutrition scientists generally hold that activity, as well as resting metabolism, decreases in the later decades, lowering energy needs. Although this adjustment has been made by the United States nutrition authorities, they have not modified downward their recommendations for intakes of the B-vitamins thiamine, riboflavin, and niacin--all of which function in the metabolism of carbohydrate foods and other energy sources. Hence, needs for these nutrients are tied to and related to caloric intake when estimates are made of amounts needed. One reason for this decision is that reducing the amount of energy eaten means that the amount of food eaten is also reduced. Most foods that supply energy--starch and other staples--also carry other needed vitamins and minerals. The older body may have somewhat increased, rather than decreased, needs for the carried nutrients. When energy intake is lower, these other requirements may properly be met by vitamin supplements, taken upon the advice of a knowledgeable professional, such as a dietician or nutritionist, unless more nutrient-dense foods can be eaten. Some authorities (Weg 1979) feel, since the older organism is less efficient than younger ones in carrying out tasks, and it needs more energy to do them, that energy intakes should not be decreased for those in the older age brackets.

It is hoped that the foregoing somewhat scientific explanation illustrates that appropriate diets, adequate in all
known nutrients, are just as important in old age as they
are for those of younger years.   It is also almost academic
to suggest that good dietary habits in younger years may
redound to the benefit of everyone growing older.   Food
habits tend to persist when other behaviors change.   If
they were somewhat eclectic in younger years, choosing
from a wide and varied food supply, continuation of such
an eating pattern should help maintain reasonably good nutrition status into later life.   Some factors over which the
individual may have little control can influence nutritional
adequacy of diets at all ages, particularly in the waning
decades.   These may be arbitrarily categorized as social
and physiological.

SOCIAL FACTORS AFFECTING NUTRITION OF THE AGING

The economic status of an individual or family has a
profound effect on their nutritional state, determining what
they can afford to buy to eat.   A study by Guthrie and
coworkers of elderly rural Pennsylvanians found that nutrient adequacy of these people's diets was directly related to
income, intakes being positively correlated to greater income
(Guthrie, Black and Madden 1972).   More recently Kohrs
and others found in a study of participants in a congregate
meal program (one in which people go or are brought to
centers where hot meals are prepared and served in a colle-
gial setting) that educational level and preretirement occupation also related positively to nutrients consumed.   Those
of higher educational and work attainments choose better
nutrient sources than those with less education (Kohrs et
al. 1979).

The longitudinal British study by Corless (1973)
showed that there is an elite group whose nutrient intakes
are high and change little with age.   Guthrie and her colleagues noted that the consumption pattern of all the elderly in their study resembled that of low income populations
of all ages, although only half their sample of households of
old people were at or below the official poverty level at the
time of the study (1970).

Other behavioral or environmental factors affecting
satisfactory eating habits of the elderly include being alone,
not wanting to eat or cook, lack of adequate or suitable
cooking equipment, and mobility problems that could hinder
self-care or interfere with shopping.   Some portion of older
citizens may have medically-related, modern folk beliefs

about foods that are either suitable or to be avoided in real or imagined health problems.

PHYSIOLOGICAL FACTORS INFLUENCING NUTRITIONAL STATE

Some physical or physiological problems may also interfere with optimal dietary practices of this age group. Older people may have few or no teeth, or poorly fitting dentures, due in part to shrinkage of tissues. Both conditions can limit the foods a person chooses or is able to eat. Altered digestion or inadequate fiber in the diet can lead to constipation, which in turn depresses appetite. The senses of taste and smell are often reduced in older people. Glanville, Kaplan, and Fisher (1964) found an exponential decline in these senses after the second decade of life. This is at least in part due to a normal involution of the taste buds. These senses too affect appetite. Taste and smell are reduced at all ages in persons whose intake of zinc is low. The best dietary sources of zinc are animal protein foods, which may be low in the diets of those of low income or of people who cannot chew. Such reduced gustatory awareness may lead to putting increased amounts of sugar and salt on food. Langan and Yearick (1976), testing the effects of improved oral hygiene on taste perceptions of elderly people, found that such treatment increased their ability to detect sweet and salt but had no effect on responses to bitter or sour food. Much earlier research (Laird and Breen 1939) suggested older people like a tart flavor much better than younger people do.

Some health problems of aged people may be directly related to nutrient status. The most common is probably osteoporosis, thinning or demineralizaton of the basic structure of bones, the trabeculae, leading to increased risk of broken or fractured bones. Although more common in older women, it also occurs in men. Prolonged low intakes of calcium (from early to middle years) are at least partially responsible for the condition. Vitamin D is also needed in its prevention, since it aids in the calcium absorption in the intestine, which decreases naturally with age. British studies suggest that some of the mental confusion seen in the aging may be due in part to a deficiency of ascorbic acid (found in fruits and vegetables), vitamin B-12 (another nutrient best contributed by animal protein foods), and folic acid (in which leafy and other green vegetables, legumes, and whole wheat products are rich.

NUTRITIONAL TREATMENT OF THE AGED CROSS-CULTURALLY

Some cultures set people apart or define their status by assigning them different types of foods or diets, according to the age they have attained. There are children's, adults', and old folks' foods in many cultures--foods one is old enough, or too old, to eat according to this cultural classification.

Preindustrial societies that are supportive of their elders include food in their care. Thus Malays and Mexican Americans almost daily take part or all of a main meal to an older relative living alone nearby. Among the Muslims of Sri Lanka, a son-in-law is obliged to give his father- and mother-in-law a rice meal every day (Yalman 1971:302). The Chinese venerate old people. Cantonese have special foods for those without teeth, a kind of concentrated essence of proteins (from beef or chicken) to substitute for the soups taken by younger people (Mo 1983). Beardsley, Hall, and Ward (1959:111) reported that in villages in Japan, grandparents cook and eat separately from the rest of the family (although living with them) as a symbol of retirement from active household headship.

There are other cultures in which people too old to function normally are discarded or discard themselves by stopping eating. Thus Fowler and Fowler (1971) quoted John Wesley Powell's nineteenth-century observations of the Numa of western North America, among whom "suicide" by starvation of its old women was held to be meritorious. Death of a well-respected family member may lead all survivors to alter food consumption temporarily to items less well liked. Widows may be singled out for longer abstention from familiar foods because these would remind them of the departed. The extreme case may be South India, where a widow eats one meal a day. It is thought that eating more in this state would be unhealthy (Katona-Apte 1975).

In some Western nations older people may appear to be set aside after retirement age by the provision of retirement centers and nursing care facilities, where they may be fed and otherwise cared for. In the United States there is a Nutrition Program for Older Americans in the Office of Human Development of the U.S. Administration on Aging, Department of Health and Human Services. This administers funds from Title VII, the Older Americans Act of 1965. This program gives education and counseling in nutrition, health, consumer protection, and shopping assistance, among other aid, and referral to health services. Food, or cash, or food stamps is distributed for this program by the U.S. Department of Agriculture. States have autonomy to choose cash or food stamps for distribution to clients, who must meet household income eligibility requirements. If a state elects to distribute food, the U.S. Department of Agriculture buys it or supplies it from surplus commodities. Other legislation (Title XX) provides social services to the aging, such as homemaker and chore services, foster- and day-care, and transportation. Home-delivered (Meals on Wheels, for example) and congregate meals served at central facilities are included under this latter law. The services and food are available to all, but those able to do so pay for the services and the food.

THE MYTHS AND REALITIES OF NUTRITION AND THE AGING PROCESS

A few words should be included about beliefs that certain dietary practices can increase life expectancy. Aside from the restrictions discussed at the beginning of this chapter, no magic treatment to prolong life or improve its quality is thus far known. The diets of longevous people tend to resemble those of their less long-living compatriots more strongly than they differ. Yogurt, said by some to be the reason the Abkhasians of the Caucasus live longer, is simply a good dietary source of calcium and some B-vitamins. The very old are, finally, a selected population of survivors. To reach this state, consumption of a varied diet in not too great amounts above needs appears to be one positive factor. Certainly, as with other aspects of aging, more research is needed on the roles of nutrition in aging and the aged.

REFERENCES

Anonymous
    1969 Old Age, Nutrition, Mental Confusion. British Medical Journal 5671:608-609.

Beardsley, Richard H., John W. Hall and Robert E. Ward
    1959 Village Japan. Chicago: The University of Chicago Press.

Corless, D.
    1973 Medicine in Old Age. Diet in the Elderly. British Medical Journal 5885:158-160.

Felstein, Ivor
    1973 Living to Be a Hundred: A Study of Old Age.
         New York: Hippocrene Books.

Food and Nutrition Board
    1980 Recommended Dietary Allowances, ed. 9, revised.
         Washington: National Academy of Sciences.

Fowler, Don D. and Catherine S., eds.
    1971 Anthropology of the Numa: John Wesley Powell's
         Manuscripts on the Numic Peoples of Western
         North America, 1868-1880. Washington:
         Smithsonian Institution, Contributions to
         Anthropology.

Glanville, Edward V., Arnold R. Kaplan and Roland Fisher
    1964 Age, Sex, Taste Sensitivity. Journal of
         Gerontology. 19:474-478.

Guthrie, Helen A., Kathleen Black, and J. Patrick Madden
    1972 Nutritional Practices of Elderly Citizens in Rural
         Pennsylvania. St. Louis, Mo.: Mosby Co.

Kahn, Alfred J.
    1972 Development, Aging, and Life Duration: Effects
         of Nutrient Restriction. American Journal of
         Clinical Nutrition 25:822-828.

Katona-Apte, Judit
    1975 The Relevance of Nourishment to the Reproductive
         Cycle of the Female in India. In Being Female:
         Reproduction, Power and Change. Dana Raphael,
         ed. Pp. 43-48. The Hague: Mouton Publishers.

Kohrs, Mary Bess, Pauline O'Hanlon, Gary Krause and
James Nordstrom
    1979 Title VII--Nutrition Program for the Elderly. II.
         Relationships of Socio-Economic Factors
         to One Day's Intake. Journal of the American
         Dietetic Association 75:537-542.

Laird, D.A. and W.J. Breen
    1939 Sex and Age Alterations in Taste Preferences.
         Journal of the American Dietetic Association.
         15:549-550.

Langan, M.J. and Elisabeth S. Yearick
    1976 The Effects of Improved Oral Hygiene on Taste
        Perception of the Elderly. Journal of Gerontology
        31:413-418.

McCay, C.M., M.F. Crowell and L.A. Maynard
    1935 Effect of Retarded Growth upon Length of Life
        Span and upon Ultimate Body Size. Journal of
        Nutrition 10:63-79.

Mo, Bertha
    1983 Personal communication.

Ross, Morris H.
    1977 Dietary Behavior and Longevity. Nutrition
        Reviews 35:257-265.

Weg, Ruth B.
    1979 Old Age: Changing Dietary Needs. The
        Professional Nutritionist 11:1-5.

Widdowson, Elsie M. and G.C. Kennedy
    1962 Rate of Growth, Mature Weight and Life-Span.
        Proceedings of the Royal Society of London,
        Series B (Biology) 156:96-108.

Yalman, Nur
    1971 Under the Bo Tree. Studies in Caste, Kinship,
        and Marriage in the Interior of Ceylon.
        Berkeley: University of California Press.

Yearick, Elisabeth S., Mei-Shan L. Wang and
Susan J. Pisias
    1980 Nutritional Status of the Elderly: Dietary and
        Biochemical Findings. Journal of Gerontology
        35:663-671.

II: INTRA-CULTURAL DIVERSITY

Introduction

There is a human tendency to classify, and forms of classification vary from one cultural context to another. In the United States and other parts of the Western world such categories as technical versus general curricula in educational institutions are regarded as discrete phenomena. The same is generally true for racial and ethnic classifications when we make generalizations about social groups. However, a tendency to group people into familiar categories may obscure important dimensions of diversity that we wish to underscore in this volume.

In this section, we emphasize diversity among the aged in the United States. There are two main problems addressed in the following chapters. (1) Stereotypical assumptions made about particular groups may structure generalizations about the aged within those groups and obscure differences found among individuals; (2) Sweeping generalizations about the aged in America may ignore dimensions of diversity that genuinely covary with ethnic identity. Our present knowledge of aging phenomena may, in fact, be inadequate for explaining the variation and dealing with the problems that we find in the United States.

Green addresses the first point forthrightly in chapter 5, emphasizing the range of diversity among aging blacks in America. She deplores studies that refer to "The Black Aged" as a monolithic group and criticizes attempts to use overgeneralized material in the formulation of policy concerning elderly black people. Green suggests several

dimensions of diversity that cross-cut that of ethnic identity among elderly blacks. These are: class stratification,
rural/urban differences, North/South regional differences,
intra-regional variation, local-level or community variation,
and individual variation. Consideration of these dimensions
in studies of elderly blacks in communities in the United
States would add complexities, but, Green believes, would
facilitate the development of practical programs where they
are needed.

Another aspect of intra-group diversity is discussed
by Drew and Waters in chapter 7. They have studied the
attitudes of low-income Puerto Rican adults and high school
seniors toward older people in the workplace. These reveal
a possible intergenerational conflict that could have a noticeable social impact. Within one ethnic group, older people are seen as dissatisfied with their work and disabled to
an extent that exceeds realistic assessment. Thus, stereotypes can be generated from within as well as from without.

With these emphases in mind, we turn to the second
problem addressed in this section: sweeping generalizations
made about the aged in America may ignore dimensions of
diversity that genuinely covary with ethnic or subethnic
group identity. We look at two groups in which we might
expect to find problematic situations for the aged. First,
there is Faulkner and Heisel's study (ch. 6) of inner-city
black aged who live with the difficulties of low incomes and
minority-group status. Second, there is Marea Teski's (ch.
8) study of the elderly among an immigrant population of
Kalmuk Mongols, a culture that has endured generations of
political oppression and forced migration. In examining
these populations, we are impressed with the extent to
which they have evolved ingenious solutions for situations
that might otherwise be problematic. As Teski suggests,
ethnicity becomes a context for experience. It becomes an
internal reservoir of cultural resources that may be used to
manage problems imposed from without.

Stack (1975) has drawn our attention to the ways in
which strategies for survival may be developed by the residents of impoverished black communities. Faulkner and
Heisel describe an informal exchange network that serves
the needs of the inner-city black elderly in their study.
They have uncovered a local system in which family and
neighbors become givers, receivers, and exchangers on a
day-to-day basis. Faulkner and Heisel do not deny that
the elderly in this community have problems and unfulfilled
needs. Their study suggests that those involved in policy
formulation and service delivery might wisely take notice of
a locally evolved adaptive strategy in planning for the
aged.

Similarly, when Teski finds healthy, serene, well-adjusted old people in the Kalmuk Mongol community, she attributes this phenomenon to the contexts in which Kalmuk culture interprets past experience and the phenomenon of aging. Old age is regarded positively. It is not considered difficult or problematic. To approach this community with the notion that aging is problematic would be to impose the views of other American communities upon this one. Using such an approach, resources could be misdirected and populations could be alienated rather than assisted. These examples underscore a point well stated by Faulkner and Heisel:

> the accumulated evidence of differences between and among the aged of this country's many ethnic and racial groups falls far short of the comprehensive inventory needed to guide policy formulation and service delivery for an expanding population.

We believe that the present state of the art also shows a need to increase the existing body of scholarship to enable useful generalizations to be made about the aged in America.

Further resources on these topics can be found in the following sections of the Annotated Bibliography: Section II.A. deals with studies of the aged in single ethnic, regional, or other groups in the United States. Included are studies on black, Hispanic, and Asian Americans. Section III.A. provides sources comparing two or more ethnic, national, or racial groups in the United States. Additionally, Section IV., which deals with residential types, is relevant to the concerns addressed by several authors.

REFERENCE

Stack, Carol B.
    1975 All Our Kin: Strategies for Survival in a
        Black Community.   New York: Harper and Row.

5

Underlying Issues of Diversity in the Study of Aging Blacks

VERA GREEN

While the elderly have been rediscovered in the last few years (Vinyard 1978), authors such as Jackson conclude that information about elderly United States blacks follows a familiar pattern:

> ...gerontological literature about Blacks, still generally sparse, fragmented and inconclusive, despite its recent proliferation, is heavily influenced by myths oozing with racial biases. Inadequate racial comparisons by some geronto-logists strengthen these myths. (Jackson 1978:15)

Jackson's statement holds true for many anthropological studies of elderly blacks as well as for studies about blacks in general. Anthropologists should know better, in view of their emphasis on specifics, or microlevel studies, that increase our understanding of macrolevel phenomena. Yet the range of variation within a given population is not always indicated. Research populations are sometimes not even introduced in such a way that the total range of variation within that specific group can be understood.

Years ago, Linton (1936), a pioneering American anthropologist, pointed out that each culture has extant as well as potential universals and specialties, alternatives and individual, idiosyncratic traits or tendencies.

A.F.C. Wallace, in his classic work on culture and personality, indicated that:

> Culture shifts in policy from generation to generation with kaleidoscopic variety and is characterized internally not by uniformity, but by diversity of both individuals and groups, many of whom are in continuous and overt conflict in one subsystem and in active cooperation in another. (Wallace 1970:24)

Wallace further stated:

> ...nor can the phenomenological world of an individual, or of a people, be assumed to be understood by the anthropologist, once he can predict the movements of their bodies; rather, he must recognize the possibility of a radical diversity of mazeways that have their orderly relationship guaranteed not by the sharing of uniformity, but by their capacities for mutual prediction. (Ibid.)

Wallace discussed the relative importance of the organization of diversity versus the replication of uniformity:

> For descriptive purposes serving only to delineate the preponderant characteristics of a group, particularly in comparing them with some other group (for example, in comparing one tribe with another, or one generation with another), the replication-of-uniformity approach is convenient and serviceable. But for the purpose of developing empirical support of theoretical analysis of the relation of socio-cultural and personality systems, the organization-of-diver-sity approach is essential; in such contexts, the replication-of-uniformity approach is actually misleading. (ibid.:123)

In order to understand the basis of an organization-of-diversity approach, the range as well as the cause of diversity within a population must be analyzed. Therefore, historical studies are of critical importance in social science research. Marxist scholars have stressed the importance of history in our understanding of sociocultural phenomena as well as the range of possibilities of given phenomena. Godelier in his Perspectives in Marxist Anthropology is not far from Linton or Wallace in considering the establishment of a range of possibilities--a basic prerequisite for the study of any social or cultural group.

DIVERSITY AMONG BLACKS

There have been few attempts to establish a range of diversity in the study of United States or Caribbean populations of African descent. Many studies select out the southern regional and/or lower class components, as Blauner (1970) pointed out. Blauner is one of the few scholars to stress that: (1) "a mechanical application of the model of immigrant ethnic group assimilation [has been applied] to a very different cultural experience" (1970:349); and (2) "the Black cultural experience more resembles an alternating current than it does a direct current" (ibid.:351). Hence the culture of black populations is often perceived as "ambiguous" or "of paradoxical nature" by outsiders (ibid.:361). Blauner further indicates:

> Compared once again to the immigrant groups upon which sociological models of ethnic group assimilation were built, the Negro minority is extremely large and highly differentiated. At the high points of immigrant ethnicity, most of these groups were small, their members concentrated in one or more cities and socially in the lower classes. During the period that Black culture has been building up (including the present) the Afro-American minority continues to differentiate itself. The middle classes grow; new political and religious movements proliferate (e.g., the Muslims). (1970:350)

Blauner's statement was made during the late 1960s. Since then, approaches to the study of United States blacks have continued in more or less the same vein. That is, the majority of scholars select one or two segments of the total reality of the life of black people for study, thereby strengthening the process of reification of certain segments. By contrast, they neglect other segments that ought to be included in the total range of possibilities. How may we insure that a broader base is incorporated in our research given the tendency to limit the field? Devons and Gluckman, for example, indicated that "limitation is vital if his [the social scientist's] study is to be manageable ... with limitation goes simplification, which also seems necessary in order to isolate what appear to be the essential features of the problem under examination" (1964:17). As more attention is drawn to the plight of elderly blacks, it is hoped that social science studies of this group, particularly those presented from an anthropological perspective, shall proceed differently.

It is possible that only some black Americans and a few others have realized that the range of norms in black America has never been established. Division into areas, such as those demarcated by scholars such as Arensberg for the United States as a whole and by Pearsall (1966) and Owlesy (1949) for the South specifically, is lacking for United States black populations. The range must first be delineated.

I offer a suggestion for overcoming the dangers of oversimplification in the study of elderly blacks, in particular, and black populations, in general, in the Americas and in other complex societies. Let us consider the levels of data that may be viewed prior to reconstructing the limited number of possibilities that may occur. Godelier (1977) stated in Perspectives in Marxist Anthropology: "We must therefore go further with our analysis in order to explain the possibilities which depart from the norm, their occurrence or lack of occurrence in other aspects of social life. We ourselves have not been able to go so far, but we have at least recognized the problem." If we prepare a basic multilevel or checklist we may overcome the arguments of those who insist on the limiting and simplifying process inherent in approaches to some modern scientific studies. These are the components of a model which may be ideal for sample consideration and data analysis of diasporan populations:

* Stratification, i.e., class and more simplified forms of ranking that may exist.
* The rural/urban dimension.
* The North/South dimension.
* The intraregional differences. These result from the interplay between variable historical and ecological factors. Examples that may apply to United States blacks are: the South--the southern Tidewater-Piedmont, the coastal Southeast, the Lowland South, areas of French tradition and Appalachia; the North--the old eastern colonial area, the Midwest, Far West, Southwest, and post-1920 ghetto constellations; areas of Indian influence, which are found in both the South and the North.
* Local or community variations. For example, in the state of Mississippi which is located in the lowland South, there are variable settlements such as Mound Bayou, which is a black town with its own administration, as compared with others that are white dominated.
* The final level of data entails individual variation in adaptive responses.

A study of any segment of the population of a community must present or place the population in terms of all of
the above considerations.   Such placement would in itself
acknowledge the existence of a range of possibilities and
the interrelationships between several levels of analysis.
Even though the scope of a specific problem would be limited or simplified, the awareness of the scope of the population affected would not be limited.

In the study of responses to change and stress and
patterns of coping behavior among the black elderly in the
Philadelphia area, Wilbur Watson indicated the difficulty that
might result from faulty use of social science terminology:

> If we permitted ourselves the convenience of con-
> ventional social science labels, it would appear
> ... that members of the "upper" economic class,
> who account for nine percent in the distribution,
> were clearly the least numerous in this popula-
> tion.   Following in order by frequency were mem-
> bers of the "lower" class, fifteen percent, and fi-
> nally, there was the "middle" class, constituting
> seventy-six percent of the total.   But, as we will
> see in the discussion that follows, such an inter-
> pretation could be grossly misleading.   It is ar-
> guable   that   our   sample   is   overwhelmingly
> lower-class black, not middle-class in characteris-
> tics.   (1980:14,15)

Some social scientists, and among these some black
scholars, resist considerations of class where blacks are
concerned.   They are of the opinion that the lower position
of blacks vis-a-vis whites within the racially perceived
United States socioeconomic order effectively places all
blacks in a lower-class position.   While this argument may
be true at the level of grand theory, it loses its power as
other than a backdrop for understanding forces operative at
the practical/applied and local levels.   Watson, as others,
illustrates that there are differential responses by class
which underscore the "significance of socio-economic class
in studies of stress and old age" (1980:15).

The historical data provided below for Virginia illustrate the basis for variable class position for United States
blacks.   Class within the diasporan context involves not
only the more or less powerlessness in the face of everyday
life events, as mentioned by many social scientists; it involves relative degrees of psychological and social isolation
and/or an inability to utilize local, regional, and national
service institutions.   Class relates generally to comparative
degrees of exposure and opportunity.

STUDYING THE BLACK ELDERLY

If we consider studies of elderly blacks to date, few if any include discussion of research populations in terms of more than two of the dimensions I have outlined. Those scholars who have discussed heterogeneity among black populations--e.g., Jackson (1978)--seldom analyze more than the rural/urban dimension, class, or North/South provenience of populations. Jackson, for example, generally qualifies her discussions of the populations under study by specifying "southern" and by providing the areal context--e.g., rural Alabama. Blake (1978-79) indicates the specific southern provenience of the population he studies as isolated rural inhabitants of the Sea Islands of coastal South Carolina and Georgia. Others, such as Meyers (1978-79), indicate the area--Jackson, Mississippi--but there is no discussion as to whether the members of the population were primarily Jackson-born and reared (i.e., urban) or whether they may have been recent migrants to the city from rural areas. Moland (1978) focuses on black aged in Claiborn, DeSoto, and Red River parishes in rural Louisiana. He does not specify the extent to which the black population is of purely English-speaking Protestant tradition, mixed French (Creole or Cajun) and English tradition or solely French-speaking Catholic tradition. Louisiana is one area in which subcultural variation clearly cuts across patterns of socioeconomic adjustment among blacks. This is especially true of the elderly as they were socialized in an era when the communication networks were more limited and regional, and divergent local groups were more clearly isolated from one another.

Moland's study, like that of Faulkner and Heisel in this volume (ch. 6), emphasizes the role of social participation and "significant others" among the elderly and the importance of this factor for social service administrators and planners. This finding has implications for all elderly populations and may even be considered a universal need.

In the Louisiana context, some discussion of the sociocultural profiles of the inhabitants of the three parishes, in addition to their education and income, may have been meaningful. My own informants in Houston, Texas, have claimed that "French" families are even more kin- and extended-family oriented than "English" southern blacks. If this were so, to what extent might factors of this type have been applicable, but simply glossed over, if the subcultural backgrounds of informants were not mentioned.

Matters may be even more complicated when considering studies that focus on populations in the North, especially those located in areas I have designated "post-1920 ghetto constellations." The populations in these areas are the most heterogeneous of all black populations despite the tendency of migrants from given areas to reside near each other. In such situations even greater care should be taken to avoid a dangerous tendency to overhomogenize what may well be distinctive black populations. A number of scholars overlook the heterogeneity in their attempts to provide insights that will benefit aging blacks. Dancy (1977), for example, in providing a guide for practitioners working with black populations, implies that since the bulk of the black population comes from the South, the black elderly per se share common food, language, and coping patterns:

> Dietary preferences of individuals vary. After allowing for individual tastes and dietary restrictions due to health, however, there are some generalizations which can be made about food habits of the black elderly. These are based largely on traditional Southern cooking, for a high proportion of the aged black population is from the South. A history of poverty and rural life is also evident in the emphasis on cheaper meat cuts, variety meats, and game. (1977:26)

> In summary, the black elderly, like all groups, have certain culturally influenced preferences in food. The worker in the field of aging should know and be sensitive to these dietary preferences. If institutions, agencies, and nutrition programs become aware of favorite food and recipes in the black community, they will provide more satisfactory service to their clientele. (ibid.:27)

If we accept the importance of the components of the model for studying diasporan populations, Dancy's first paragraph cannot be accepted without outlining the points of variation, specifically those pertaining to region and class. The second paragraph, as it lacks specific reference to types of variation, would appear to add to the impression of homogeneity among elderly blacks.

In 1978, Carter discussed the need "for a study of the condition of the Black aged in Florida" (1978:42a) in an editorial for Black Aging. If simplistic lumping of black populations as "southern" were sufficient at the basic level of understanding and planning, surely there would be no need for specific studies of Florida blacks.

It is believed that blacks had progressive living conditions in pre-Civil War Virginia, with conditions varying ac-

cording to social and economic status. There were 58,042
free blacks in the state of Virginia in 1860. It should be
noted that during this period, 37 percent of the free black
population was mulatto as was 8 percent of the slave population. This information is provided to offset the idea that
free blacks were predominantly mulatto. That there was a
percentage of free individuals versus freedmen, the former
having often purchased their own freedom by utilizing por-
tions of their time to earn money for this purpose, allows
us to understand the possible basis for a middle
class—descendants of independent farmers, successful arti-
sans, mechanics, etc. This is in spite of the fact that
one-fourth of the blacks in the North and West compared to
only one-eighth in the South could be classified as middle
class during the earlier periods.

Class within the diasporan context is often related to
the degree of exposure and opportunity. The higher the
class, the more exposure and, consequently, the broader
the cultural inventory. For example, if diet were under
discussion, the point would not be that the diet of the
wealthier of a specific area of the South does not include
soul foods. The point is, rather, that it may include these
as well as a variety of other foods. If we were to follow
Dancy's recipe for satisfaction of the food preferences of
either blacks in the South or those who are residents of
any inner-city ghetto, the chances are high of limiting the
diets instead of responding to actual preferences. Again,
this might occur precisely because the ranges of dietary
preferences, even for the poor and consequently more isolated elderly blacks, have not been established. Rather
than implying blanket acceptance of statements such as offered by Dancy's "guide for paractioners," considered judg-
ment (Troll 1975:93) should involve not only specification of
the part of the South or North from whence the elderly
residents came but also their previous patterns of exposure
and participation. Thus the first four levels I have listed
would be employed.

In a similar fashion, the discussions of the role of religion and grandparenting among blacks may also be over-
emphasized when considering the black populations as a
whole as well as when comparing blacks to whites of similar
socioeconomic status (Jackson et al. 1977-78). Even when
comparing blacks to whites of similar backgrounds, problems
arise since the black samples of "northerners" are often not
of persons who are the descendants of people who have
been residing in the area for three or more generations.
Frequently the sample is either of mixed northern and
southern descent or of northern residents of southern descent. These factors are frequently not discussed ade-

quately. There is no need to state that the bulk of blacks
are of southern extraction. For resolution of this argument
the specific sectors of the South, whether rural or urban,
should be delineated. It should be remembered that old
Yankee cities such as New York, Philadelphia, Providence,
Boston, and even Newark had established black communities
by the 1790s.

The potential importance of intraregional data has been
pointed out in Moland's (1978) discussion of black elderly in
Louisiana. The historical factors, the interplay between
physical attributes of the land, and the cultural patterns of
the early settlers in a region, combine to color the adjustment patterns of long-time residents of given areas. To
what extent would there be variation in the religious and
grandparenting patterns of those residing in New England
of New England ancestry versus those of rural Georgia of
roughly the same socioeconomic status? To what extent
would "isolation" be found versus "desolation" in these two
communities? Would isolation be found more frequently
among the aged in New England? Would desolation be found
more frequently among the southern blacks? Troll defines
isolates as:

> those who live alone and like it and desolates as
> those who live alone but don't like it. Many iso-
> lates have lived alone and been "loners" most of
> their lives. The desolates are the ones who have
> loved and lost. Their spouses have died; their
> children live far away; and they haven't adjusted
> to the loneliness yet--if they ever will. (1975:92)

The majority of the discussions in the social science literature dealing with religion in black populations have focused
on southern evangelical, or free forms of, Protestant
churches. Few studies of the role of what is called the
"Institutional Church" in areas in which black populations
lived prior to the 1820s in either the North or the South
have been undertaken; nor are there many, if any, studies
of the Catholic churches in parts of Maryland and Louisiana
or Episcopalian churches in the southeastern part of the
United States. Is it reasonable to expect the basic
expression of religiosity of elderly persons reared within
the structure of the invisible versus the Institutional
Church to be the same? Since authors rarely distinguish
either among or between their populations, it becomes difficult to interpret the real significance of church attendance
statistics. For example, understanding the degrees of
alienation and/or change which Watson discusses, may be
increased by comparing the church structure of northern

descendants, i.e., Institutional church versus southern Institutional versus southern unstructured, i.e., the invisible church.

While the importance of considering regional variation with black populations is stressed, individual responses and coping strategies must not be overlooked. The following three cases represent widows who reside in one of the small towns in the lowland South. All three are Baptists. They were born in rural areas, then they migrated to town as young adults. They have subsequently spent the majority of their lives in the town and would be considered exceptionally handsome women by local standards.

Miss A, a long-time widow, is the mother of two children and grandmother of five. Her education is limited in terms of local norms, and she frequently uses nonstandard English. Miss A was formerly employed in both domestic and skilled labor and until recently rented her home. Both children are professionals, and each moved out of the state shortly after graduating from high school. Miss A seldom visits others and receives almost no visitors. She is extremely active at home and takes extended trips to visit her children who live across the country. An avid television watcher, she only attends church periodically. Even though the children have been away for more than forty years, her life, as revealed in conversations with her, revolves around the children and the grandchildren. The latter visited frequently and periodically lived with Miss A when they were small. She has few friends and relatives but is highly self-sufficient and in robust health.

Miss B, the mother of one child and the grandmother of three is a recent widow. Her education would be considered standard in local terms, and she generally uses standard as well as nonstandard English, depending on the occasion. Miss B, who was more economically advantaged because of the previous existence of two incomes in the family, occasionally engaged in domestic work. She and her husband owned their home. Their child is a professional and lives out-of-state in a distant part of the country. Miss B enjoys visiting although she has few visitors. She is a joiner, is active in church and in local associations. She is both active within as well as outside of the home. Miss B makes some local excursions; however, her visits to her child are few and brief. An avid television watcher, Miss B has many friends and relatives even though few actually visit her, and she is in comparatively good health.

Miss C is a long-time widow who has four children and six grandchildren. She is educationally advantaged according to the norms of the region. As a teenager she was teased regarding her educational advantages and thereafter became a user of nonstandard English. Miss C was employed in both domestic and skilled occupations in order to support her children. She owns the home in which she lives alone. Her children are college-educated professionals. She seldom visits others and visitors to her home are primarily relatives. She is not active in or out of home, and she rarely attends church. She watches a few television programs. All the grandchildren and two of the children lived with Miss C when the grandchildren were small. She has few friends who are not also relatives. Miss C has frequent complaints of feeling ill, but a number of medical examinations have failed to reveal any specific illness.

According to local opinion, of the three widows, Miss B, the oldest one, has made the best adjustment to the aging process, while Miss C has simply folded her hands to be "waited on." It is clear from discussions with her that from her point of view the elderly are to be catered to, never disagreed with, never left to their own devices, but always surrounded by family members. They are to be ushered to and from weekly shopping as well as for more important medical visits. Her vision of old age, which differs from that of her children, is of virtually total dependence.

Miss B is highly independent and is not dependent upon children and grandchildren. Her visits to the children are fewer, and her conversations are all inclusive even though she has more reason to boast than Miss A. Her child was, in the local view, a "first" in several areas and a model for many of the local youths. The interesting factor in all three cases is that there has been little actual change in their coping and adjustment strategies in the last forty years. Miss B was always outgoing, Miss A was always involved with self and the immediate extensions of self--her children; and Miss C was always involved with her parents, siblings, children and, to a lesser extent, with her extended kin network. Even when young, she rarely went to church. A common reason given was the lack of appropriate garb. She seldom visits and is virtually without friends. In an area where there are few recreational avenues available, she was always seen as excessively retiring and family bound. Forty years later the pattern is simply more entrenched. The more retiring she becomes the less activity she engages in, which, in turn, means the less she becomes physically able to be active. Within a relatively short period of time, she has entered the ranks of the frail elderly. This pattern solidifies her dependence on her children. At the same time, she is constantly verbalizing the wish to "remain independent" of them as "you know they have no time for me," implying a tendency for them to neglect her, which observation reveals is not the case.

The brief sketches of the behavior patterns of the three widows located in the lowland South illustrate a need to consider idiosyncratic and alternative behavior along with possible subcultural or area norms. If, as is frequently stated, the family is a major vehicle for social participation among elderly southerners, we find that Miss B is an exception. If immediate family is considered, Miss A conforms to the pattern. She is an exception, however, as (1) she has fewer relatives, and (2) she does not interact with any other than a sister-in-law and her children. Only Miss C conforms completely to the supposed pattern; it should by stressed that by local standards and her peers, Miss C's behavior is considered excessive even though it is simply a continuation of her earlier behavior. It is an overextension or overexpression of a form of appropriate behavior for the elderly in that area. These cases illustrate the need to be aware of the various forms of diversity that may be found at the local or community levels, as well as at the individual level.

CONCLUSION

The checklist model for studying elderly or general black populations would tend to ensure against generalizations that apply only to one sector. It emphasizes the need for knowledge of exactly where an element or tendency fits within the range of behavior possible for a population. Hopefully scholars would be induced to broaden their spectrum by selecting additional areas for research. This approach may also provide a useful database for testing developmental and symbolic interaction theories of aging.

Defining developmental theory, Carroll Estes (1978: 44) states it as:

> Essentially a theory of psychological or personality processes associated with successful aging, the key variable here is continuity, i.e., the maintenance of a stable integrated "self" according to one's own standards. The major difficulty with this theory is its solipsistic bias--there are potentially as many paths to happiness in later life as there are old people. The research question ultimately becomes, what are the conditions of consistency, which may not be a psychological query.

Estes indicates that "many" developmentalists argue that "old age is characterized by enhanced consistency, and by a turning inward [interiority] rather than concern with the reaction of others" (1978:44). These characteristics are definitely shared by Miss C. However, the consistency or continuity of a "stable integrated self," according to her own standards, is not considered successful aging in the late 1970s and the early 1980s. She does not really operate according to "her own standards" but in accord with one of the available norms to which she has elected to conform. Anthropologically speaking, even idiosyncratic behavior is culturally patterned. Given an awareness of the history of the era and place in which Miss C was socialized, it becomes immediately clear that her mode of adaptation may have been considered highly appropriate and successful in the past.

From 1915 to 1935, among poorer rural families of the deep South, all social activity was group oriented. Transportation was difficult; therefore, several individuals always traveled together, and the elderly were considered not up to walking long distances or riding in trucks, wagons, or on horseback. To live alone was most unusual and to be "delicately" ill after rearing a family, especially if one was widowed, was if not actually ladylike, at least appropriate within the expected range of local behavior. What are the conditioning patterns for such a consistency?

As a child, Miss C, the youngest child in a sizable family, was sent off to boarding school alone. She was homesick, and she cried for a solid week. Her parents, instead of supporting her through this period, brought her home permanently. She was widowed during her mid-twenties and for various family reasons stayed close to her parents when she was not living with them. When one parent died, the other, a very dominant, independent individual, moved in with Miss C and lived to a relatively advanced age. The pattern for dependency--consistency in this case--was established quite early. Had the pattern been broken earlier, possibly Miss C would have achieved independence earlier, would have developed interests which encompassed other than her family and extended kin, and very probably would have continued to lead a more active life by local standards.

Behavior which is currently seen as unsuccessful or successful only in an isolated or multiproblem-poor context, may be modified for the mutual benefit of the elderly and their relatives, especially if the population is comparatively heterogeneous and flexible. One of the problems in coping with adaptive strategies within black populations, given the inappropriate stress on homogeneity, for example, has been the fear of "changing their cultural values." This in many instances has simply been a crutch upon which the status quo is maintained. Use of the checklist model prepares the way for the range of variation within a given situation to be documented and analyzed. Planning and service personnel as well as scholars would have better ideas of the culturally and situationally acceptable alternatives that exist within a given black population. This framework--allowing for inherent variability--may result in more accurate analysis of United States elderly black populations.

NOTES

[1]A regionalism whereby women are addressed as "Miss" plus their given names, regardless of marital status.

[2]The rural schools generally provided education up to the "eighth reader" when these women were young. Some of the older and/or brighter children might have finished the eighth reader, but continued to attend or repeat the grade because of the lack of other local educational facilities.

REFERENCES

Blake, J. Herman
     1978-79 Doctor Can't Do Me No Good. The Black
          Sociologist 8:6-14.

Blauner, Robert
     1970 Black Culture: Myth or Reality? In
          Afro-American Anthropology. Norman E. Whitten,
          Jr. and John F. Szwed, eds. Pp. 347-366. New
          York: The Free Press.

Carter, J.L.
     1978 Editorial. Black Aging: 429.

Dancy, Joseph
     1977 The Black Elderly: A Guide for Practitioners.
          Detroit Mich.: Institute of Gerontology.

Devons, E. and M. Gluckman
1964 Conclusion: Modes and Consequences of Limiting a Field of Study. In Closed Systems and Open Minds: The Limits of Naivety in Social Anthropology. M. Gluckman, ed. Chicago: Aldine Publishing.

Estes, C.
1978 Political Gerontology. Society 15:43-49.

Godelier, Maurice
1977 Perspectives in Marxist Anthropology. Cambridge: Cambridge University Press.

Jackson, J.J.
1978 Special Health Problems of Aged Blacks. Aging 287-288:15-20.

Jackson, J.S., J.D. Bacon, and J. Peterson
1977-78 Life Satisfaction among Black Urban Elderly. International Journal of Aging and Human Development 8:169-179.

Linton, Ralph
1936 The Study of Man. New York: Appleton-Century-Crofts.

Meyers, L.W.
1978-79 Elderly Black Women and Stress Resolution. The Black Sociologist 8:29-37.

Moland, J.J., Jr.
1978 The Quality of Life among Older Blacks. The Black Sociologist 8:14-29.

Owlesy, F.L.
1949 Plain Folk of the Old South. Baton Rouge, La.: Louisiana State University Press.

Pearsall, D.
1966 Cultures of the American South. Anthropological Quarterly 39:2-8.

Troll, L.
1975 Early and Middle Adulthood. Monterey, Calif.: Brooks, Cole Publishers.

Vinyard, Dale
1978 Rediscovery of the Elderly. Society 15:24.

Wallace, Anthony F.C.
    1970 Culture and Personality.   New York:
        Random House.

Watson, Wilbur H.
    1980 Stress and Old Age.   New Brunswick, N.J.:
        Transaction Books.

6

Giving, Receiving and Exchanging: Social Transactions among Inner-City Black Aged

AUDREY OLSEN FAULKNER and MARSEL A. HEISEL

Increases in knowledge about the process of aging and the state of being old has led to a new recognition of the diversity of the aged population and its division into many subgroups, each with its own unique cultural characteristics (Clark and Anderson 1967; Keith 1982; Holmes 1983). Research addressing the issue has provided documentation of cultural variation (Faulkner, Heisel and Simms 1975; Sterne, Phillips and Rabushka 1974; Gelfand 1982). However, the accumulated evidence of differences between and among the aged of this country's many ethnic and racial groups falls far short of the comprehensive inventory needed to guide policy formulation and service delivery for an expanding population. As a further complication, myths about those whose color, language, or traditions are different from the majority are grafted onto myths about aging, so that stereotypes frequently crowd out the limited factual material available.

In this chapter we present the results of research carried out with a group of older black men and women residing in the inner city of Newark, New Jersey. We present information about their attitudes toward themselves and their neighbors, and about their social interaction, with special attention to the informal family and neighborhood transactional system through which they give and receive support in their day-to-day lives.

THE STUDY SAMPLE

The study sample consisted of 208 black persons aged forty-five to ninety-five. The rationale for inclusion of persons whose chronological ages were less than those usually designated as the dividing line between middle and old age--sixty, sixty-two, or sixty-five--was based on our understanding of mortality, morbidity, and life expectancy for blacks, and upon discussions with scholars and practitioners who have worked in the black community. Manton and Poss, among others, have argued that the eligibility for age-related benefits should be adjusted downward for minorities, in view of their shorter average life span and the earlier onset of the accumulated disabilities associated with old age (Manton and Poss 1978). Since life expectancy for blacks is less than that of whites it follows that if old age is to be considered roughly as the last trimester of life, our sample would have to dip further into the younger chronological ages to have a sample that truly reflects old age among blacks.

For this reason our first dip was to age fifty-five, to take account of shorter average life spans. Our second dip was to age forty-five, provided that the individual had been in the labor market, and was now permanently out of the labor market for reasons related to health.[1] This allowed us to use functional health status related to employability, as well as the adjusted chronological age, in our sample of "aged." These adjustments in our sample's chronological age permitted us to approximate the definition of age that fit the subcultural context in which we expected to gather data.

The sampling frame was established by a house-to-house canvass of two inner-city census tracts to locate the households that contained an older person meeting the age-disability-labor market criteria. The research sample then drawn was stratified to oversample men, those with limited mobility, and persons living in households with others.[2] The age distribution of the sample was as follows:

Age Category	N	Percent
45-54	13	6
55-64	69	33
65-74	85	41
75-96	41	20
	208	100

There were 66 men and 142 women. Forty-seven percent lived alone, 22 percent lived with a spouse, and the balance with spouse and children, children, or other relatives, and in two cases with friends. More men than women were married. Fewer than half in the sample had a child residing within the same urban area. Twenty-four percent had impaired mobility; 76 percent described themselves as mobile, i.e., they were able to get around to do such things as shop, go to the doctor, and do the errands of daily living without undue hardship because of physical health.

Two-thirds resided in low-income, high-rise public housing, with the remaining third occupying dwellings in the surrounding neighborhood. The area, adjacent to that where the Newark riots of the sixties occurred, presented many threats to health and safety. Grocery stores, service establishments, and professional offices had fallen victim to civil disorder, to fire, to urban clearance, and to other hazards of the inner-city environment. The primary local social service agency was a poorly funded neighborhood center. It was necessary to travel outside the neighborhood for public or private health care, and residents of the area saw ambulance, police, and other city services as generally unresponsive to the area's needs.

Among other objectives, the study sought to determine the effect of social services, delivered through vigorous outreach, on the health and well-being of the study population. A random assignment of approximately two-thirds of the participants was made to an experimental group to whom outreach services would be given, and one-third to a control[3] group whose members were not to receive the service. The findings and conclusions presented in this chapter are based on the interviews with the 137 experimental group participants.

CULTURAL SIMILARITIES AND DIFFERENCES

Racial, cultural, and class differences between researchers and the persons whose lives they study create methodological problems of considerable magnitude. Social and political tensions add to the difficulties. Recognizing this, we made determined attempts to carry out the data collection process in[4] such a way as to maximize the cultural validity of the data.

The research operated under the aegis of the local neighborhood house whose board, staff, and committees were actively involved in personnel and program decisions. Family consultants, paraprofessionals who served both as

interviewers and as service delivery personnel, were selected from applicants who lived in the same neighborhood as
the research participants. They came from the same cultural milieu as the research population and, therefore, we
accepted as expert their knowledge about their neighborhood elderly and the family, friends, and neighbors who in-
teracted with them. In addition to cultural and socioeconomic factors, the family consultants were selected for their
personal warmth, their empathy, and their interest in the
older people of their neighborhood. The family consultants
were an integral part of the project's research team, partic-
ipating in the selection of questionnaire topics, the style
and wording of questions, the identification of sensitive
subjects, the piloting and revision of the instruments, and
interpretation of the responses (Faulkner, Heisel and Simms
1975).

DATA COLLECTION METHODS

The data collection was designed to facilitate the application of the research findings to the administration of services. The primary instruments used to assess the characteristics of the sample population were detailed questionnaires focusing on the self-concept of the respondents,
their life situation and their satisfaction with it, their degree of social participation, and their knowledge about and
use of the institutionalized social services in the Newark
community. Believing that interviewer-respondent rapport
was more than usually important in this study, two outreach
visits to establish the beginnings of a helping relationship
were made by the family consultants before the first of the
formal questionnaires was administered.

Our premise, following Mazlow, was that persons of all
racial, ethnic, and language groups have the same basic
physiological, psychological, and spiritual needs. Because
of varying life styles embedded in cultural, economic, and
educational differences, the types of services desired to
meet these needs and the structure and techniques of service delivery that would be considered acceptable will differ
from group to group (Cantor 1979). We collected information about needs and patterns of informal delivery among
our respondents for three reasons: (1) to identify any
unique services individuals required but might not have
available if they were socially isolated; (2) to identify any
specifics of our respondents' informal service delivery practices that might be incorporated into our outreach services;
and (3) to establish what services were available on an informal basis so that we would not supplant them, but could

target our efforts to situations and individuals where service did not exist.

We first asked our family consultants about what families, friends, and neighbors did for each other in the neighborhood. Their answers served as the basis for determining the scope of questions about informal exchanges. Their initial list was piloted--with opportunities for additions to be made by the family consultants and the older persons interviewed in the pilot test--revised, and grouped into six domains of health, death, happy events, financial assistance, religion, and personal activities. Respondents were asked which of the following things they did for others, and which had been done for them by others within the past year. They were asked to specify whether the giving or receiving transaction was with a member of their family, friends or neighbors, or both.

Health:

1. Go with someone to the doctor/have someone go with you when you were sick.

2. Visit someone who is sick/have someone visit you when you were sick.

3. Visit someone who is feeling poorly and do for them/ have someone visit you when you were feeling poorly and have them do for you.

4. Fix food for someone who is sick/have food fixed for you when you were sick.

5. Help around the house when someone is sick/have someone help around the house when you were sick.

Death:

1. Went to a wake when somebody passed/somebody came to a wake when someone in your family passed.

2. Took food to the house when somebody passed/someone brought food to the house when somebody in your family passed.

3. Stayed at the house during services/had someone stay at your house during services.

4. Helped serve food at the house when somebody passed/

had someone help serve food at your house when someone in your family passed.

5. Gave money to the family when somebody passed/ received money from others when somebody in your family passed.

Religion:

1. Prayed with someone/had someone pray with you.

2. Read the Bible to someone/had someone read the Bible to you.

3. Went to church with someone who could not go alone/had someone go to church with you when you couldn't go alone.

Financial:

1. Fixed a meal for someone who didn't have money for food/had someone fix a meal for you when you didn't have money for food.

2. Lent money to someone who needed it/had someone lend you money when you needed it.

Personal Activities:

1. Go to the store for someone/had someone go to the store for you.

2. Baby sat for someone/had someone keep you company when you needed it.

3. Lent food, such as a cup of sugar, to someone/ borrowed food, such as a cup of sugar, from someone.

4. Shared a bottle with someone/had someone share a bottle with you.

5. Knocked on the door to see if someone was o.k./had someone knock on your door to see if you were o.k.

6. Watched for the mailman and picked up someone's check so it couldn't be stolen/had someone watch for the mailman and pick up your check so it couldn't be stolen.

Happy Events:

1. Helped at the time a baby was born/had someone help you with a happy family event.

2. Gave or helped with a birthday party/gave you or helped with a birthday party for you.

3. Helped with a wedding or graduation/received help with a wedding or graduation in your family.

4. Shared something special with someone else/had someone else share something special with you.

These transactions were those that embodied an element of service, as distinct from purely social activity such as visiting someone, attending a movie or a senior program with someone, or going fishing with someone.

Each individual was assigned a score for each giving transaction that involved family and for each such transaction with friends or neighbors. This score was doubled if the giving transaction had taken place with both family and friends and neighbors. The same system was used to develop a score for receiving transactions. The lowest possible score for either giving or receiving was 0, for those persons who reported no transactions; the highest possible score was 104, cases in which individuals had every listed transaction, all of them with both family and friends and neighbors. Actual scores ranged from 0 to 96 on giving, and from 0 to 100 on receiving.

THE CONCEPT OF EXCHANGE

The high volume for informal services to family, friends, and neighbors confirmed our expectations. The wide range in receiving and giving scores, however, led us to an interest in the equivalency of the transactional volume, i.e., whether some individuals were primarily givers and some primarily receivers, or whether a high volume of service in one direction was associated with a similar volume in the other direction. Such reciprocity has been shown to be an important element in social support networks (Meyerhoff 1978; Goodman 1982).

To answer these questions, both receiving and giving scores were divided into high, medium, and low categories, based on inspection of the frequency distribution of these scores. A cross-tabulation of the frequency distribution was used to classify respondents into three groups: (1) receivers, whose receipt of service was greater than their provision of service; (2) givers, who gave more than they got; and (3) exchangers, whose giving and receiving score categories were equivalent. While the giving and receiving scores took account of the volume of activity, this second classification was based on the equivalency of scores. Thus an individual would be characterized as an "exchanger" if support were given and received to an equivalent extent, regardless of how many or how few transactions he or she engaged in. A person who gave very little, but received even less would be placed in the "giver" category, and those who received more than they gave were placed in the "receiver" group. The resulting classification placed almost half (46 percent) in the exchangers category; 25 percent were in the receivers category; and 29 percent were designated as givers.

We wished to explore the association between the exchanger, receiver, and giver characteristics of the respondents, and certain of their psychological and social characteristics. Since we were attempting to avoid placing on the black community a template cut from prior research on predominantly white groups, we again sought the assistance of the family consultants to help us devise questions that would explore our conceptual areas in as culture-fair a way as possible. We told them we wanted to learn how people felt about themselves, how they viewed themselves in relation to their community, and how satisfied they were with their present stage of life. Together the family consultants and the researchers discussed the kinds of questions we thought might work, prepared tentative ones, and tested them in the field. We asked the family consultants in the field test to report back the responses to the questions, as well as the answers. In some cases, the field test respondents provided curtly succinct criticism of our queries: they told the family consultants they thought the questions were "ridiculous."[6] The final questions were the result of researcher-family consultant-community informant collaboration. All questions were presented as a statement to which the person was asked to respond in the categories of (1) very true for me; (2) somewhat true for me; and (3) never, or almost never true for me. We used factor analysis to isolate the clusters of related questions that formed our indices of Age-Related Self-Concept, Self as a Good Person, Enjoyment of Life, Alienation, Abandonment, Loneliness, and Self as Victim. The three response categories were assigned a numerical value, and a total score for each was computed. Scores, where necessary, were transformed into the appropriate direction, i.e., a high score on Age-Related Self-Concept was viewed as positive, but a high score on

Alienation represented a negative direction. Frequency distributions were inspected, and scores were assigned to high, medium, and low categories for chi-square analysis.

The data attest to a large amount of informal service. The greatest volume of transactions took place in the domains of health, religion, and personal service. Eighty-six percent of the respondents were both recipients and donors of sickness-related service. Almost everyone (97 percent) had received personal service assistance, and eighty-seven percent had looked after others in this manner. Sixty-eight percent of the sample had given support in relation to religious activity, and an even higher number (77 percent) had been receivers in this domain. More than half (59 percent) had provided aid at the time of someone's passing, 47 percent had provided financial assistance to others, and a little less than half of the respondents (45 percent) had participated in celebrations of happy occasions.

More transactions took place with friends and neighbors than with relatives, probably reflecting a proximity factor. Respondents who lived in senior citizen housing, for example, were unlikely to have a relative also living in the building. The next-door neighbor/friend was, by housing policy, another older person. Many of the persons in the sample had children and grandchildren who lived in the area but not in the neighborhood, and a number of the respondents had no living children at all.

DEMOGRAPHIC OF GIVING AND RECEIVING

As expected, the younger age groups were responsible for more acts of giving, with the oldest age group, those seventy-five to ninety-six, having the lowest total number of giving transactions. Age was not significantly related to receiving service, contrary to expectations that the old would be the recipients of more informal services from family, friends, and neighbors. Living alone or with others was not significantly correlated with giving or receiving scores, and while the nonmobile were low in giving transactions (less than .01), lack of mobility did not increase the receipt of service. Sex was significantly related to both giving and receiving transactions, with women having higher scores on giving (less than .04) and on receiving (less than .01). Only 15 percent of the men reported a high rate of involvement in helpful activities, but 40 percent of the women had high scores on giving. Fifty-eight percent of the men were in the low category for receipt of service, whereas almost three-fourths of the women (71 percent) were in the medium or high category for receiving service.

There were some surprises for the researchers. The study population, in spite of a lifetime of the dual deprivations of racism and poverty, had a predominantly high age-related self-concept, and a view of themselves as good people who accepted their lives as they were and had been, and who enjoyed living in old age. On our measures of integration into society--alienation, loneliness, abandonment, and a view of self as a victim--scores were lower than expected. While some individuals had relatively high scores, the total scores distributed more toward the lower end of the possible range. Men reported less integration than women.

The black elders' scores on enjoyment of life tended to be high: as a group, they were generally glad to be alive, viewed old age as a reward, and were joyful about families, friends, and the meager comforts of their old age. Enjoyment of life was strongly associated with giving, and exchangers also fell into the higher life-enjoyment categories. While far more receivers reported low enjoyment of life than did givers or exchangers, over half of the receivers were also in the high-enjoyment category (less than .01). The altruism effect is the strongest one, and the equality of transaction is also important, but the receipt of a high volume of service is also related to a high enjoyment of life for many persons in the sample.

Although receivers were somewhat more likely to score lower on both the Age-Related Self-Concept Index and the Self-as-Good-Person Index, neither self-concept measure had a statistically significant relationship to classification as a giver, receiver, or exchanger. Associations on the transactional measures showed similar results. Although givers tended to have lower scores on Abandonment, Loneliness, and Alienation, and receivers were somewhat more likely to have a higher score on Self as Victim, none of these relationships reached statistical significance in the chi-square analysis.

Myth, stereotype, and reality about black culture and black community are often difficult to separate. Propositions put forth about the way blacks behave and the reasons they do so are always subject to challenge by other blacks and by nonblacks. Because of our close day-to-day involvement with many individuals in our study, and because we had the opportunity to observe them in interaction with each other, we were in many cases able to buttress our quantitative results with qualitative observations. When we did not find the expected simple one-to-one relationship between high scores on self-assessment and community integration measures and high scores on giving and exchanging, we looked for an explanation that fused numerical-score data and observational data.

Our perception of the dominant community ethos among our workers and our respondents was based in the biblical adage that "it is better to give than to receive." These were, in the main, men and women who were generous with the little they had. We also perceived less resistance to accepting help when it was needed than we had observed in some elderly in the majority culture--feelings of self-worth did not appear to be negatively affected by acknowledging need. We assumed this had its genesis in a cultural norm evolved over the centuries, that if blacks are to survive in a society that gives them meager entitlements, they must develop their own self-help mechanisms. Membership in the black community becomes the basis of entitlement; those who are in need can expect to receive without a lessening of status because they are a receiver rather than a bestower. Whether or not this feeling is stronger in the late age cohort of blacks than in the younger ones awaits further research.

SUMMARY AND CONCLUSIONS

We have sought to contribute to knowledge about the black aged, and especially to explore the questions of the diversity and homogeneity of a group of blacks whose social, economic, educational, and residential characteristics would lead us to consider them as essentially homogeneous if we used yardsticks from other socioeconomic analyses.[7] We concentrated on intragroup analysis, with the guidance of black family consultants who were members of the community we studied. We looked at a measures of self-assessment, community integration, and enjoyment of life; while we found a wide range of scores on these indices, the black aged's view of self were predominantly positive. Most saw themselves as integrated into their community, and the majority of them enjoyed old age.

The black aged in our study participated in an active system of informal service delivery and exchange. More exchanges of service took place with friends and neighbors than with family, probably a result of their physical isolation from families in the suburbs and the South. Women were more active than men in this system, and those who delivered and exchanged service were more likely to have higher life-enjoyment scores. A norm of entitlement appeared to operate in the community so that those in need, who had their needs met by others, did not suffer impairment of their feelings of self-worth. Our findings support a conclusion that the inner-city black elderly we studied have developed active mechanisms for dealing with the stressful realities of their lives. We believe their transactional system of informal social service delivery, together with their sense of entitlement, activates a sense of coping. This, in turn, reinforces and contributes to the development of positive conceptions of themselves as strong and competent individuals.

NOTES

[1]This group turned out to be so small that in this chapter we have not made any comparisons between those under fifty-five and those over that age.

[2]Since the sampling frame was dominated by females, the mobile, and those living alone, we wished to obtain a larger number of individuals with the nondominant characteristics for analysis of diversity within the population.

[3]Any control group member found by our interviewers to be in crisis was assisted in obtaining services from appropriate community agencies. Once the referral connection had been made, our workers did not continue to be involved in the service aspects of the case. The effect of this decision was to render more conservative findings of positive change related to our services, but ethical considerations required that the interests of the participants receive priority over the interests of the researchers. Results of the experiment have been reported elsewhere (Faulkner and Heisel 1974; Graves 1981).

[4]In addition to procedures to protect the quality of the data, we also operated under an exchange philosophy whereby value was returned to the community by the university researchers as a quid pro quo for the provision of data.

[5]These persons were not in the sample, but were in the original sampling frame.

[6]Such frank feedback is not always available to the social scientist; we tried to swallow our chagrin with grace, and either reworded or eliminated questions that evoked

that response.

[7]Data for the research reported in this chapter were gathered with support received from NIMH Grant No. 18051.

REFERENCES

Cantor, Marjorie H.
    1979 The Informal Support System of New York's Inner City Elderly: Is Ethnicity a Factor. In Ethnicity and Aging: Theory, Research and Policy. Donald E. Gelfand and Alfred J. Kutzik, eds. New York: Springer Publishing Company.

Clark, Margaret and Barbara Gallatin Anderson
    1967 Culture and Aging. Springfield, Ill.: Charles C. Thomas.

Faulkner, Audrey; Marsel A. Heisel and Peacolia Simms
    1975 Life strenghths and Life Stresses: Explorations in the Measurement of the Mental Health of the lack Aged. The American Journal of Orthopsychiatry 45:102-111.

Fry, Christine L.
    1980 Aging in Culture and Society. Brooklyn, N.Y.: Bergin Publishers, Inc.

Gelfand, Donald E.
    1982 Aging: The Ethnic Factor. Boston: Little, Brown and Company.

Goodman, Catherine Chase
    1982 Reciprocity and Responsibility: Help Exchange among Elderly Neighbors. Paper presented at the 35th Annual Meeting of the Gerontological Society of America, Boston, Massachusetts.

Graves, Conrad
    1981 Family and Community Support Networks and Their Utilization by the Black Aged. Doctoral Dissertation, Rutgers University.

Heisel, Marsel A. and Audrey O. Faulkner
    1974 Evaluation of an Outreach Project with Elderly
        Blacks. Paper presented at the 27th Annual
        Meeting of the Gerontological Society of America,
        Portland, Oregon.

Holmes, Lowell D.
    1983 Other Cultures, Elder Years. Minneapolis,
        Minn.: Burgess Publishing Company.

Keith, Jennie.
    1982 Old People as People: Social and Cultural
        Influences and Old Age. Boston: Little, Brown
        and Company.

Manton, Kenneth and Sharon Poss
    1978 The Black/White Mortality Crossover: Possible
        Racial Differences in the Intrinsic Rate of Aging.
        Black Aging 3:43-52.

Meyerhoff, Barbara
    1978 Number Our Days. New York: Simon and
        Schuster.

Sterne, Richard S.; James E. Phillips and Alvin Rabushka
    1974 The Urban Elderly Poor. Lexington, Mass.:
        D.C. Heath and Company.

7

Aging and Work: Perceptions of Low-Income Puerto Rican Adults and High School Students

BENJAMIN DREW and JUDITH WATERS

In these times of economic crisis, we find an increasing number of groups (e.g., adolescents, women, minority groups, and the aging) competing for a constantly decreasing number of jobs. The technology that contributed to advances in medical care, extending lifespan, and improving the quality of life, has also led to the development of sophisticated robotics, replacing both skilled and unskilled workers. The continued emphasis on a technology that promises to keep reducing the number of jobs performed by humans has become a major concern, particularly for labor unions and workers involved in light and heavy industry.

Over the past thirty-five years, retirement has been institutionalized as a socially expected phase of life (Blau 1973). However, a steadily rising rate of inflation has eaten away at the value of pension funds and social security payments making it necessary for large numbers of older people to find part-time employment or to remain on the job past the time they had anticipated retiring. Many able-bodied people must keep working whenever possible because private pension funds are not available to the vast majority of unskilled workers and they simply cannot afford to retire. Of almost equal importance is the concept that occupation is a vital element in one's identity and that it strongly influences self-esteem. Social stratification most often occurs along occupational lines so that without a job-defined role, there is a decrease in social status for most unemployed workers or retirees (Streib 1976; Puner 1974). Job loss can lead to an increasingly poor self-image and feelings of uselessness, loneliness, aimlessness, demoralization, and isolation (Streib and Schneider 1971; Blau 1973; Freese 1977).

Subjects responding to a survey conducted by Louis Harris and Associates (1976) listed the major problems attributed to most people over sixty-five years old. In order of priority they said that "not having enough to live on" was the most serious issue. Financial need was followed by "loneliness," "not feeling needed," "fear of crime," "poor health," "not enough job opportunities," "not enough medical care," "not enough to do to keep busy," "poor housing," and "not enough friends." More than half of these problems are either directly or tangentially related to work. Increased income can solve the problems of paying bills, housing, and better medical care. The psychological needs for a support group and having something to do are also filled by working at meaningful tasks in the company of others. Since occupational status is considered to be a master status in our society, the loss of occupational identity, even for a person who is not suffering economic pressures, may threaten self-esteem to the point of developing stress reactions, depression, and physical and psychological symptoms (Holmes and Rahe 1967). Thus, providing work for the competent older man or woman, while not a universal panacea, does solve many problems.

Employers may not be willing to retain older employees with seniority who represent higher costs than younger workers in the form of salary increments and fringe benefits accumulated over the years. On the other hand, retired workers are also perceived to be a financial burden, this time to taxpayers in terms of medical insurance costs and federal, state, and municipal programs for the ailing and/or poverty-level aged. Clearly, even the most creative solutions to problems raised by the "graying of America" will lead to difficulties for other segments of the population, chiefly the working class.

Ageism spreads its insidious influence through all arenas of life, but it is particularly vicious in the workplace where it results in job discrimination against many of the elderly who can least afford to be out of work. Women are subjected to a "double standard of aging" that defines the physical manifestations of aging as "distinguished" in men, but as evidence of loss of capability as well as sexual desirability in women. Many elderly workers experience the double jeopardy of being old and a member of a racial or ethnic group already exposed to the consequences of prejudice in the society. Older women in such minorities suffer the unique but unfortunate distinction of being exposed to the triple jeopardy of minority group, age, and sex discrimination.

One of the most serious barriers to the acceptance of older people in the workplace, outside of the economic issues, is the existence of strong, deeply embedded stereotypes of aging. The success of policy changes involving retirement age or the establishment of programs for hiring older workers depends, in part, on understanding the beliefs of various segments of society concerning the capabilities of older men and women. Toward this end, we conducted a survey of the attitudes of low-income Puerto Rican adults and high school seniors, a group likely to be affected by an increase in the numbers of older people in the job market.

The model of lifespan development that seems most appropriate for these issues is related to the cultural milieu and the economic value placed upon individuals at various times in their lives. Conceptually, the human lifespan can be divided into four chronological categories. The first includes the youngest members of the society for whom the resources of the family and the community at large are mobilized in order to transmit, through the enculturation process, the accepted norms, values, and mores and the occupational and social skills needed to succeed in that society. The potential of children exceeds or at least equalizes their high cost to society; and the investment in time, energy, and economic wealth will eventually result in accrued benefits, hopefully to the family and the maintenance of the group as a whole.

The second category comprises those individuals in the most productive period of their lives. The productivity of these adults must exceed or at least equalize their cost, for it is these people who are called upon to be responsible for the well-being of the dependent groups of the society: the ill, the disabled, the young, and the elderly. The third group is what the French call the "troisieme age." Many members of this group who have been employed in occupations outside the home have experienced retirement. Others, mainly traditional housewives, point out that for them there is no demarcation between work and retirement. They continue in their roles even if the setting is changed. Many in this category are in good health but are no longer viewed with the respect accorded the "productive members of society." They receive little reinforcement for the tasks they do perform and are sometimes treated as if they are mentally, physically, and sexually incapacitated. The compensation that is granted to this group is based on, at least in the United states, either a fraction of what they have earned during their working years or "what is derived from the humanitarian aspects of the society" (Eisdorfer 1983).

The last category includes the majority of the elderly whose cost exceeds their economic return to the society. These are the weakened survivors who become increasingly more needy and dependent and who are usually perceived as a burden to the society as a whole. In their case, the risk-payoff ratio has become unbalanced with little or no hope of retrieval of costs. Generally speaking, the position of the aged in any given society, preliterate or otherwise, can be expressed in terms of their gender and position in society prior to old age and in terms of how much they, as old people, contribute to the resources of the group, balanced by the cost they exact and compounded by the degree of control over valuable resources (Simmons 1945; Cowgill 1972; Amoss and Harrell 1981; Eisdorfer 1983).

Beyond the cost-benefit approach it must be recognized that the experience of aging often does have emotional impact and can be idiosyncratic. Dissatisfaction is great when the reality of the situation does not match one's expectations of how the later years would be. Many older Americans thought that social security and other retirement benefits would enable them to live a respectable old age. Inflation has, however, destroyed many dreams of financial security. For some people, disorders associated with old age, such as Alzheimer's disease, have led to a precipitious decline in functions where the expectation had been for the gradual waning of capabilities (Sinex and Merril 1982). These atypical forms of aging may contribute heavily to the negative stereotype associated with the elderly.

Some thirty years ago, Tuckman and Lorge (1953) conducted a study of stereotypes of the elderly. They found that there was "substantial acceptance of the misconceptions and stereotypes about old people." What made this result even more important to them was the nature of the subjects. They were, according to Tuckman and Lorge, "sophisticated young adults, many of whom had had a good grounding in psychology, who presumably were well acquainted with individual differences and who have shown sufficient interest in the problems of the older adult to register for a course in the area (ibid.:259). The investigators concluded it was obvious that the subjects had had limited contact with older relatives and were not familiar with the experimental literature or they would not have expressed such negative attitudes about aging. The opinions expressed by the subjects may, in fact, have been close to the truth. The authors state that the subjects believed that old age was a time of life marked by "economic insecurity, poor health, loneliness, resistance to change and failing physical and mental powers." Given the data collected in recent years on the poor living conditions of many elderly, these perceptions may have been reasonably accurate.

Eight years later, Kogan (1961) found that subjects were more willing to express negative feelings toward the elderly than toward members of ethnic groups or the physically and mentally disabled. In the late fifties and early sixties, there was a heightened awareness that prejudicial comments directed against racial or ethnic groups and the handicapped should not be expressed. At the same time, there was a relative insensitivity to the status of the elderly in a youth-oriented culture. The results were probably heavily influenced by social desirability (the response set based on the wish to give the socially "correct" answer or in this case, not to give the socially "incorrect" answer). In addition, there is often a defensiveness apparent in discussions of aging and death and dying that is manifested in humor and facetious comments about the ravages of time that make it easier to express negative attitudes toward the elderly.

Kogan and Shelton (1962) found that younger subjects thought that one of the greatest fears of many old people was "death or dying" whereas older subjects focused on "lack of money" and "financial insecurity." The older men in the group most often cited a general condition of "dependence" as their greatest fear. The results may reflect a certain amount of denial when it comes to the topic of death. On the other hand, it is also possible to infer that the older subjects were reporting very real and immediate concern with the inadequacy of their financial resources and the need for assistance.

The discrepancy in perceptions between older and younger subjects may be particularly important, if, as Rosow (1962) suggests, "the crucial people in the aging problem are not the old, but the younger age groups." It is his contention that the latter control the position of the aged in the social order.

SAMPLE SELECTION

There were several important considerations that had to be made in selecting the subjects for a study on perceptions of aging. Since even a superficial review of the literature on attitudes is enough to demonstrate the over-representation of college students as subjects, we were determined not to use a sample of our own college students for this study.   Having considered a number of possibilities we selected a Puerto Rican blue-collar sample of high school students and working adults employed in low-income but not necessarily unskilled jobs.   We felt that the attitudes of high school students of Puerto Rican heritage would be critical to the project because they are a group that would be most likely to experience the immediate impact of competition with older people remaining in the work force.   This was determined by giving careful consideration to the concept of the "dual labor market" that was developed (although not originated) by Doeringer and Piore (1971). This concept involves two labor markets: the primary and the secondary.

The primary labor market is one that contains hierarchical job sequences and in which employers invest resources in the training of workers, periodically rewarding them with promotions and salary increases for improved skills (Kaufman and Spilerman 1982).   The secondary labor market is more important because it influenced the choice of subjects for the study.   This sector consists of jobs requiring minimal skills and training for which employers invest few resources for training.   Employees with experience are really no more attractive to employers than are inexperienced ones, and salaries are relatively low with few prospects for promotion.   Seniority counts for little, and in a very real sense these low-status positions (e.g., gas station attendant, dishwasher, messenger, food service worker, office boy, night watchman or janitor, among many others) are dead-end jobs.   Because these kinds of jobs are easy to enter, with new entrants very quickly as competent as veterans, they often become the focus of second careers for many elderly workers who are forced into retirement or compelled to change jobs because they can no longer fulfill the requirements of their old jobs.   Unemployed older workers often find job opportunities severely limited because they either lack education, have obsolete skills, or have worked in a declining industry.   Even minor health problems may be enough to keep them unemployed and unable to follow a new job market because of decreased mobility (Rhine 1978).   These factors coupled with discriminatory practices emphasizing chronological age rather than functional ability constitute the foundations underlying the unemployment problems of elderly workers.   Under these circumstances, the secondary labor market becomes, if not particularly attractive, certainly necessary.

Jobs in the secondary labor market also appeal to many very young adults who are not yet committed to a career or a line of work and who are only looking for temporary or intermittent employment (Kaufman and Spilerman 1982).   So it is in the arena of the secondary labor market that many older workers find themselves competing with very young individuals for low paying dead-end jobs because they need to survive. Sheppard (1977) has found that low-income workers are more vulnerable to loss of employment during periods of economic recession and that there is as a strong interaction between health, minority status, and unemployment. Members of minority groups who are unemployed, unskilled, and in poor health are those most likely to withdraw from the labor force.

The study's adult sample of mainly blue-collar workers were employed, but at jobs that require relatively few skills or skills that are available in the community (i.e., secretarial). The positions of some of these adults are vulnerable to inroads into the labor market made by each succeeding high school graduating class and by older members of the population seeking employment in the secondary job market. None of the adults in this group was retired or unemployed, although the unemployment rate in the community often runs as high as 25 percent.

Eventually, a broad spectrum of opinions from all socioeconomic levels of society and from a variety of ethnic and racial groups should be examined to clarify differences in attitudes toward older people in the workplace. It is equally important to establish the relationships between these perceptions and the actual performance of the older worker. In this study, the focus is on the attitudes toward older workers of a segment of the American population who are already finding themselves in competition with these older workers for scarce employment opportunities.

The profile of the population from which our sample was drawn is based upon a survey of the Hispanic community in Morris County, New Jersey, made by Greene and Curran (1982a). Their data indicate that of 377 respondents, about 42.9 percent of the adults are under thirty years of age while 13.6 percent are fifty years of age or over, 27.5 percent are between thirty and thirty-nine, and 16 percent are between the ages of forty and forty-nine. In terms of education, 37.3 percent reached various levels of elementary school up to and including the first year of high school, 49.3 percent completed from two to four years of high school, and 13.4 percent indicated some college education. About 75 percent of the respondents were blue-collar workers (one-third unskilled) and 25 percent were white-collar workers (i.e., supervisors, clerks, secretaries, or beauticians). More than 57 percent of them earned under $15,000 per year (almost 35 percent earned under $10,000 per year and 18 percent earned under $6,500 per year). In 75 percent of the households with married couples, both husband and wife were wage earners. In response to questions concerning major problems in the community, both the younger, lower income individuals and the older group saw limited employment opportunities as a problem (Greene and Curran 1982a).

Interestingly, non-Hispanic leaders in Morris County did not see limited employment opportunities and the lack of job and career counseling as very serious problems for the Hispanic population (Greene and Curran 1982b). Instead, they saw the problems as stemming from personal deficiencies caused by an inability to communicate fluently in English, the lack of job skills, and the low level of education. The non-Hispanic leaders did not see the personal needs of the Hispanic population as having developed as a result of inadequacies in the social, economic, or educational systems (ibid.).

In 1914, Arthur F. Yager, the appointed governor of Puerto Rico, submitted to President Wilson and the War Department a proposal advocating the planned emigration of Puerto Ricans to the United States as a way of resolving serious social problems on the island which, in the governor's considered opinion, resulted from serious overpopulation and widespread unemployment (Campos and Flores 1978). The proposal was eventually accepted and implemented over the following decades. At the time it was recommended, the program was attacked by Jose de Diego, Puerto Rican poet and political lawyer who expressed outrage at the very idea of negotiating the emigration of Puerto Ricans as one would negotiate some business transaction (ibid.) The first giant wave of migrants followed almost three decades later at the close of World War II when about a million people settled in New York and a number of other large northern cities (Bray 1983). Almost all of them were unskilled agricultural workers, largely motivated to emigrate to the mainland by high rates of unemployment resulting from the collapse of the sugar industry. By now, almost two million people, or about a third of the entire population of Puerto Rico, has moved to the United States (ibid.). The early migrants tended to concentrate in the New York area, and by 1970, 64 percent of them were living in New York State. Today, only half of the two million live there and the percentage continues to drop (ibid.). Although Puerto Ricans face no immigration barriers, because they are United States citizens, they move to the mainland not as citizens from another state in the "Union," but as if they were immigrants from a "foreign" country (Campos and Flores 1978).

Unfortunately, there are relatively few data on the Puerto Rican elderly in the United States. According to

Bengtson (1979), the census data provided by the U.S. Bureau of the Census in 1976 counted approximately 382,000 individuals of Spanish descent over the age of sixty-five in this country--Mexicans and Cubans as well as Puerto Ricans. Minority leaders complain that the number of minority elderly over sixty-five have probably been undercounted because many of them are reluctant to make their presence known to those whom they view as respresentatives of authority and therefore objects of suspicion and distrust. Since members of minority groups tend to have a lower life expectancy than whites (Puerto Ricans and blacks among others for example), minority leaders allege that aging occurs more rapidly because of the hardships imposed upon them throughout a lifetime subjected to social and economic bias (Jackson 1970). Since the census data only includes those sixty-five and over, it is claimed that the numbers of the minority populations who function as elderly are not reflected in the census figures (Bengtson 1979). Puerto Ricans may be defined as elderly, not only by chronological age, but by virtue of the fact that they have adult children and grandchildren and that they may exhibit the kinds of functional impairments and disabilities usually associated with age (Zambrana, Merino and Santana 1979).

The proportion of Puerto Rican elderly in the United States may be low for another reason. Many of these Puerto Rican "elderly " in New York are willing and able to help spouse and children (especially as caretakers of grandchildren) in the hopes that they will earn enough money to permit them to return to their island. It is difficult to assess problems among these "elderly" because they choose to return to Puerto Rico as soon as they feel, as they put it, "very sick," because they want to die in their homeland (ibid.).

Many researchers have suggested the older members of minority groups experience the impact of double jeopardy, the negative effects of being both old and a member of some ethnic or racial minority (Cantor and Mayer 1975; Cantor 1979; Dowd and Bengtson 1978; Jackson 1980), or even triple jeopardy if they also happen to be female. In contrast, others have hypothesized that age exerts a leveling influence and that, regardless of cultural background, the aging individual is subject to a range of influences that cut across ethnic or racial lines and mediate, or level, the differences in patterns of aging (Kent and Hirsch 1969; Kent 1971; Bengtson 1979). Our sample is an economically and socially disadvantaged group that is probably more likely to see their own elderly as suffering multiple hazards not only because they are elderly and Puerto Rican but because they have language problems, minimal job skills, and low educational levels.

THE STUDY

There were several important considerations that contributed to the planning of this project. First, in the social sciences especially, results of past studies must constantly be updated and revised. Second, policy decisions demand current material based on the needs and perceptions of specific groups in the population. Third, there were still issues in the study of attitudes concerning aging that could be clarified by utilizing a technique reflecting the variability within and between subject groups.

A thorough examination of the literature yielded few studies that had assessed the impact of the double standard of aging on respondent's attitudes (Green 1981; O'Connell and Rotter 1979). Not only did we consider the sex of the stimulus person (older man as compared to older woman) to be a major variable for study, but we also felt that the sex of the respondents would affect their beliefs. If, as Simic and Myerhoff (1978) point out, "The fact is inescapable that male and female life trajectories differ markedly," then we could expect an interaction between the sex of the older person and the sex of the subject.

While the number of investigations focusing on minority groups has increased in recent years, there continues to be a lack of data on the attitudes of the Puerto Rican population, one of the fastest growing groups in the United States. Ours was a sample of working class Puerto Rican subjects. Although studies comparing the attitudes of different age groups have been conducted, the findings have been inconclusive--older generations sometimes being more negative in their opinions and sometimes less negative than either children or young adults. Since the position of the elderly in any society is dependent upon the attitudes of the younger generations, those perceptions become critical to the welfare of older people and must be examined.

All other factors being equal, attitudes do guide behavior. Stereotypes of the elderly affect the way that they are treated at home and, perhaps a more critical issue for survival, how they are regarded in the workplace. In order to assess current perceptions of the level of functioning in older men in comparison with older women, we designed a survey dealing with several areas of functioning. A series of statements (thirty-nine in all) focusing on work-related issues, physical and cognitive ability, and sources of irritation between the generations was formulated based on various sources in the literature (Palmore 1980; Arnhoff, Leon and Lorge 1964; Kogan 1961), discussions with professionals in the field of gerontology, observations of the images of the elderly in the media, and suggestions from our students (see Table 1). We predicted that the following patterns would occur:

* All subjects would rate the majority of older men and women as having some form of disability and some loss in physical or cognitive functioning. Consequently many older workers would be seen as more costly to their employers than younger employees.
* The younger subjects, the high school seniors, would be more critical of older men and women than the adult working subjects would be.
* There would be evidence of the double standard of aging; attitudes toward older women would be more negative than attitudes toward older men.
* The sex of the subjects would also influence perceptions of aging. The women upon whom the care of the elderly may depend would perceive older people as needing more love and reassurance than any other age group.

The change in methodology involved the type of responses that subjects are often asked to give to survey questions. In many previous studies, the usual procedure has been to show the subjects a series of statements concerning the process of aging and request that they either "agree" or "disagree" with each statement (Arnhoff, Leon and Lorge 1964). In similar studies, subjects have been asked to determine if the statements were "true" or "false" (Palmore 1980). The data were then analyzed by comparing the frequency of responses in each category. There are two problems with these instruments. When the focus is on the subject to express agreement or disagreement with a general statement, responses are more likely to be influenced by response bias in the form of social desirability than by the person's attitude. The second issue concerns the data analysis. With only two choices possible, the entire range of opinions cannot be evaluated.

In order to deal with both issues, the subjects in this study were asked to judge the percentage (from 0 to 100 percent) of older men and older women who exhibit a particular behavior or have a disability. For example, when presented with the statement, "Older men are forgetful," subjects could respond by saying, "Twenty-five percent of them are forgetful." The emphasis was shifted from the subject's simple agreement or disagreement with the state-

TABLE 1

Questions Concerning "Older Men" and "Older Women"*

What percentage of older men (women):

1. can put in a full day's work?
2. are paid too much for the work they do?
3. lose too much time from work because of illness.
4. have reaction times that are slower than that of younger workers?
5. are more interested in job security than raises?
6. have problems learning new methods of doing things?
7. are more costly for their employers than younger workers?
8. have some physical disability?
9. worry more about their health than younger people?
10. avoid physical activity?
11. have poor physical coordination?
12. get into more accidents than younger workers?
13. are forgetful?
14. are mentally alert?
15. can manage their own affairs?
16. are afraid of death and dying?
17. like to give advice to others?
18. are conservative?
19. complain about the younger generation?
20. are "different" and hard to understand?
21. bore people with talk about the "old days?"
22. grow wiser as they grow older?
23. expect others to take care of them?
24. should only live with others their own age?
25. need more love and reassurance than anyone else?
26. have a lot of power in business and politics?

*   There were 13 additional questions concerning social relationships and sexual behavior that will be discussed elsewhere.

TABLE 2

Summary of Responses of Subjects (High School Students and Working Adults) to "Older Men" and "Older Women"

Questions	Sex of Older Person							
	Older men				Older Women			
What percentage of older men/women:	Adult Males	Adult Females	H.S. Males	H.S. Females	Adult Males	Adult Females	H.S. Males	H.S. Females
1. can put in a full day's work?	58*	60	63	65	58	63	60	59
2. are paid too much for the work they do?	50	36	57	60	44	36	57	61
3. lose too much time from work (illness)?	59	44	60	61	60	49	59	59
4. have slow reaction times?	61	58	59	62	53	50	60	59
5. are interested in job security over pay raises?	68	56	57	62	59	71	59	65
6. have problems learning new things?	58	45	65	60	58	37	59	58
7. are more costly...than younger workers?	50	51	52	58	51	33	56	62
8. have some physical disability?	53	49	65	54	58	48	59	60
9. worry more about their health than younger workers?	65	70	66	64	65	70	62	62
10. avoid physical activity?	49	59	59	56	56	56	57	56
11. have poor physical coordination?	56	48	62	66	56	56	65	65
12. get into more accidents than younger workers?	49	37	53	38	54	47	54	38
13. are forgetful?	51	45	60	62	54	53	56	59
14. are mentally alert?	54	60	57	59	58	56	50	58
15. can manage their own affairs?	60	59	66	64	62	63	59	60
16. are afraid of death and dying?	59	68	65	64	60	71	54	62
17. like to give advice to others?	66	78	57	60	65	78	59	63
18. are conservative?	63	64	65	62	63	71	57	58
19. complain about the younger generation?	58	70	57	61	65	72	62	62
20. are "different" and hard to understand?	49	46	62	62	52	46	65	60
21. bore people with talk of the old days?	49	47	56	61	56	60	60	63
22. grow wiser as they grow older?	38	45	54	56	52	50	56	59
23. expect others to take care of them?	51	46	66	65	54	44	62	63
24. should live only with others their own age?	56	37	59	62	60	34	57	60
25. need more love and reassurance than anyone else?	63	79	63	62	68	72	63	59
26. have a lot of power in business and politics?	60	56	59	61	55	42	57	58
27. would like to work for younger supervisors?	58	44	65	63	50	47	54	57

* Responses in percentages.

ment to an assessment of the proportion of the older male population who are perceived to be forgetful. It was expected that this type of response would not be as influenced by response set as one requiring simple agreement or disagreement. The other advantage to be gained from the numerical data collected, is that they could be analyzed in a way that would demonstrate variability within and between groups.

The samples of Puerto Rican working-class adults and high school students came from a suburban community in northwestern New Jersey. The total group of ninety-eight subjects was composed of twenty-four working men, eighteen male high school seniors, nineteen working women, and thirty-seven female high school seniors. Each person was interviewed individually in the language of his or her choice (English or Spanish). In order to obtain the most reliable and valid results, the interviewers were trained to take sufficient time to establish rapport with the subjects and to "close graciously" (Valle and Mendoza 1978). Subjects were assured that their responses were anonymous.

An analysis of variance (repeated measures) was performed on each statement utilizing subject group (working men and women versus high school seniors), sex of subject and sex of older person (older men versus older women) as the independent variables. The dependent measure was the percentage of older men and older women perceived as exhibiting the behavior in each statement.

Although many of the findings indicated significant differences in perceptions between the subject groups (adult working men and women and high school seniors) and between the sexes for older men versus older women, there was also common consensus on several important issues (see Table 2).

For example, subjects generally agreed that approximately half of all older people have some physical disability and lose more time from work than younger employees. It is possible to explain the high percentage of estimated disability in a number of ways. First, the results may reflect the negative stereotypes held by the general population. A second possibility is that the subjects may have divided the elderly into two groups, the young-old who are primarily healthy and the old-old, many of whom are chronically ill or disabled. Their responses may refer mainly to the old-old segment of the population. Third, if the study conducted by the Social Security Administration stating that 39 percent of their sample was handicapped in some manner represents the incidence of disability in the population, then the perceptions of these working class subjects may only be an exaggeration of reality. Fourth, since one of the conse-

consequences of being a member of a disadvantaged group is the early development of physical disorders that often go untreated until they are serious (Zambrana, Merino and Santana 1979), the perceptions reported here may not even be an exaggeration.

The major differences were between the adult working people and the high school students. The adults thought that more older people were "afraid of death and dying" than did the students. The working men and women also thought that more older people were "conservative," and given to dispensing advice than did the high school students. In general, high school students were more negative in their assessments of older men and women than the working adults. Not only did the students estimate higher percentages of older people as having "poor coordination," "accidents," "slow reaction time," and "being forgetful," "difficult to understand," and "having problems learning new methods," they also said that more of them were "paid too much," "lost too much time because of illness," and were "too costly for their employers" than did the adult working subjects. The students felt that the majority of the elderly "worry about their health too much," and that most older people "expect others to take care of them." In addition, the students felt that large numbers of the elderly "bore people with talk of the old days" and that many of them "should live only with others their own age." At the same time, the high school students said older people have "power in business and politics." All subjects saw older men as more powerful than older women. It should be noted that while differences between the subject groups were statistically significant, both samples usually estimated that approximately 50 to 60 percent of older men and women exhibited deficits in function or stereotypic behavior.

As one of the indices of intergenerational conflict, subjects were queried about the proportion of older men and women who complain about the "younger generation." On first examination, the findings were somewhat surprising. It was expected that the students would respond more negatively than the adults. However, the opposite results occurred: the working men and women stated that more of the elderly complain than did the students. The female students, as a group, thought more older people complained about the younger generation than did the males. If we think about the household structure in the Puerto Rican community, it may be that the older members of the family complain about the children to the parents or to whomever is available. Many Puerto Rican households are managed by a female without a male present or with males who take little or no responsibility for children (Glazer and Moynihan 1963;

LaRuffa 1971; Seda 1973; Blatt 1979; Cruz-Lopez 1980). When the mother works, the oldest daughter at home generally assumes the household duties, with all girls usually required to look after younger siblings. Many widowed, separated, divorced, or deserted females often join their parents' household so it is most likely that the person available to receive the complaints will be female (Glazer and Moynihan 1963; LaRuffa 1971; Seda 1973; Blatt 1979; Cruz-Lopez 1980).

While beliefs about the ability of older people to contribute to the productivity of society are unquestionably important, we also wanted to evaluate attitudes concerning the needs of the elderly. Subjects were asked, for example, what percentage of older men and women had strong needs for "love and reassurance." All subjects saw high percentages of the elderly as having stronger emotional needs than any other age group. The adult women saw 72 to 79 percent of the aging population as having emotional needs. The attitudes of these subjects may be derived from their traditional position in the home. The nurturant role of women in Puerto Rican society requires that they continue to fulfill the personal needs of all family members despite the fact that most of them may be working (Burma 1954; Glazer and Moynihan 1963; La Ruffa 1971; Sanchez-Hidalgo and Sanchez-Hidalgo 1971; Seda 1973; Blatt 1979; Cruz-Lopez 1980). These needs may be seen as demands that press heavily on their shoulders.

CONCLUSIONS

The sample of Puerto Rican working-class subjects for this study comes from a culture in which the emphasis on family relationships remains strong. We might have expected the influence of family interdependency to reduce the impact of ageism on perceptions of older men and women in this group. The results, however, indicate that, despite some significant differences, all subjects estimated that at least half of the aging population was forgetful, not as mentally alert as younger workers, and disabled in some way. Only half of all older people were perceived to be capable of doing a full day's work. The variations in attitude between male and female subjects and the differences in perception of older men versus older women, while clear evidence for the double standard of aging, were not as pervasive as the gap between the high school students and the working men and women. The high school students held views that were distinctly more negative toward older people than the adult sample.

Working class Puerto Ricans suffer from the hazards of discrimination as well as from being forced to compete with all the formerly disenfranchised groups in American society for many jobs that may soon be filled by machines.   At the present time, those high school seniors who wish to become gainfully employed are likely to find themselves in competition with women and blacks of all ages as well as with older Puerto Ricans in their own community.   The impact of economic exigencies plus the acceptance of negative stereotypes of the aged were probably stronger influences than cultural norms in the community and may account for the results. It is also possible that, despite generally unfavorable perceptions of large numbers of the faceless elderly in the population, close interpersonal contact between the young and the old in the Puerto Rican community may be characterized by respect and positive regard for elderly people. Other researchers have noted that subjects can and do distinguish between the elderly in the general public, older people as depicted in the media, and individuals in their own social sphere (Green 1981).

Holzberg (1982) has pointed out that one of the major research problems in studying ethnic groups in the United States is that the investigators have confused the influence of socioeconomic class and minority group identity with other cultural factors.   In order to evaluate the contribution made by cultural factors, the next logical step should be to study attitudes in middle- and upper-income Puerto Ricans on the mainland as well as in Puerto Rico and to compare these results with evidence from cultural groups with different traditions of behavior toward older men and women.

NOTES

The authors wish to thank Rosa Sanabria and Wilfredo Rodriguez for their assistance in the data collection and Anthony Rao for processing the information.   We also wish to thank Linda Boyer for typing the manuscript.

REFERENCES

Amoss, P.T. and S. Harrell
1981 Introduction: An Anthropological Perpective on aging. In Other Ways of Growing Old: Anthropological Perspectives. P.T. Amoss and S. Harrell, eds. Stanford, Calif.: Stanford University Press.

Arnhoff, F., H. Leon, and I. Lorge
1964 Cross-cultural Acceptance of Stereotypes toward Aging. Journal of Social Psychology 63:41-58.

Bengtson, V.
1979 Ethnicity and Aging: Problems and Issues in Current Social Science Inquiry. In Ethnicity and Aging. D. Gelfand and A. Kutzik, eds. New York: Springer Publishing Co.

Blatt, I.B.
1979 A Study of Culture Change in Modern Puerto Rico. Palo Alto, Calif.: R and E Research Associates, Inc.

Blau, Z.
1973 Old Age in a Changing Society. New York: New Viewpoints.

Bray, H.
1983 The New Wave of Puerto Rican Immigrants: The Island's Recessions has Forced a New Middle Class to Start Out Again on the Main Land. New York Times Magazine: 22, 26, 33, 34-35.

Burma, J.H.
1954 Spanish-Speaking Groups in the United States. London: Cambridge University Press.

Campos, R. and J. Flores
1978 National Culture and Migration: Perspectives from the Puerto Rican Working-Class. New York: Research Foundation of the City University of New York.

Cantor, M.
1978 The Informal Support System of New York's Inner City Elderly. In Ethnicity and Aging. D. Gelfand and A. Kutzik, eds. New York: Springer Publishing Co.

Cantor, M. and Mayer M.
    1975 Factors in Differential Utilization of Services
        by Urban Elderly. Paper presented at 28th
        meeting of the Gerontological Society.
        Louisville, Kentucky.

Cowgill, D.
    1972 A Theory of Aging in Cross-Cultural Perpective.
        In Aging and Modernization. D. Cowgill and
        L.D. Holmes, eds. New York: Appleton-
        Century-Crofts.

Cruz-Lopez, M.A.
    1980 Puerto Rican Elderly: Analysis of the Support
        Systems of Two Age Cohort Groups. Ph.D.
        dissertation, Syracuse University.

Doeringer, P. and M. Piore
    1971 Internal Labor Markets and Manpower Analysis.
        Lexington, Mass.: D.C. Heath.

Dowd, J. and V. Bengtson
    1978 Aging in Minority Populations: An Examination of
        the Double Jeopardy Hypothesis. Journal of
        Gerontology 33:427-436.

Eisdorfer, C.
    1983 Conceptual Models of Aging: The Challenge of a
        New Frontier. American Psychologist 38:197-202.

Freese, A.
    1977 Adjustments in Later Life. Dynamic Years 1977:
        37-39.

Glazer, N. and D.P. Moynihan
    1963 Beyond the Melting Pot: The Negroes, Puerto
        Ricans, Jews, Italians, and Irish of New York
        City. Cambridge, Mass.: MIT Press.

Green, S.
    1981 Attitudes and Perceptions about the Elderly:
        Current and Future Perspectives. International
        Journal of Aging and Human Development
        13:99-119.

Greene, K. and J. Curran
    1982a The Hispanic Community in Morris County: A
        Needs Assessment. New Jersey: Morris County
        Organization for Hispanic Affairs.

Greene, K. and J. Curran
  1982b The Hispanic Community in Morris County:
      Non-Hispanic Leaders' Perceptions. New Jersey:
      Morris County Organization for Hispanic Affairs.

Harris, L. and Assoc., Inc.
  1976 The Myth and Reality of Aging in America.
      Washington, D.C.: National Council on Aging.

Holmes, T.H. and R.H. Rahe
  1967 The Social Readjustment Rating Scale. Journal of
      Psychosomatic Research 11:213-218.

Holzberg, C.
  1982 Ethnicity and Aging: Anthropological
      Perspectives on More Than Just the Elderly.
      The Gerontologist 22:249-257.

Jackson, J.
  1970 Aged Negroes: Their Cultural Departures from
      Statistical Stereotypes and Rural-Urban
      Differences. The Gerontologist 10:140-145.

  1980 Minorities and Aging. Belmont, Calif.: Wadsworth
      Publishing Company.

Kaufman, R. and S. Spilerman
  1982 The Age Structures of Occupations and Jobs.
      American Journal of Sociology 87:827-851.

Kent, D.
  1981 The Negro Aged. Gerontologist 11:48-50.

Kent, D. and C. Hirsch
  1969 Differentials in Need and Problem Solving
      Techniques Among Low Income Negro and White
      Elderly. Paper presented at the 8th
      International Congress of Gerontology,
      Washington, D.C.

Kogan, N.
  1961 Attitudes toward Old People: The Development of
      a Scale and an Examination of Correlates.
      Journal of Abnormal and Social Psychology
      62:44-54.

Kogan, N. and F. Shelton
1962 Beliefs about "Old People": A Comparative Study of Older and Younger Samples. The Journal of Genetic Psychology 100:93-111.

LaRuffa, A. L.
1971 San Cipriano: Life in a Puerto Rican Community. New York: Gordon and Breach.

O'Connell, A. and N. Rotter
1979 The Influence of Stimulus Age and Sex on Person Perception. Journal of Gerontology 34:220-228.

Palmore, E.
1980 The Facts on Aging Quiz: A Review of Findings. The Gerontologist 29:669-671.

Puner, M.
1974 To the Good Long Life: What We Know About Growing Old. New York: Universe Books.

Rhine, S.
1978 Older Workers and Retirement. New York: The Conference Board, Inc.

Rosow, I.
1962 Old Age: One Moral Dilemma of an Affluent Society. Gerontologist 2:182-191.

Sanchez-Hidalgo, E. and L. Sanchez-Hidalgo
1971 La Psicologia de la Vejez. Rio Piedras, P.R.: Editorial Universitana.

Seda, E.
1973 Social Change and Personality In a Puerto Rican Agrarian Reform Community. Evanston, Ill.: Northwestern University Press.

Sheppard, H.L.
1977 Factors Associated with Early Withdrawal from the Labor Force. In Men in the Pre-Retirement Years. S. Wolfbein, ed. Philadelphia, Pa.: Temple University.

Simic, A. and B. Meyerhoff
1978 Conclusion. In Life's Career: Aging, Cultural Variations on Growing Old. B. Myerhoff and A. Simic, eds. Beverly Hills, Calif.: Sage Publications.

Simmons, L.
1945 The Role of the Aged in Primitive Society.
London: Oxford University Press.

Sinex, E.M. and C.R. Merril, eds.
1982 Alzheimer's Disease, Down's Syndrome, and
Aging. New York: New York Academy of
Sciences.

Streib, G.
1976 Social Stratification and Aging. In Handbook of
Aging and the Social Sciences. R. Binstock and
E. Shanas, eds. New York: Van Nostrand and
Reinhold.

Streib, G. and C. Schneider
1971 Retirement in American Society. New York:
Cornell University Press.

Tuckman, J. and I. Lorge
1953 Attitudes toward Old People. The Journal of
Social Psychology 37:249-260.

Valle, R. and L. Mendoza
1978 The Elder Latino. San Diego, Calif.: The
Campanile Press.

Zambrana, R., R. Merino, and S. Santana
1979 Health Services and the Puerto Rican Elderly. In
D. Gelfand and A. Kutzik, eds. Ethnicity and
Aging. New York: Springer Publishing Co.

8

Culture, Aging and Stress among Elderly Kalmuks

MAREA TESKI, with Computer Data by KRZYSZTOF TESKI

Aging and stress are two universal experiences which have become increasingly interesting subjects for research in the past two decades. This augmented attention is the result of the larger proportion of the United States population that is elderly, and the demonstrated effects of stress upon the health of all age groups. In both areas of interest, culture plays a significant role. The question of the relationship of culture to aging--a biological, psychological, and social process--is a vital one. Different individuals and different groups experience aging in dissimilar ways. Many factors associated with successful or unsuccessful aging--such as life satisfaction, perception of health status, and identification of stressful events--are culturally conditioned.

Culture is an ecological-historical adaption through which a group's way of life emerges in response to conditions and events. Definitions and perceptions of aging and stress, like definitions and perceptions of life itself, grow out of the long-time cultural experience of the group. This approach takes issue with the view that culture or ethnicity can be considered as a "compensator," "mediator," or "buffer" in solving the problems of aging (Holzberg 1982). Rather, we see culture as expressed in ethnicity, as a matrix which not only solves problems, but identifies and describes them. There are some universal aspects of the aging process, but culture may well have a primary role in determining even physical aging; it has a key role in providing the context in which psychological and social aging are realized.

Declining physical strength, certain experiences (becoming less active, losing a spouse or friends, etc.) happen to people in all cultures, but our understanding of aging may be better served by clarifying the particular ways in which the total cultural context of different groups directs the manifestation of these experiences in individual lives. For bicultural populations, it is possible to imagine ethnicity being used as a resource, when needed (Cool 1979). For the deeply identified ethnic, it is not possible to separate oneself from ways of thinking evolved in the group which give events and experiences their definition. Ethnicity is not a filter for experience, but a total inescapable context in which aging (the course of life), life events, and life satisfaction are defined, experienced, and expressed to others.

In the twentieth century, war, disasters, migration, and resettlement have been a part of the experience of many ethnic groups. As with aging, there are some universal features of these events, but the total response of any group to these stressors is dependent upon the culture of that group.

A good analysis of universal problems of involuntary migration and the resettlement process has been provided by Scudder and Colson (1982:267-71). They have outlined the main aspects. Two types of relocators are distinguished: refugees and development relocators. Both kinds of relocators are characterized as being primarily low income, low status people who have relatively little political power. Multidimensional stress is identified as a major feature of relocation. The stress is subdivided into physiological, psychological, and sociocultural stress. Since all of these types of stress affect a single individual, it might be expected that illness of a physical or psychological nature could emerge as a reaction.

The Kalmuk Mongols of the United States are a group with an extended history of migration--both voluntary and involuntary. The experience of relocation is part of their history, and the idea of moving is part of their culture. The older adults of the Kalmuk community of Howell Township, New Jersey, were part of a study which examined self-reported health status, general well-being, and attitudes toward past stresses of life. The effects of physiological and psychological stress were sought. These adults had experienced their last relocation in 1951 after having had much difficult in finding a country that would accept them as a group. By the 1980s many who had relocated were over sixty-five years of age.

THE KALMUK MONGOL PAST

The history of the Kalmuk Mongols, which lives in the memories of the remnant population in the United States, is rich with adventure but fraught with unimaginable hardship. Although it is not possible to determine with absolute certainty whether the New Jersey Kalmuks are closely connected to the Mongol hordes of Genghis Khan which brought destruction and terror to Europe in the fourteenth century, it is fairly certain that they are related to groups of Mongol tribes that migrated to Russia in the seventeenth century. These tribes settled in the area between the Caspian Sea and the Volga River. Grousset (1970) calls the Kalmuks Oirat, which means "confederates"--indicating that there was an alliance of tribes. These migrating tribes were probably trying to escape the power of the Manchu Ch'ing dynasty in China and the Manchu allies among the eastern Mongolian tribes. Although the transition to Russia was accomplished over several years, 1616 is the traditional date for the move.

Once established in Russia, the Kalmuks sought to maintain their traditional pastoral way of life. They concluded treaties with the Russians in which they provided cavalry to the Russian army and defense of the country's southern regions in exchange for security and the right to live in their own way. Living in their own way included the maintenance of contacts with the East. They retained contact with the Chinese Imperial Court and with the Dalai Lama of Tibet who was the head of the Lamaist Buddhist religion (Nembirkow).

The next major upheaval for the tribes occurred in 1770-71 when the Kalmuk leaders decided to return East to western Sinkiang Province from Russia. This migration has been discussed by Fathor Amiot (1776), Benjamin Bergmann (1804), and M. Moris (1925). Reasons for the migration probably were related to the growing power of the Russians, the Kalmuk's desire to be closer to the center of their religion, and their sense that there was much space to be occupied in the East.

At a date in the Year of the Tiger, 1771, said to have been determined by the Dalai Lama, the migration began. An early thaw of the Volga River left some Kalmuks stranded on the western side of the water. They did not accompany the 400,000 who left Russia, and their descendants are the modern Russian Kalmuks. The approximately 80,000 Kalmuks who survived the migration to China were accepted by the Emperor Chien Lung and given land and animals. They were gradually assimilated into Chinese culture as other minorities before them had been.

The Kalmuks who stayed in Russia maintained their own culture and their pastoral way of life. In the nineteenth century some of them moved into the Don River area. When the Russian Revolution erupted, the Kalmuks, along with the Don Cossacks, fought against the Bolsheviks in the White Army. After the Red victory, many fled to Yugoslavia and other Eastern European countries. When the Communists took over Kalmuk areas, the people were starved into submission or sent to Siberia in large numbers. They were forbidden to practice their religion and all temples were closed (Rubel 1971).

The history of poor relations with the Soviet government led some of the Kalmuk people to support the invading Germans in World War II. Many left Russia with the retreating German army. Of those who were left behind many were sent to Siberia as collaborators and not allowed to return to their homes until 1957-58 (Nembirkow n.d.). After the war, about 900 Kalmuks who had survived the labor camps were placed under the control of the United Nations international refugee organization. The Kalmuks were put into displaced person camps in the area of Munich, West Germany. Although the Soviets wished all nationals to be repatriated, this group came to the United States in the 1950s after much waiting and searching for a country that would accept them.

Relative to our interest in the stress experienced by Kalmuks who are now elderly, each of these historic relocations has been characterized by group involvement in the decision to move, even though it seems that there was often little choice but to move. The Kalmuks see themselves as decision makers and feel responsible for what has happened to them. They also see themselves as a powerful people. Alton Khan, a past leader, is said to have made this statement: "We, Mongols are powerful because our ancestral race descended from the sky" (Shakabpa 1967). Indeed, many of the difficult political situations that the Kalmuks have experienced are the result of daring choices made at crucial times.

When the attorney general of the United States ruled that Kalmuks were eligible for admission to the United States in July 1951, and the Tolstoy Foundation became active on their behalf, the United States sojourn of the group began. About 900 arrived in the United States settling mainly in the areas of Philadelphia, and Howell Township and Medford in New Jersy. An attempt to relocate some of the Kalmuks on New Mexican ranches where they could live a pastoral life was unsuccessful. Most returned to the East to be near their friends and relatives.

In the 1980s many of the adults who came to the United states in 1951 were over sixty-five years of age. Many were older than their recorded ages because of the unwillingness of the United States government to accept immigrants over the age of fifty. The older members simply subtracted enough years from their age to qualify for admission. The older members of the community had behind them not only years of difficulty as an ethnic group, but years of personal experience of hardship, uncertainty, and deprivation. In view of their extraordinary past and the dearth of work done concerning the aged of smaller minority groups, we decided to begin a study of as many elderly people as possible in the Kalmuk community. The study was done in Howell Township in the Freewood Acres community where Paula Rubel had done research thirteen years earlier (Rubel 1967).

Rubel's study concentrated on looking at the continuity of culture from the Kalmuk past and on the question of the maintenance of cultural identity in a large host society. She found that the small size of the Kalmuk community, their settlement as a group, and their frequent social interaction with other Kalmuks seemed to encourage the persistence of distinct ethnic identity and a separate Kalmuk community.

THE KALMUK COMMUNITY OF HOWELL TOWNSHIP

After thirteen years, the Howell Township area was still the "crossroads hamlet" that Rubel (1967) described. The land is flat and sandy, and scrub pines are the main large vegetation. Although some evidence of development--gasoline stations, stores, and restaurants--has changed the highway that runs through the community, a semirural feeling remains. There are no large buildings and the small, often colorfully painted houses have ample space around them for gardens. The three temples are the most colorful buildings, one of which, the Red Temple, is actually painted in brilliant shades of red. The atmosphere is quiet; to the casual observer, it appears that nothing is happening.

As in the time of Rubel's study, Kalmuk households are interspersed with non-Kalmuk housholds. Many of these houses are occupied by other immigrants, mostly from Russia and Eastern Europe. The Kalmuks have been on particularly good terms with the Russians because of their shared language (older Kalmuks speak both Kalmuk and Russian) and their shared dislike of the Soviet government. The three Buddhist temples are important foci for the older people in particular. One of the men in our study spent most of his time at the prayer wheel of the temple nearest his home. Praying there daily was his main occupation.

Two of the three temples in the community have been built since the time of Rubel's study. Three years ago one was also completed in the Philadelphia Kalmuk community. On holy days, we were told, the devout of Howell Township visit all three temples. The rhythm of social contact around the temple holidays remains very important to older residents. Almost none of the elderly Kalmuks lived alone. They lived with younger relatives or, in the case of monks (six in the study), with other monks. All were in constant social contact with people outside their homes.

Many of the Kalmuk elderly could understand and reply to questions in English. When language was a problem, sons, daughters, or grandchildren served as interpreters. The presence of a family member did not seem to inhibit the elderly, and replies from those who were interviewed directly and alone were very similar to replies of those who used an interpreter. About half of the the people over age sixty-five were seen and/or interviewed, and respondents ranged in age from sixty to ninety years. There were four females and nineteen males. The high proportion of men to women in this small sample can be partially explained by the presence of many monks in the community. However, since only six of the men interviewed are monks and the rest of the men are widowers, the lack of older women still cannot fully be explained. It may be that women were less in evidence when interviews were set up. The only person we were not allowed to interview, because of the objections of relatives, was a woman. Many of the men even asked to be interviewed, so it is also possible that women were selected out of the process by themselves or their families. Nevertheless a casual walk around a Kalmuk neighborhood reveals the presence of many active and vigorous older men at work on outdoor tasks.

The interview instrument was divided into five sections: the first three being of special interest in regard to culture and stress; the last two addressing questions of aging and intergenerational relations. The first section aims at determining the health status of the elderly as it is self-reported. The section directly confronts the question of stress and the respondents' views about their lives and the world. The third section gives information on the group's use of physicians and hospitals and seeks information on traditional Kalmuk health practices. In sections four and five, which deal with aging and intergenerational relations, we wished to discover the elderly Kalmuks' attitudes about growing old and their relationships with younger people. We hoped to find out how important it was to them to maintain a distinct cultural identity. The answers gained for all sections suggest that Kalmuk elderly display distinct solutions to the stressful past and to the future in which they will continue to live and grow old in a culture very different from their own. The scheduled interview was answered by twenty-three elderly Kalmuks in their own houses.

The first section, which dealt with health and health practices, showed an amazingly healthy group. Ninety-five percent of the respondents either "strongly agreed" or "agreed" that they were quite healthy. The same percentage reported that they feel active each day. When asked if they had colds, allergies, digestive problems, headaches, or fatigue, 91.3 percent reported that they had none of these problems. They were asked about several major health problems--heart, arthritis, cancer, stroke, kidneys, and diabetes--and 87 percent reported that they had experienced none of these. Two persons complained of heart problems and one person had arthritis. In response to a statement "I should exercise each day," 47.9 percent "strongly agreed" and 47.8 percent "agreed." They were also asked to respond to "I like physical work." Fifty-two and one-half percent "strongly agreed" and 43.5 percent "agreed." In response to "I believe a person should be outside a part of each day," 65.2 percent "strongly agreed" and 34.8 percent "agreed." Conversations and observations confirmed that walking, gardening, and doing outdoor chores were a part of the routine of most Kalmuk elderly. If recent findings about the importance of physical activity in maintaining good physical functioning are true, it would seem that Kalmuks have traditionally maintained good health into old age this way.

Section two begins with a statement "I have had a hard life." A surprising (to us) 52.2 percent "strongly disagreed" and 13 percent "disagreed" that this was the case for them. It would also seem that these people are generally pleased with their community, for 100 percent "strongly agreed" that "I like living in the community where I live." One hundred percent also responded "never" to a statement "I try to make changes in my life." Seventy-eight and eight-tenths percent "strongly agreed" that "I enjoy being with friends," and 100 percent either "strongly agreed" or "agreed" that they liked doing what they do each day. There seemed to be a sense of satisfaction that they are close to other Kalmuks and that there are agreeable ways of spending time. During the research it became obvious that there was a great deal of casual visiting between homes every day. People feel that they are part of a community and that there is always someone to talk with.

Since the Kalmuks were greatly affected in the past by events that seemed largely to be outside their control, we were interested in the reaction of the elderly to the things that had happened. They were asked to respond to the statement "I feel angry about some of the things which have happened to me." Seventy-eight and eight-tenths percent responded "never," 4.3 percent "seldom," 17.4 percent "sometimes"; no one responded "often." The lack of anger about the past and the real pleasure in the present seem to indicate that the respondents have effectively coped with all the vicissitudes of life. In response to "I feel I have no control over things which have happened to me," 52.2 percent reported that they "never" felt that way, 4.3 percent "seldom," 26.1 percent "sometimes," and 17.4 percent "often." Many of the Kalmuks perceive their lives in a different way from the outsider who might see much more governing by forces beyond individual control. The lack of anger over the past may well contribute to their good health; for anger caused by stress is a well-known cause of disease. Serenity, good health, and adequate exercise are probably also reflected in the responses to "I sleep well all night." Seventy-eight and seven-tenths percent reported that they "always" slept well and 21.7 percent reported "sometimes." No one said that they "seldom" or "never" slept well all night.

In response to questions about physicians and hospitals, 56.4 percent said that they had "never" been in a hospital as a patient. Most agreed that they should go to a hospital when very ill, and most had a good relationship with a physician or clinic. Most of the respondents were not in the habit of regularly visiting a physician or clinic. Their reported good health would make frequent visits unnecessary. Only 26.6 percent said that they "sometimes" took medicine prescribed by a physician. Thirty-four and eight-tenths percent said that they "seldom" did, and 34.6 percent said that they "never" took such medicine. Sixty-nine and nine-tenths percent said that they "often" or "sometimes" used natural medicines such as herbs and teas to treat themselves.

A recent Harris Poll commissioned by the National Council on Aging reports that among people over age sixty-five, only 8 percent consider the sixties and seventies to be optimal years in a person's life. Section four of our scheduled interview indicates a different response on the part of the Kalmuk elderly. They appear to be comfortable with the thought of growing older. Eighty-seven percent "strongly agreed" or "agreed" that this was the best time of their lives. One hundred percent "strongly agreed" or "agreed" that they have interesting ways of spending their time, and 100 percent either "strongly disagreed" or "disagreed" with the statement "I am often bored." This points to their active social life and their sense of belonging to a community as a significant determinant of present satisfaction. There was no indication that older people felt they were less a part of the community than younger people. Sixty-nine percent felt that they were happier at present than when they were younger.

The questions in section five looked at the elders' attitudes toward their traditions and religion. Here we must agree with Rubel's assertion (1967:243) that religion and religious ceremonies connect the group with their history and past and reaffirm the symbol system that expresses the ethnic identity of the group. We had a unique opportunity to witness such an occasion when the Dalai Lama visited the Freewood Acres temples on October 13, 1979. About 1500 Kalmuks gathered to welcome the principal figure of their religion who visited each of the three temples and had lunch at one of them. We were told that the crowd was made up of Kalmuks from the Howell Township area, from Philadelphia, and from small enclaves in other parts of the country. The obvious joy and respect with which the Dalai Lama was received showed how important a source of identity religion was for a large number of Kalmuks. On this occasion, older members of the community were given special consideration and for each of the talks of the Dalai Lama they were given seats close enough to assure that they could both see and hear him.

Ninety-five and seven-tenths percent of the older Kalmuks interviewed "strongly agreed" that religion was important to them, and 91.4 percent "strongly agreed" that religion helped them to face life. It was also obvious that religion gives all Kalmuks who participate a strong sense of group identity. There was some feeling among the younger Kalmuks that there was a slipping away from strict adherence to the religious observances. Some felt that their children would not be strongly motivated to cling to the old customs. Yet the religion was of great importance to the older Kalmuks and it appears that their Buddhism, with its emphasis on acceptance and working to improve oneself rather than to change the world, has helped the elderly to remain confident and happy--although their lives in many ways have been challenging and difficult. For example, many well-educated Kalmuks had to work at blue-collar jobs in the United States because they did not speak enough English to function in other jobs. From all reports, they made the best of this situation and tried to do well in whatever jobs were available. In old age they appear to have satisfaction with whatever work they have done in the past.

In sum, the elderly Kalmuks we interviewed and observed, far from showing any ill effects of the many moves and many changes in their life situations, seemed to be extraordinarily healthy, serene, and well-adjusted to their lives. The small number of health problems reported, the absence of anger about the past, the reported satisfaction with their lives, all indicate that the Kalmuks as a group see old age as a positive time of life. Aging is accepted and not thought of as a difficult period of life. There is a general agreement among the old that there are interesting things to do. We note that none of the elderly interviewed could in any way be described as affluent. Their houses are small and often totally without conveniences such as toasters, electric mixers, can openers, washers, dryers, and other items that some people regard as necessary. Most of the elderly do not own cars and walk when they wish to visit a friend. Some of the elderly have no telephones, and many have no radio or television set. Visiting and seeing family are important ways of spending time. There is a social club where many of the men go, and almost all of the men reported that they tended gardens in the summer. The way of life of the elderly is not keyed into mainstream or national culture; rather it has established its own rhythm and is centered around the individual's contacts with people who are important in their lives.

Judging by the self-reported health status and general satisfaction with life it would appear that forced migration and resettlement, which some had experienced as many as three times, had done no harm to the Kalmuk elderly. The fact that the concept of moving is a part of their cultural heritage must be considered when noting the lack of stress that the elderly now report after experiencing great changes in their lives. One older man said casually, "Kalmuks are nomads," in answer to a question about the hardship of relocation. Far from showing any ill effects as a result of many moves and changes, the elderly we observed and interviewed seemed to be extraordinarily healthy, serene, and well-adjusted to their lives. The small number of health problems reported, the absence of anger about the past, and the reported satisfaction with their lives all point to Kalmuk culture as being a context within which stressors are perhaps differently defined and experienced than in the larger culture. Certainly these experiences are expressed differently than they might have been by a mainstream group. The Kalmuk context is one in which aging and the turbulent past are differently understood. Ethnicity is not an aid to coping with life events, but rather the definer of life events. The good health and good spirits of the Kalmuk elderly are simply an indicator that stress, like aging, is not experienced the same way in every culture. It is the context in which the aging and stress are experienced which is the most significant determinant of whether the effects will be extreme or negligible.

REFERENCES

Amiot, le Pere
1776 Monument de la Transmigration de Torgouths des Bordes de la Mer Caspienne dan l'Empire de la Chine. Memoires Concernant l'Histoire de la Chine par les Missionaires de Pekin, Vol. #I.

Baldwin, C.S., ed.
1898 De Quincey's Revolt of the Tartars. New York: Longman's, Green and Co.

Barkman, C.S.
1955 The Return of the Torghuts from Russia to China. Journal of Oriental Studies, II.

Beaver, Marion
1979 The Decision-Making Process and its Relationship to Relocation Adjustment in Old People. The Gerontologist 19 (6):567-574.

Bergmann, Benjamin B.
1804 Nomadische Streiferien unter den Kalmuckenin den Jahren 1802 und 1803. Versuch zur Geshichte der Kalmukenflucht von der Volga, Riga.

Cool, L.E.
1979 Ethnicity and Aging: Continuity through Change in Elderly Corsicans. In Aging in Culture and Society: Comparative Viewpoints and Strategies. C.L. Fry, ed. South Hadley, Mass.: James Bergin Publishers.

Eichenbaum, J
1975 A Matrix of Human Movement. International Migration 13(I/2):21-40.

Grousset, Rene
1970 The Empire of the Steppes: A History of Central
     Asia. New Brunswick, N.J.: Rutgers University
     Press.

Holzberg, C.S.
1982 Ethnicity and Aging: Anthropological
     Perspectives on More Than Just the Minority
     Elderly. The Gerontologist 22.

Moris, M.
1825 Essai sur la Fuite de Kalmuks des Bords du
     Volga, traduit de L'Allemand (Bergmann).
     Chatillon-sur-Seine.

Nembirkow, Basan
     n.d. History of the Kalmuks. Unpublished paper.

Rubel, Paula
1967 The Kalmuk Mongols: A Study on Continuity and
     Change. Bloomington, Ind.: Indiana University
     Press.

1971 Ethnic Identity Among the Soviet Nationalities.
     In Soviet Nationality Problems. Edward Allworth,
     ed. New York: Columbia University Press.

Scudder, T. and Colson, E.
1982 From Welfare to Development: A Conceptual
     Framework for the Analysis of Dislocated Peoples.
     In Involuntary Migration and Resettlement. A.
     Hansen and A. Oluin-Smith, eds. Boulder,
     Colo.: Westview Press.

Shakabpa, Tsepon W.D.
1967 Tibet: A Political History. New Haven, Conn:
     Yale University Press.

CONTRIBUTORS

Vera Green, associate professor of anthropology at Rutgers University, was more than a contributing author to this volume. It was she and Heather Strange who together decided that a book combining original articles and an annotated bibliography would be useful on a theme embracing both anthropology and gerontology. Toward that end, they requested articles from several scholars, and a focus on diversity began to emerge. Vera Green died during the winter of 1982, before her ideas for the book could be developed. She had, however, drafted the article that appears herein, which the editors have revised for publication. After Dr. Green's untimely death, Michele Teitelbaum joined Heather Strange in editing this volume. The book has changed considerably since Vera Green began discussing the idea. However, the editors hope that the book is in the spirit of what Vera Green intended, and they dedicate it to her memory.

***

Benjamin Drew is an associate professor of anthropology at the Florham-Madison campus of Fairleigh Dickinson University. Recently, his research has focused on attitudes toward the elderly in the workplace and issues of aging and sexuality. He has just completed a study with his coauthor, Judith Waters, investigating the possibility of using video games as a natural therapy for the improvement

165

of perceptual-motor skills and cognitive functioning in the elderly.   Professor Drew's broad research interests have included a study of the relationship of sex and aggression in Poecilia reticulatus.   He also ran a primate laboratory at Fairleigh Dickinson for nine years.

Audrey Faulkner has been director of the Institute on Aging at Rutgers University and is a professor in the School of Social Work, Rutgers University.   She has had extensive practice, and administrative, teaching, and research experience in community organization and in the field of gerontology.   She is the principal investigator of a ten-year longitudinal study dealing with the mental health of inner-city black aged in Newark.   Other research interests include older women, and community development in urban America and the Third World.   Dr. Faulkner is coauthor, with Dr. Heisel, of When I Was Comin' Up, an oral history of aged blacks in the Newark study.

Marsel A. Heisel is an assistant professor in the School of Social Work, Rutgers University, where she teaches methods of social research and gerontology.   She has taught and done research on family life and adult education in Kenya and was a coinvestigator with Dr. Faulkner on the longitudinal study in Newark.   She has published a number of articles on black aged in the United States and on aging in developing countries.   Currently doing work on aging in Turkey, her research interests center on older women and social change.

Bonnie McCay is an associate professor of human ecology and anthropology at Rutgers University.   She received her Ph.D. in anthropology from Columbia University in 1976.   Her fieldwork has focused on fishing communities in Newfoundland, New Jersey, and Puerto Rico.   Dr. McCay has published extensively in the areas of ecological, evolutionary, and maritime anthropology.

Heather Strange is an associate professor of anthropology and director of the Graduate Program in Anthropology at Rutgers University.   She has worked in Trengganu, Malaysia, for three extended periods beginning in 1965. Dr. Strange served as senior Fulbright lecturer in Malay studies and in the Southeast Asia Program at the University of Malaya, Kuala Lumpur, during 1978-79; she was appointed to a three-year term as external examiner for sociology/anthropology in Malay studies in 1982.   Her diachronic study, Rural Malay Women in Tradition and Transition, was published in 1981.

Michele Teitelbaum is managing editor of Society magazine and a consultant in social medicine. She received her Ph.D. in anthropology from Rutgers University in 1977. Dr. Teitelbaum has conducted field research on political cognition in West Africa; and she has published work on social organization, sex roles, and methodology. Previously, she taught anthropology at Rutgers University and Hamilton College.

Krzysztof Teski is a member of the Computer and Informations Sciences Program at Stockton State College. He was trained as a mechanical engineer at Warsaw Technical University in Poland, and he worked as an engineer in the United States where he developed his interest in computer technology in industry. He invented several computer-aided solutions to bearing design problems. He has also delivered several papers on the subject of the immigrant professional in American industry.

Marea Teski is an associate professor of anthropology at Stockton State College. Her major interest is in aging and the evolution of culture and the adjustment to aging of different groups of elderly people. She has worked with American elderly, Uganda Asians in Britain, and elderly of a small community of Kalmuk Mongols. She is the author of: Living Together: An Ethnography of a Retirement Hotel and A City Revitalizes: The Elderly Lose at Monopoly, with R. Helsabeck, F. Smith, and C. Yeager--a study of changes in lives of the elderly in Atlantic City after casino gambling was introduced.

Judith Waters is an associate professor of psychology at the Florham-Madison campus of Fairleigh Dickinson University. She has written about the impact of physical attractiveness on the income of women from the ages of twenty to over sixty. She has also studied the relationship of retirement and other job stressors to the physical and mental health of members of such high risk occupations as law enforcement. Recently, Professors Drew and Waters have completed an investigation of the efficacy of utilizing video games to improve the perceptual-motor skills and cognitive functioning of a sample of noninstitutionalized elderly men and women.

Christine Wilson is a nutritionist-anthropologist in the Department of Epidemiology and International Health and the Program in Medical Anthropology of the University of California, San Francisco. Dr. Wilson holds degrees from Brown University and the University of California,

Berkeley. Her research has included dietary and sociocultural aspects of human behavior, particularly as they relate to food, dietary epidemiology of cancer, maternal and child nutrition crossculturally, and effects of modernization on traditional health and other behavior patterns.

PART II
Annotated Bibliography

I. GENERAL WORKS

A. OVERVIEWS, THEORETICAL AND METHODOLOGICAL WORKS

Anderson, Nancy N. 1967. The Significance of Age Categories for Older Persons. **The Gerontologist** 7 (3):164-167.

This review article deals with age categories among older people. Three major expositions of Barron, Rose, and Rosow are presented implying three hypotheses: older people interact with each other more than people of other age categories; older people identify with age categories; and age roles are developing their own values and norms. The author suggests that there is insufficient evidence to accept or reject these hypotheses and proposes that development of age consciousness, group characteristics, and role expectations based on age should first be explored.

Barron, Milton L. 1953. Minority Group Characteristics of the Aged in American Society. **Journal of Gerontology** 7 (4):477-482.

The author discusses the ways in which the social psychology of the aged in urban, industrial society resembles that of ethnic minorities.

Brennan, Michael J., Phillip Taft,and Mark B. Schupack.
1967. **The Economics of Age.** New York: W.W.
Norton and Co.

Using direct surveys and theoretical models, the authors' intent is to present a complete analysis of the economic problems associated with age. Part I explores the
topic of age with a discussion of the historic evolution of
the aging problem and concludes that more research in this
area is needed. In Part II, income and employment problems are investigated from the perspective of various industries. Age groups within given industries are compared,
and comparisons are made among industries for each age
group. The authors' objective is to identify common factors
operating across industries which produce employment patterns by age and to determine the extent to which industries differ in their hiring patterns regarding age.
Geographic migration, differences in mobility by age,
and the effects of migration upon the distribution of income
and employment by age are examined in Part III. Part IV
investigates various occupations in order to determine the
factors that explain the age structure within each occupation and which occupations provide employment opportunities
for older workers. In Part V, conclusions are drawn and
used as a basis for a discussion of public policy with regard to different age groups. Throughout this volume particular attention is paid to determining and examining the
concerns of the older worker.

Butler, Robert N. 1975 **Why Survive? Being Old in
America.** New York: Harper and Row.

An overview of the problems of the aged in America is
offered with recommendations about ways of solving them.
It is referred to by The Washingtonian as "The Encyclopedia Britannica of American Aging." Poverty, pensions, and
work; housing; physical and mental health; nursing homes;
government programs; victimization; the politics of aging;
and death; are among the subjects discussed in a clear and
comprehensive way.

Clark, Margaret M. 1973. Contributions of Cultural
Anthropology to the Study of the Aged. In **Cultural
Illness and Health.** Laura Nader and Thomas W.
Maretzki, eds. Pp. 78-88. Washington, D.C.:
American Anthropological Association.

Anthropological studies of any society would be incomplete if the aged in that society are not studied. In this article dealing with anthropological contributions to gerontological studies, the author notes the lack of literature in the field and feels the need for developing an "ethnography of adult life." The suggestions for studies include culture and personality of the aged, cognitive changes and nonverbal communication patterns within the adult life span, age and sex role studies, occupational socialization patterns, and changes in personal integration styles.

Clark, Margaret and Barbara G. Anderson. 1967.
**Culture and Aging: An Anthropological Study of
Older Amer- icans.** Springfield, Ill.:   Charles C.
Thomas.

The book opens with "An Anthropological Approach to Aging" which has been reprinted in several other works during the past decade. The subjects of the study, their San Francisco milieu, history and characteristics of the sample, measures of personal and social function among the aged, dynamics of the personal and social systems of the aged, and the process of aging adaptation in American culture are examined. Some cross-cultural data are included. Most of the nine chapters end with brief conclusions or summaries. The two appendices deal with characteristics of the study sample and the measurement of morale.

Cumming, Elaine, Lois R. Dean, David S. Newell, and Isabel
McCaffrey. 1960. Disengagement--A Tentative Theory
of Aging. **Sociometry** 23 (1):23-35.

In the absence of sociopsychological theories of aging, there seems to prevail an implied theory of the aging process in which the society withdraws from the aged, leaving them isolated and stranded. As an alternative to the implied theory, the authors suggest a tentative theory in which the individual cooperates in a process of disengagement and is not forced into it. The authors suggest that the disengagement process may be viewed as primarily intrinsic and secondarily responsive, leading to disengagement. The result of the disengaging process is seen as more self-centered and idiosyncratic behaviors on the part of ambulatory adults.

The disengagement theory is refined and elaborated in **Growing Old: The Process of Disengagement,** by Elaine

Cumming and William E. Henry, published by Basic Books in 1961.

Cumming, Elaine.   1963.   Further Thoughts on the Theory
    of Disengagement.   **International Social Science Journal**
    15:377–393.

    In amplifying and elaborating the disengagement theory
of aging, the author hopes to deal with some of the diversity observed among men and women in old age.

Curtin, Sharon R.   1972.   **Nobody Ever Died of Old Age.**
    Boston: Little, Brown and Company.

    This collection of vignettes offers the author's per-
spectives of growing old based on the lives of relatives and
friends as well as encounters with many other elderly.   She
discusses the biological as well as the social aging process.
Examining the indignity the elderly experience in hospitals
and in other institutions, Curtin states that our inefficient
social welfare system--including professionals such as doc-
tors, nurses and administrators--does not understand the
needs of the elderly and causes them much undue suffering.   Living in a culture that does not wish to concern itself with death and dying, the elderly are ignored and,
worse, they are treated inhumanly in an effort to deny
their existence.

Eisele, Frederick R., ed.   **Political Consequences of Aging.**
    Philadelphia Academy of Political and Social Science.
    (The Annals of the American Academy of Political and
    Social Science, V. 415).

    The volume is concerned with how the aged in the
United States affect politics now, with the aged and the future of American politics, and pensions.   One chapter concerns the National Center on the Black Aged, black aged,
and politics.

Foner, Anne.   1986   **Aging and Old Age: New
    Perspectives.**   Englewood Cliffs, N.J.:   Prentice-Hall.

    The age stratification perspective is the broad theoret-
ical approach used in this book.   Three underlying themes
about the aged and aging are: the age structure of so-

cieties, including the behavior and attitudes associated with each stratum; the dynamic age process of individuals and cohorts; and the intimate relationship between structure and process. The author emphasizes history and social change, and how aging processes vary among people born in different eras. The book concludes with a view toward future perspectives.

It is unfortunate that the publisher chose to print the chapter notes in small print that is difficult to read. This is especially so because the references are in the notes rather than in a separate list.

Hochschild, Arlie Russell. 1975. Disengagement Theory: A Critique and Proposal. **American Sociological Review** 40 (5):533-569.

This is a critical examination of the disengagement theory central to the study of the aged. The disengagement theory does not account for the many changes that have taken place since its formulation. It does not account for distinctive patterns of engagement of old women, and it cannot cope with the changing role of women and its effects on older women subsequently. it also cannot deal with problems of measuring social and normative engagement of older people. The author feels that research stemming from this theory is inconclusive and outmoded. In an attempt to avoid these problems he sketches an alternative theory in which he redefines disengagement and proposes new structural determinants of it.

Kalish, Richard A. 1971. A Gerontological Look at Ethnicity, Human Capacities, and Individual Adjustment. **The Gerontologist** 11:78-87.

The focus of this article is ethnicity as a factor in the individual capacities and adjustment of the aging and the aged. The author discusses variability within ethnic communities. Kalish suggests priorities in future research, emphasizing research into ethnic differences in performance on simple sensory, motor, and cognitive tasks; on performance on more complex cognitive tasks; on individual adjustment; on the meaning of age-related changes to various ethnic groups; on how each ethnic group defines good adjustment; and on people now in their fifties and sixties who will be the concern of social gerontologists of the future.

Keith, Jennie. 1980. The Best is Yet to Be: Toward an Anthropology of Age. In **Annual Review of Anthropology**, Volume Nine. B.J. Siegel, ed. Pp. 339-364. Palo Alto, Calif.: Annual Reviews Inc.

This review article is organized under the topics "old age in anthropology, anthropology of old age, and...anthro- pology of age." It includes recommendations about research directions.

Kiefer, Christie W. 1971. Notes on Anthropology and the Minority Elderly. **The Gerontologist** II (1, part 2):94-98.

Kiefer asks how acculturation affects the elderly, and whether all old people are culturally marginal in a rapidly changing society. She offers cultural relativism as an explanation for attitudes.

Lane, William C. 1978. The Aged as a Minority Group: The Controversy and Some Implications for Social Policy. Paper presented at the American Sociological Association Meeting, September, 1978, San Francisco.

In this paper, four specific issues concerning minority elderly are discussed: the point of entry issue; prejudice and discrimination; stereotyping; and sense of group identity. Some policy implications of viewing the aged as a minority group are also discussed.

LeVine, Robert A. 1978. Adulthood and Aging in Cross-Cultural Perspective. **Social Science Research Council Items** 31/32 (4/1):1-5.

In such areas of adult life as work and family roles, mid-life changes, and retirement, both theory and policy are often based on culture-bound concepts. LeVine advocates an empirical approach, using information systematically gathered from other cultures, and transcultural categories of analysis.

Linton, Ralph. 1942. Age and Sex Categories. **American Sociological Review** 7 (5):589-603.

This comparative study of age and sex categories examines the status "old women," postmenopausal women and
power, and the passage from "adult" to "aged," when there
is often a removal of ritual and social taboos. Even where
old age confers additional formal prestige, it is doubtful
that this amounts to additional prestige in daily living.

McGee, Jeanne and Kathleen Wells. 1982. Gender Typing
    and Androgyny in Later Life: New Directions for
    Theory and Research. **Human Development** 25 (2)
    116-139.

    The authors provide a sociological framework to bal-
ance   the   more   prevalent   psychologically-oriented
gerontological studies. Gutmann's role reversal theory and
Sinott's role blurring theory are examined. Suggestions for
the study of gender typing in later life include considerations of sexism, agism, continuity and change in gender
typing in old age, and the impact of demographic change.

Payne, Raymond. 1960. Some Theoretical Approaches to
    the Sociology of Aging. **Social Forces** 38 (4):359-362.

    An attempt is made in this article to approach the phe-
nomenon of aging in contemporary society through theories
of socialization, decision making, prestige age groups, and
social roles. The focus of the article is the process by
which the aging male assumes and maintains (or fails to assume and maintain) appropriate statuses and roles in his
social world.

Riley, Matilda White. 1973. Aging and Cohort Succession:
    Interpretations and Misinterpretations. **Public Opinion
    Quarterly** 37 (1):35-49.

    The two processes of aging and cohort succession un-
derlie many of the changes and trends of concern to social
scientists. As the relevant data accumulate, better understanding of both individuals and social change becomes more
attainable. The purpose of this article is to further such
understanding by providing guideposts for the analysis of
data that often appear to be deceptively simple.

Riley, Matilda White and Anne Foner. 1968. **Aging and
    Society, Volume One: An Inventory or Research
    Findings.** New York: Russell Sage Foundation.

This inventory brings together and summarizes the results of social science research on middle-aged and older
people.   It is a reference work of carefully selected, con-
densed, and organized findings intended as a tool for advancing theoretical understanding and enhancing professional practice.
    The volume is divided into four major focuses.   Part
1--the societal context: describes society as it provides a
setting for the aging individual;   Part 2--the organism:
deals with the health of older people, indluding age-related
behavioral changes in perception, motor skills, intelligence,
memory, and learning;   Part 3--personality: outlines relevant research on personality characteristics and basic attitudes of the individual as he or she reacts to circumstances, defines the self as old, and takes a negative or positive
view of the self;   Part 4--social roles: concerns political,
economic, religious, and familial roles that are available to
older persons including retiree, widow, and inmate of an
institution.   **Aging and Society** consists of three volumes:
Volume II is on Aging and the professions; Volume III is on
the sociology of age stratification.

Rose, Arnold. 1965. The Subculture of the Aging: A
    Framework for Research in Social Gerontology.   In
    Older People and Their Social World. A. Rose and W.
    Peterson, eds. Pp. 3-16. Philadelphia: F.A. Davis.

This article presents a theoretical framework for research in social gerontology.   Current trends revolve
around loss of social roles, adjustment and maladjustment,
and disengagement.   The author deals with aging as a subculture and points to the fact that there is no particular
age when people start participation in the subculture--
rather aging is a continuum.   Individuals participate in
varying degrees.   The parallel alternatives suggested by
the author include studying the characteristics of people
and conditions under which they start participation as well
as the extent and form of participation.   The aim of the
theoretical framework is to enable the development of
nomothetic generalizations rather than merely presentations
of empirical facts.

Rosow, Irving. 1967. **Social Integration of the Aged.**
New York: Free Press.

Rosow examines basic dimensions related to the extent of integration of the elderly in society. He considers social roles, social values, and formal and informal group membership. The following factors are related to positions occupied by the elderly: ownership of property; command of strategic knowledge and skills; religiosity and sacred traditions; kinship and extended family bonds; and low productivity, dependence and reciprocal aid. It is noted that some of the elderly may experience alienating effects.

Rosow, Irving. 1962. Old Age: One Moral Dilemma of an Affluent Society. **The Gerontologist** 2 (3):182-191.

An excellent essay, this deals with aging as a moral dilemma rather than a social one. The author suggests that insulating the aged from the insults and rebuffs of a youth-oriented affluent culture is just a temporary measure in order to alleviate the problem. A deeper level of analysis is suggested in which there is a "shift from materialistic obsessions to a richer quality of life and a corresponding respect for creativity, excellence and beauty for its own sake as well as a practical concern." If such a shift can be made, only then will there be a deeper understanding and respect between old and young.

San Diego Center on Aging. 1977. **Minority Aging and the Legislative Process.** San Diego, Calif.

These proceedings of the 3rd National Institute on Minority Aging examine some of the ways in which legislators, policymakers, and administrators have developed programs and policies that may have an impact on older minority persons.

Soldo, Beth J. 1980. America's Elderly in the 1980s.
Population Bulletin 35 (4):1-48.

This includes an overview by a demographer covering the age structure of the United States population since 1910. The author considers the quality of life and help for the elderly as well as death and illness. Two pages are devoted to "Aging in International Perspective."

U.S. Senate Special Committee on Aging. 1971. **A
Pre-White House Conference on Aging.** Summary of
Development and Data. Senate Report on Public Bills,
92nd Congress.
Rep.505, Abs. 502.

This report was submitted by Idaho Senator Frank
Church. It is extensive and covers almost all aspects of
aging and related problems. It consists of nine chapters
and nine appendices. Some key issues presented are retirement income, health and rising costs, and reduced programs for the elderly. Important emphasis is placed on minority aged and social attitudes toward them. Appendices
include important reports on retirement roles and activities,
planning, education, transportation, employment, and retirement. An interesting area-wide model program is also
suggested.

U.S. Superintendent of Documents. 1979. **Developments in
Aging.** (In two parts.) Washington, D.C.: U.S.
Government Printing Office.

The problems and opportunities of this ever-increasing
segment of the population are examined. Issues covered include health, income, home care, and housing. Background
material and agency reports on issues related to elderly citizens are also included.

B. <u>COLLECTIONS</u>

Amoss, Pamela T. and Steven Harrell, eds. 1981. **Other
Ways of Growing Old: Anthropological Perspectives.**
Stanford, Calif.: Stanford University Press.

This volume is intended to bring a cross-cultural perspective to the study of the aged and to distinguish between those factors related to age that are universal and
those that are shaped by sociocultural circumstances. Various authors included discussions of such factors as evolutionary variables, demography, subsistence economies,
property, and politics. They cover geographic areas including Africa, Asia, the Pacific, and North American Indi-

an communities. Amoss and Harrell explain variation by consideration of the degree of control achieved by the aged and the balance between costs to the community for their care and contributions made by the elderly in turn.

Contributors in addition to the editors are: Megan Biesele and Nancy Howell, Elizabeth Colson and Thayer Scudder, Carl Eisdorfer, Paul G. Hiebert, Sarah Blaffer Hrdy, James D. Nason, M. Nazif Shahrani, Henry S. Sharp, Peter W. Van Arsdale, and Kenneth M. Weiss.

Bengtson, Vern L. and Joan F. Robertson, eds. 1985.
Grandparenthood. Beverly Hills, Calif.: Sage
Publications.

The articles represent a variety of scholarly and professional perpectives on grandparenthood as a social role and as a phase of life; they provide insights into intergenerational relations. Anthropological, sociological, and psychological approaches as well as religious views, psychiatric issues, and policy matters are included.

Berghorn, Forrest J. and Donna E. Schafer. 1981. **The Dynamics of Aging: Original Essays on the Processes and Experiences of Growing Old.** Boulder, Colo.: Westview.

This interdisciplinary collection includes thirty essays grouped under seven topics: imperatives of aging; meeting health needs of older people; social parameters of aging; service delivery networks; personal dimensions of aging; creative pursuits in later life; and environmental aspects of aging. The last section includes an article about nursing home environments. The contributions most germane to the subject of cultural diversity are: "An Interdisciplinary Perspective on Aging" by Berghorn and Schafer; "Physical Aging: A Cross-Cultural Perspective" by Mary Jane Moore; and "The Ethnic Factor" by Linna Funk Place.

Binstock, Robert H. and Ethel Shanas, eds. 1976.
Handbook of Aging and the Social Sciences. New
York: Van Nostrand-Reinhold.

The book is divided into five parts. The first provides an overview of the development of social gerontology. Part Two, Aging and Social Structure, deals with the age structure of populations, intergenerational relations, and social stratification. Part Three, Aging and Social Systems, includes chapters on age strata, housing, the economy, work and retirement, leisure, law and politics. Part Four, Aging and Interpersonal Behavior, covers the topics of social networks, isolation, role change, and death and dying. The last part, Aging and Social Intervention, examines dilemmas, research, and issues including the future of social intervention.

Borgatta, Edgar F. and Neil G. McClusky, eds. 1981. **Aging and Society.** Beverly Hills, Calif.: Sage Publications.

The nine articles relate to the central theme of how the aged operate within our society. They are organized into five sections: economic perspectives; biological and psychological perspectives; health and welfare perspectives; political perspectives; and a conclusion. Articles cover such subjects as economic roles of the elderly, biological and psychological factors of aging, mental health, and support systems and old age politics.

Contributors in addition to the editors are: Marjorie H. Cantor, Carol Eisdorfer and Donna Cohen, Martin B. Loeb, Raymond Harris, Robert B. Hudson, Eugene Litwak, Abraham Monk, Charlotte F. Muller, and Harry Posman.

Busse, Ewald W. and Eric Pfeiffer, eds. 1977 (second edition). **Behavior and Adaptation in Late Life.** Boston: Little, Brown and Company.

With the great amount of new information about the aging process and the rapid obsolescence of present skills and knowledge, Busse and Pfeiffer found it practicable to present updated information by every author who appeared in their first edition in 1969. Recognizing that no single discipline offers a comprehensive explanation of how aged people act, the editors offer a collection of essays by authors who are either members of a common faculty at Duke University or who shared committee and organizational work.

Examining psychiatry, sociology, biology and economics, the authors are: Kurt W. Bach, Ewald W. Busse, Carol Eisdorfer, E. Harvey Estes, Jr., Alvin I Goldfarb, Dorothy K. Heyman, Frances C. Jeffers, Juanita M. Kreps, George L. Maddox, Erdman Palmore, Eric Pfeiffer, Grace H. Polansky, Ethel Shanas Joseph J. Spengler, Virginia Stone, Adriaan Verwoerdt, F. Stephen Vogel, and H.S. Wang.

Cox, Harold, ed. 1980. **Aging, Second Edition.**
Guilford, Conn: Annual Editions. The Dushkin
Publishing Group,
Inc.

This volume, which may be most useful on a secondary
school level, includes forty-four articles on topics relevant
to aging. These come from a wide range of publications,
including popular and semi-popular media, government publications, and scholarly journals. The book is divided into
sections on the American population, the phenomenon of aging, aging in other cultures, societal attitudes toward old
age, problems and potentials of aging, retirement, the experience of dying, social policies, programs and services
for older Americans. The book has a useful topic guide
which cross-references the articles.
    Contributors in addition to the editor include: Robert
C. Benedict, Fred Best, E. Virginia Beverly, Robert N.
Butler, Francis D. Glamser, Anita S. Harbert and Carroll
W. Wilkinson, Richard A. Kalish, Robert Kastenbaum,
George L. Maddox, Bernice L. Neugarten, Erdman Palmore,
Phyllis K. Snyder, and Ann Way. Several popular authors
are included.

Davis, Richard H. and William K. Smith, eds. 1973.
    Drugs and the Elderly. Los Angeles, Calif.: U.S.C.,
    Ethel Percy Andrus Gerontology Center.

    A collection of eight papers focuses on aspects of drug
use by the elderly, including self medication, side effects
of various drugs, influence of drugs on behavior, drug administration from two viewpoints--that of a physician administrator and that of a family nurse practitioner--clinical
pharmacy, and interaction between drugs and the changing
physiology of the aged.
    Contributors in addition to the editors are: Edward
S. Brady, Frank J. Briganti, Alan Cheung, Linda E.
Jessup, Ronald C. Kayne, Paul Lofholm, Bertram Moss, Eric
Pfeiffer, Ruth B. Weg.

Derber, Milton, ed. 1950. **The Aged and Society: A
    Symposium on the Problems of an Aging Population.**
    Champaign, Ill.: Industrial Relations Research
    Association.

    Concerned with the impact of greater life expectancy
on society, the Industrial Research Association held its first

research symposium in 1950. This volume of fifteen articles is dedicated to an awareness of this basic problem and to a concern for effective remediations.

Part I reviews the distribution of the aged in the new industrial society. An age profile of the population is followed by research on the aged in industrial and rural societies. In Part II, the authors examine social patterns and older workers with studies concerning labor force participation, industry, union policies, and retirement, including social provisions and self-help for a successful retirement. Topics of concern including personal and social adjustment, politics, psychology, employability, mental health, and medical and social aspects of aging are discussed in Part III.

The list of contributors includes: Clark Kerr, Edwin E. Witte, Solomon Barkin, J. Douglas Brown, Ernest W. Burgess, Lloyd H. Fisher, Oscar Kaplan, Elon H. Moore, Wilbert E. Moore, Otto Pollak, J.H. Seldon, Nathan W. Shock, Henry S. Shryock, Jr., Sumner H. Slichter, T. Lynn Smaith, D. Speakman, and A.T. Welford.

Fry, Christine, L. and Jennie Keith, eds. 1986. **New Methods for Old Age Research.** South Hadley, Mass.: Bergin and Garvey.

The results of a 1980 workshop on cross-cultural research on old age are updated to reflect new findings. Nine participants offer anthropological perspectives on the methods needed for the successful, "more adventurous" study of old age. Advantages of participant observation, life history approaches, social network and age grade analysis, holocultural studies (e.g., using data from sources such as the Human Relations Area Files) as well as cognitive anthropological techniques for the study of older populations are all discussed in detail. The importance of role transitions during the life course and the most useful means for measuring the morale of the aged in an anthropological context are explored. As methodological approaches are stressed, there are comparatively few ethnographic examples of elderly populations.

Other contributors in addition to the editors include: J. Kevin Eckert and Cynthia Beall, Gelya Frank, Anthony P. Glascock, John T. Hinnant, Corrinne N. Nydegger, and Jay Sokolovsky.

Fry, Christine L., ed. 1980. **Aging in Culture and Society: Comparative Viewpoints and Strategies.** Brooklyn, N.Y.: J.F. Bergin Publishers Inc.

The book contains sixteen selections about various aspects of aging, including a summary by L.D. Holmes and a foreword by Paul Bohannan. In her opening article, Fry discusses the origin and development of "an anthropology of aging, methodologies, and contemporary issues, particularly the need for significant theory." In another article, she shows the use of multidimensional scaling analysis as a method for discovering hidden structures within empirical data and pressing them in a geometric picture. Biological factors in aging are addressed by Beaubier. Four articles deal with problems and strategies of aging in America; two of them are based on research carried out in six public housing projects in Milwaukee. Another examines kin relations among Polish-American aged in Chicago; the fourth analyzes death anxiety among middle-class Protestants in a semirural midwestern community. Aging and/or the aged in a Colombian peasant village, among Native Americans in Oklahoma, among the Black Carib, in India, among Niolan Corsicans living in Paris, among the Chinese in Hong Kong and China, and among construction workers in a retirement residence near Paris, France, are the subjects of other articles.

Contributors in addition to the editor are: Eunice Boyer, Linda Cool, Charlotte Ikels, Karen Jonas, Diane Kagan, Jennie Keith, Virginia Kerns, Carol M. Schultz, Maria Siemaszko, Sylvia Vatuk, Edward Wellin, Gerry C. Williams.

Fry, Christine L., ed. 1981. **Dimensions: Aging, Culture and Health,** Brooklyn, N.Y.: J.F. Bergin Publishers.

This volume collects research on the relationship of aging to health in both industrialized and nonindustrialized cultures. Chapters in the first part deal with aging in many geographical areas including Africa, New Guinea, China, England, and the United States. The second part of the book deals with research on the subjects of health and medicine. A third part explores generally the relationships between the fields of gerontology and anthropology.

Other contributors in addition to the editor are: Pamela T. Amoss, Arnold Arluke and John M. Peterson, Barry Bainton, Paul Bohannan, Margaret Faulwell and Rhoda S. Pomerantz, Valerie Fennell, Doris Goist Francis, Anthony P. Glascock, Susan L. Feinman, David I. Kertzer and Oker B.B. Madison, Jeanie Kayser-Jones, Jennie Keith, Helena Z. Lopata, Otto von Mering, Corinne N. Nydegger, Andrea

Sankar, Jay Sokolovsky and Carl Cohen, Peter W. Van Arsdale, and Jack M. Weatherford.

Gelfand, Donald E. and Alfred Kutzik, eds. 1979.
Ethnicity and Aging: Theory, Research, and Policy.
New York: Springer Publishing Company.

Most articles in this volume were originally prepared for the National Conference on Ethnicity and Aging at the University of Maryland in 1978. Part I deals with theory and policy issues in the area of ethnicity and aging. Part II focuses on ethnic factors influencing the relationship of younger family members to the aged. Part III includes research in a variety of additional areas relevant to ethnicity and aging. In brief concluding remarks, the editors reiterate the continuing significance of ethnicity in the study of the aged.

Other contributors in addition to the editors are: William Bechill, Vern L. Bengtson, David E. Biegel and Wendy R. Sherman, Marilyn R. Block, Marjorie H. Cantor, Bertram J. Cohler and Morton A. Lieberman, David Guttman, Robert Kastenbaum, John Lewis McAdoo, David Maldonago, Jr., Elizabeth W. Markson, Darrel Montero, Danuta Mostwin, Rolando Merino and Sarah Santana, Jody I. Olsen, Donald C. Snyder, James E. Trela and Jay H. Sokolovsky, Raju Varghese and Fred Medinger, Ruth E. Zambrana, and Irving Kenneth Zola.

Goldsmith, Jack and Sharon S. Goldsmith, eds. 1976.
Crime Against the Elderly. Lexington, Mass.: D.C. Heath and Company.

There are sixteen chapters dealing with crimes against the elderly and how crime and the fear of it affect the quality of life of elderly Americans. The book is divided into three parts: patterns of crime against the elderly, criminal victimization of the elderly, and the criminal justice system and the elderly victim. Papers were delivered at the National Conference on Crime Against the Elderly in Washington, D.C., and include psychological aspects of crime; fear of crime in urban and public housing environments; American views of aging; and police responses to criminal acts against the elderly victims.

Contributors in addition to the editors are: Phyllis Mensh Brostoff, John E. Conklin, Carl L. Cunningham, John P. J. Dussich, Charles J. Eichman, Steven Feldman, David M. Friedman, Gilbert Geis, M. Powell Lawton, James

T. Mathieu, Lucille Nahemow, Anne D. Nelson, Evelyn S. Newman, Jeffrey H. Reiman, James B. Richardson, Edmund A. Sherman, Richard A. Sundeen, Richard E. Sykes, David P. Van Buren, Emilio C. Viano, Silvia Yaffe, and Evelle J. Younger.

Gubrium, Jaber F. ed. 1974. **Late Life: Communities and Environmental Policy.** Springfield, Ill.: Charles C. Thomas.

Focusing exclusively on environmental issues, this collection of twelve papers examines physical, formal, and cross-cultural factors and their impact on the aged. The physical environment is examined in the first section; community structure and demography are included among the reports. Nursing homes and a French retirement residence are investigated in the second section which is entitled "Formal Communities." The third section concentrates on cross-cultural environments and includes aspects of aging and modernization as well as an examination of old age among the Baganda of Nganda and the Issei (Japanese immigrants to the United States). In the final section, environmental policy is examined vis-a-vis the aspects of matching environments to needs, relocation, stress, institutional life, and the dimensions of adult learning and spiritual well-being.

The contributing authors are: Bert N. Adams, Gordon L. Bultena, Albert Chevan, Donald O. Cowgill, Marshall Graney, Jaber L. Gubrium, Tom Hickey, James W. Hodgson, Eva Kahana, Christie W. Kiefer, Morton Lieberman, David O. Moberg, Nina Nahemow, John O'Rourke, and Jennie Keith-Ross.

Hareven, Tamara K. and Kathleen J. Adams, eds. 1982. **Aging and Life Course Transitions: An Interdisciplinary Perspective.** New York: Guilford Press.

The life course approach is used in this collection of ten articles, which are introduced by Hareven's analytic historical overview. The approach challenges traditional gerontology, placing emphasis on how earlier experiences shape individual attitudes toward aging as well as examining collective sociocultural experience such as the impact of the Great Depression. The book combines theory, methodology, and new research about aging in the United States, Great Britain, France, and Japan.

Contributors in addition to the editors are: Daniel Bertaux, Glen H. Elder, David Eversley, Anne-Marie Guillemard, Gisela Labouvie-Vief, Leonard I. Pearlin, David W. Plath, Leopold Rosenmayr, and Lars Tornstam.

Hess, Beth B. and Elizabeth W. Markson, eds. 1985 (third
    edition). **Growing Old in America: New Perspectives
    on Old Age.** New Brunswick, N.J.: Transaction
    Books.

A demographic overview is followed by thirty-seven articles, most of which have been previously published. While the focus is on aging in America, a section is included on cross-cultural perspectives. Other sections deal with historical perspectives; cultural stereotypes; bodies, minds, and life-course perspectives; the family setting; residential settings; economic status and public policy.
    Contributors in addition to the editors include: Brian Gratton, Jill Quadagno, John B. Williamson, Corinne N. Nydegger, Paul M. Baker, Linda Cool and Justine McCabe, Kryiakos S. Markides, Charlotte Ikels, Arnold Arluke and Jack Levin, Andrea S. Walsh, Barbara F. Turner, Lois M. Verbrugge, Ruth B. Weg, Jaber F. Gubrium and Robert J. Lynott, Marjorie Chary Feinson, David A. Karp and William C. Yoels, Leonard I. Pearlin and Clarice Radabaugh, Matilda White Riley, Maximiliane E. Szinovacz, Gary R. Lee, Charles H. Mindel, Nancy Foner, Claire Pedrick-Cornell and Richard J. Gelles, Jeffrey P. Rosenfeld, Anne Woodward, Deborah A. Sullivan and Sylvia A. Stevens, Marea Teski, Ellen J. Langer and Jerry Avorn, John Cumming, Martin Hochbaum and Florence Galkin, Robert H. Binstock, John Myles, Nathan Keyfitz, Maxine Forman, and Carroll L. Estes.

Kart, Cary S. and Barbara Manard, eds. 1976. **Aging in
    America: Readings in Social Gerontology.** New York:
    Alfred Publishing Company, Inc.

The book is divided into seven sections, each of which contains from four to six chapters. The first two sections deal with theoretical approaches and methodological issues. These are followed by biological and psychological aspects of aging; work, retirement and leisure; living environs; institutionalization; and death and dying. Each section is prefaced by an introductory overview.

Kenny, Michael, ed. 1979. The Ethnography of Old Age.
Anthropological Quarterly, Special Issue 52 (1).

This issue offers seven articles on the subject of old
age, including a discussion of conditions affecting the organization of two mobile home communities in Arizona; role
diversity among members of a Sephardic home vis-a-vis
community development; the relationship between roles outside a housing project for the elderly and roles within the
project; adjustments of black and white elderly to the same
adaptive niche--namely, public housing for the elderly;
friendship and factionalism in a triethnic (black, Cuban,
white English-speaking) housing complex (Miami, Florida):
comparison and comment regrding age sets (such as those
found among the Nyakyusa) and retirement communities in
western societies.
    Contributors are: Eunice Boyer, Christine Fry,
Marion Heider, Giselle Hendel-Sebestyen, Karen Jonas,
Randy Frances Kandel, Jennie Keith, Asmarom Legesse.

Kertzer, David I. and Jennie Keith, eds. 1984. **Age and
Anthropological Theory.** Ithaca, N.Y.: Cornell
University Press.

The thirteen essays in this collection examine "the implications of a focus on age for theoretical development in
the various realms of anthropology," such as social organization, kinship, power and politics, the interrelationship
between biology and culture, and ritual and religion. The
volume is divided into three major parts: age, evolution
and biology; age and society; and age and culture.
    Contributors in addition to the editors are: Cynthia
M. Beall, Ronald Cohen, Phyllis Dolhinow, Penelope Eckert,
Nancy Foner, Meyer Fortes, Rhoda Halperin, Eugene A.
Hammel, David Maybury-Lewis, Barbara Myerhoff, Akos
Ostor, and Andrea Sankar.

Lesnoff-Caravaglia, Gari, ed. 1982. **The World of the
Older Woman: Conflicts and Resolutions.** Frontiers in
Aging Series. New York: Human Services Press,
Inc.

Lesnoff-Caravaglia has put together writings about the
particular needs, interests, and concerns of older women.
She examines legal problems; harassments such as abuse
and rape; employment distinctions; attitudes; and social
status. The authors also discuss the problem of

institutional life which older women often face alone. Suggestions are provided for the resolution of some of these problems and for the development of appropriate services.

Contributors in addition to the editor are: Stefanie S. Auslander; Adele Cooperband, Nancy Knapp, Paul S. Nathanson, Eloise Rathbone-McCuan, Phyllis R. Silverman, Marcia B. Steinhauer, Natalie P. Trager, Lillian E. Troll.

McNeely, R.L. and John L. Colen, eds. 1983. **Aging in Minority Groups**. Beverly Hills, Calif.: Sage Publications.

Issues, implications for policy and programming, and community and individual intervention strategies for helping minority-group elderly are the underlying concerns in this collection of twenty-three articles organized into five major (and several minor) parts. Part I deals with the problems of minority aging and lack of information about the topic. Part II on the demography of minority aging, has articles about Asian-Pacific elderly, blacks, elderly of Cuban origin, Mexican-Americans, and Native Americans. Part III is on exemplars of aging in a cultural context: three minority groups--Asian-American, black, Mexican-American. Part IV focuses on social problems of minority aged--housing, crime, health and mental health, employment and income maintenance, local decision making, and political involvement. The last section, Part V, covers the topic of service delivery.

Contributors in addition to the editors are: Josephine A. Allen, Elena M. Bastida, Rosina M. Becerra, E. Daniel Edwards, Adam W. Herbert, Robert B. Hill, Hisashi Hirayama, Barbara Jones Morrison, Paul H.K. Kim, Doman Lum, John Lewis McAdoo, Gaylene Perrault, Megaly Queralt, Gilbert L. Raiford, Nellie Tate, Fernando Torres-Gil, Ramon Valle, Robert O. Washington, Wilbur H. Watson, Shirley Wesley-King, Maria Zuniga-Martinez.

Myerhoff, Barbara G. and Andrei Simic, eds. 1977. **Life's Career--Aging: Cultural Variations on Growing Old**. Beverly Hills, Calif.: Sage Publications (Cross-cultural Research and Methodology Series, Vol. 4).

In order to discover common themes in the lives of informants and similar threads of experiences, the authors studied the process and patterns of aging among: the Chagga people of Kilimanjaro, the elderly in Yugoslavia and

Central Mexico, Jewish senior citizens in Venice, California, and older Mexican-Americans.

Contributors in addition to the editors are: Jose Cuellar, Sally Falk Moore, and Carlos G. Velez.

Nydegger, Corinne N., ed. 1983. Special Issue on Anthropological Approaches to Aging Research: Applications to Modern Societies. **Research on Aging—a Quarterly of Social Gerontology and Adult Development** 5 (4):451-492.

Nydegger introduces this collection of seven articles by noting the methodological eclecticism found among the anthropologists. What ties the papers in this volume together is the cultural phenomenology approach applied to modern societies. The problems examined and the specific methods used are quite different, ranging from the use of genealogies to analyze caretaker selection among two ethnic groups in Boston, to the use of topical oral biographies to provide insights into the friendship process.

Contributors in addition to the editor are : J. Kevin Eckert, B. Lisa Groger, Haim Hazan, Charlotte Ikels, Colleen Leahy Johnson, Sarah H. Matthews, Linda S. Mitteness, and John O'Neil.

Orbach, Harold and Clark Tibbits, eds. 1963. **Aging and the Economy**. Ann Arbor, Mich.: University of Michigan Press.

Reports presented at the University of Michigan's 15th Annual Conference on Aging comprise the contents of the book. Several objectives served as guidelines and goals of the conference: (1) To achieve understanding of the relationship of national income and wealth to the capacity to support the expanding older population; (2) To examine the work roles of older people in light of the rising population, national security, and trends in productivity; (3) To evaluate current methods and adequacy of supporting the retired population and to consider probable and desirable trends; and (4) To study expenditure patterns and needs of older people in relation to varying circumstances and styles of life.

The reports are divided among six sections that address the following topics about the economy and the aged: supporting the older population, work and employment opportunities, income and resources of the aged, the older person as consumer, implications of pension funds, social policy and social values. Among the numerous authors and discussants are representatives of government agencies, private industry, unions, academia, and senior citizens' organizations.

Palmore, Erdman, and Frances C. Jeffers, eds. 1971.
    Prediction of Life Span—Recent Findings. Lexington,
    Mass.: Lexington Books.

The twenty articles present data on different physiological, psychological, and social predictions of longevity. The groups studied include middle and older age community residents, as well as the institutionalized aged. Although most of the populations are in the United States, a few studies consider intra-class variables, and Gutmann discusses Navajo populations in comparison to Kansas City and Druze populations. The general conclusion is that there are many variables such as heredity and physiology which "significantly predict longevity, as no one variable in itself offers a sufficient explanation."

Rifai, Marlene A. Y., ed. 1977. **Justice and Older
    Americans.** Lexington, Mass: D.C. Heath and
    Company.

This is a collection of nineteen articles dealing with the victimization of older Americans. There are three general headings, "The Victimization of Older Americans," "Society's Response to the Victimization of Older Americans," and "The Politics of Providing Justice to Older Americans." Articles cover such topics as crime and urban elderly and various ethnic groups; nursing homes as social victimization; legal services for the elderly; law and public policy.
    Contributors are: Sheila A. Ames, Vern L. Bengtson, Albert D. Buford III, Mary Lou Calvin, Marilyn W. Culp, Neal E. Cutler, Gilbert Geis, George A. Hacker, Carol Ann Holcomb, Michel P. Jones, Paul A. Kerschner, Morton Leeds, Paul S. Nathanson, Lt. Richard Piland, Pauline K. Ragan, Vikii L. Schmall; Anne L. Schneider, Peter R. Schneider, William Simonson, Richard Sundeen, Doris A. Weaver, Terrie Wetle, and Nancy Whitelaw.

Simpson, Ida H. and John C. McKinney, eds. 1966. **Social
    Aspects of Aging.** Durham, N.C.: Duke University
    Press.

Four problem areas associated with the elderly in the United States are examined: retirement, the family, community, and perceptions about life. The interplay of demographic changes with industrialization is analyzed in Section I to explain the institutionalization of retirement and unemployment among older Americans. Section II focuses on family relationships vis-a-vis reactions to retirement. The ways in which community structure and social activities affect attitudes toward retirement by senior and by younger adults are the subjects of Section III. Section IV compares personal perspectives of the elderly to those of younger adults. The studies make clear that the problems and concerns of the elderly are as varied as their social relationships and values.

Contributors in addition to the editors are: Kurt W. Bach, Kenneth F. Gergen, Carleton S. Guptill, Alan C. Kerckhoff, Howard P. Myers, Joel Smith, Joseph F. Spengler, and Herman Turk.

Sokolovsky, Jay, ed. 1983. **Growing Old in Different Societies: Cross-Cultural Perspectives.** Belmont, Calif.: Wadsworth.

The book offers a collection of nineteen articles with an introduction about comparative sociocultural gerontology by the editor. It is organized under these headings: culture, society and aging; age boundaries and intergenerational links; aging, modernization and societal transformation; the ethnic factor in aging; networks, community creation, and institutionalization: environments for aging. There are overview articles, including one on women; some articles are based on research in one cultural context, and others are cross-cultural. Some of the societies or social contexts examined are: Inuit, Baganda, Samoan, Irish, Japanese, Oklahoma Indians, several other ethnic groups in the United States, inner-city elderly and nursing home residents in the United States, and the elderly in British New Towns. Ten of the articles were written for this volume; the others are reprints from a variety of sources. The mix is, on all counts, very good.

Contributors in addition to the editor are: Vern L. Bengtson, Pierre van den Berghe, Carl Cohen, Linda Cool, James Dowd, Lee Guemple, Lowell Holmes, Barbara Hornum, Colleen Leahy Johnson, Jennie Keith, Robert Maxwell, Justine McCabe, Leslie A. Morgan, Barbara Myerhoff, Nina Nahemov, David Plath, Ellen Rhodes, Nancy Scheper-Hughes, Marjorie M. Schweitzer, Philip Silverman, Andrei Simić, Marea Teski, and Maria Vesperi.

Spencer, Marian G. and Caroline V. Do, eds. 1975.
Understanding Aging: A Multidisciplinary Approach.
New York: Appleton-Century-Crofts.

This collection of articles, reflecting multidisciplinary approaches to aging, is an outgrowth of a Boston University experimental course. In addition to focusing on service and social welfare, aspects of the sociology and economics of aging, the technical, nutritional, mental, medical, and spiritual aspects are considered. The articles vary from a guide-lines approach to research and policy issues. The book focuses on the United States.

Tibbitts, Clark and Wilma Donohue, eds. 1960. **Aging in Today's Society.** Englewood Cliffs, N.J.: Prentice-Hall.

Eleven topics are selected in this attempt to view aging as an achievement. Twelve articles are followed by selected passages, primarily from the work of noted figures such as Aristotle and Kipling, to illustrate aging as a social achievement, aging creativeness, comprehension, questions of retirement and citizenship. One essay, by Simmons, is concerned with aging cross-culturally and diachronically.

Tibbitts, Clark, and Wilma Donahue, eds. 1962. **Social and Psychological Aspects of Aging.** New York: Columbia University Press. The proceedings of the Fifth Congress of the International Association of Gerontology.

The papers and their critiques are devoted to studies of the dynamics of aging and the subsequent ramifications-- economic, social, recreational, as well as the physical and psychological aspects of health. While there is a theme of "aging around the world," attention was given primarily to populations in the United States, Europe, and Asia, in de-scending order of importance.

Williams, Richard H.; Clark Tibbitts, and Wilma Donahue, eds. 1963. **Processes of Aging: Social and Psychological Perspectives, Volumes I and II.** New York: Atherton Press.

Containing a total of fifty-nine articles concerned with the psychological, psychiatric, psychosocial, and socioeconomic aspects of aging, Volumes I and II are the result of studies prepared for an international seminar on psychological and social aging in relation to mental health. A joint undertaking of the Social Science Research Committee of the International Association of Gerontology, the Professional Services Branch of the National Institute of Mental Health and the Division of Gerontology of the University of Michigan, the seminar attracted sixty-six research works with the aim of increasing understanding of the processes of aging and providing a basis for social planning.

Part I, Psychological Capacities, includes studies on cognition, psychophysiological problems, and psychological environment. In Part II, Successful Aging, the authors concentrate on aspects of adjustment, both personal and social as well as the personality and style of living. Part III, Psychopathology of Aging, includes discussions on diagnosis and classification, institutionalization influence of age on schizophrenia, and coping strategies. Part IV examines implications for future research on the topics discussed in the first three parts.

In Part V, Relations with Family and Society, the authors discuss some national studies of older people, social change and its impact, and special settings for the aged. Part VI, Social Factors in Psychiatric Disorders, contains articles on the epidemiology of psychiatric disorders of old age including suicide, adjustment of the normal aged and hospitalization of elderly psychiatric patients. Part VII, Economic, Health and Retirement, discusses work patterns, seniority, and occupational health. In addition, several authors from other countries examine retirement-related topics from their countries' perspectives. In Part VIII, implications for future research are discussed regarding the last four topics.

Woodruff, Diana S. and James E. Birren, eds. 1975.
Aging: Scientific Perspectives and Social Issues. New York: Van Nostrand.

The eighteen articles are grouped under six topics: "Aging in Broad Perspective" (including Woodruff's introduction about multidisciplinary perspectives and Birren and Clayton's "History of Gerontology"); three sections dealing with sociological, psychological, and biological perspectives; "Issues in the Physical Environment," and "Social Issues." Demography, the family, learning and memory, brain function, cellular biology, aspects of the physiology of aging, planning in microenvironments and in urban neighborhoods, economics, television, political behavior, and analytic approaches to public policy are some of the specific subjects pertaining to aging and the aged.

Contributors in addition to the editors are: Vern L. Bengtson, Vivian Clayton, Neal E. Cutler, Richard H. Davis, Paul Denny, Herbert A. deVries, David A. Haber, Robert A. Harootyan, Christopher Hertzog, Ira S. Hirshfield, Paul A. Kerschner, Victor Regnier, K. Warner Schaie, John R. Schmidhauser, Arthor N. Schwartz, Judith Treas, James Walker, David A. Walsh, Robin Jane Walther, and Ruth B. Weg.

C. SOCIAL ROLES AND ATTITUDES

1. Physical and Mental Health

Alington-MacKinnon, Diane and Lillian E. Troll. 1981. The Adaptive Function of the Menopause: A Devil's Advocate Position. **Journal of the American Geriatrics Society** 29 (8) 349-333.

Menopause is viewed as a normal adaptation rather than as a deficiency disease or as a symptom of decline. The authors question the appropriateness of estrogen replacement therapy as a response to biological events and life stress in middle age.

Anderson, Barbara G. 1964. Stress and Psychopathology among Aged Americans: An Inquiry into the Perception of Stress. **Southeastern Journal of Anthropology** 20 (2):190-217.

Patterns in the perception of stress are studied among a population of 127 men and women above the age of 60. The subjects had been admitted to a California state hospital's psychiatric ward two years earlier.

Butler, Robert N. and Myrna I. Lewis. 1973. **Aging and Mental Health: Positive Psychosocial Approaches.** St. Louis, Mo.: The C.V. Mosby Company.

An extremely positive approach to old age runs throughout this book. The losses faced by the elderly are treated in a frank manner, and it is demonstrated how these losses can be an aid to strengthening rather than diminishing one's mental health in old age. The authors suggest an approach that entails people not looking upon aging as a defeat, but as a series of victories. They also suggest that most older people can be rehabilitated and become involved in constructive work. Involvement is the basic theme of this book, noninvolvement leading to rapid mental and physical deterioration. An excellent book recommended for students of gerontology.

Chown, Sheila M., ed. 1972. **Human Aging: Selected Readings.** Middlesex, England: Penguin Books.

Human aging is a complicated process. Physiologically the person becomes less effective in performing certain functions with old age. Many biologists are constantly looking for a key to the aging process, e.g., failure of the sex hormones or failure to get enough oxygen to the brain. Much progress has been made in the area of cell biochemistry, but there is yet a long way to go. It has been observed that even if physiological aging did not occur, psychological aging would still go on. Psychological aging centers around the theme of adaptability. This book deals with the psychological aspects of aging with two main themes--cognition and personality. A collection of short articles deal with various aspects of normal aging as opposed to pathological problems encountered by few members of a society.

Douvan, Elizabeth. 1982. Data Reveal Older Women More Satisfied with Jobs, Family. **The Committee for Gender Research** 1:1-5.

A brief research report about two identical studies carried out at the Survey Research Center using random samples of 2,500 American adults in 1957 and in 1976. The most striking changes for people sixty to eighty are improvements in health and economic status. Also, those surveyed in 1976 were more independent than respondents who were in the sixty-to-eighty category twenty years earlier.

In 1957, "the older a woman was, the less satisfied she was with her marriage and the less good she felt about herself." Older women in the 1976 sample had higher self-esteem and were as happy with their marriages as younger women. Older women in the work force are more likely than any other group to report job satisfaction, with interpersonal pleasures ranking higher for them than power gratification (which males in the same cohort mentioned more frequently).

Erdwings, Carol J.; Jeanne C. Mellinger and Zita E. Tyler. 1981. A Comparison of Different Aspects of Self-Concept for Young, Middle Aged, and Older Women. **Journal of Clinical Psychology** 37:484-90.

Two major themes underlie this study: (1) the different roles that women assume influence the evaluation of self-concept, and (2) the negative and positive feelings are interrelated with various stages of life. The self-concepts of women in four age groups were compared (18-22, 29-30, 40-55 and 60-75). The Tennessee self-concept scale was used to measure attitude toward self.

The results of this study indicate that the 40-55 group had the most positive feelings of self-concept while the 18-22 and 29-39 were still establishing their moral value systems and thus had the lowest self-concept. The 60-75 cohort appeared most defensive and least open to self-criticism. Self-esteem did not vary significantly in all age groups. The findings of this study supported Neugarten's theories of "interiority" and "withdrawal of interpersonal relations" by the oldest age group. On the second theme it was suggested that the roles a woman assumes during her lifetime do not influence her self-concept.

Friedman, Eugene A. and Robert J. Havighurst. 1954. **The Meaning of Work and Retirement.** Chicago: University of Chicago Press.

This book reports the findings of a set of studies about the significance of work in the lives of people, and work and attitudes toward retirement. It aims to lay a partial basis for a retirement policy that is both satisfactory to the individual and wise for the general welfare.

Gelfand, Donald E. 1979-80. Ethnicity, Aging, and Mental Health. **Aging and Human Development** 10 (3):289-298.

This discussion of ethnicity and the mental health of the elderly considers the "dumping" of the elderly on inadequate facilities (long-term treatment in institutions) as well as the inadequacy of community mental health services for the ethnic elderly. The author suggests the need for major changes in the manner in which mental health services for the elderly are being delivered. He also suggests a need to rethink the appropriateness of the treatment methods now being employed because many ethnic elderly find that mental health services are in conflict with the values of their particular culture; they perceive traditional therapy as negative to their culture and a means for indoctrinating them into an alien one.

Hall, G. Stanley. 1922. **Senescence: The Last Half of Life.** New York: D. Appleton & Co.

In 1922, acknowledging the great and growing interest in the subject of old age and death, psychologist Hall compiled this volume of data and became one of the first contributors to the new science of gerontology. He ended a career devoted to the study of the life-cycle with a focus on old age. In this work, he explores the "youth of old age," and the history of old age, and discusses the literature by and on the aged, "whereby old people can fortify themselves against depressions and remissions of old age by familiarizing their minds with quotations." He deals with statistics, medical views and treatments, and biological and physiological studies and experiments. He also discusses the results of a questionnaire that was sent to "distinguished old people," and he ponders some of the questions that are still being asked in the 1980s. The psychology of death is the final topic addressed.

Lazarus, Richard S. and Anita De Longis. 1983. Psychological Stress and Coping in Aging. **American Psychologist** 37:245-254.

This article explores the dynamics of stress and coping as they interact with the processes of aging. The difficulties of systematically investigating this subject are discussed. The authors emphasize the importance of examining stress and coping longitudinally, rather than just cross-sectionally.

Lebo, Dell. 1953. Some Factors Said to Make for
    Happiness in Old Age. **Journal of Clinical Psychology**
    9:385-90.

This report is a study of degree of happiness in old people based on factors of health, financial security, hobbies, friends, living with spouse, age, and sex.

Leveen, Louis and David Priver. 1963. Significance of
    Role Playing in the Aged Person. **Geriatrics** 18 (1).

This article addresses the loss of social, econonomic, family, and physical roles in the aged person as well as their having to make drastic revisions in living conditions at a time when they are least adaptable to change. This can be the cause of intense anxiety, dependency, and regression leading to physical and emotional breakdown. The aged find themselves in a paradoxical situation when they shift to a group that has no concrete norms or approved roles.

McCord, William T. 1983. The Pressure to Conform: A
    Study of Foster Grandparents at a State Institution.
    Human Organization 42 (2): 162-166.

Members of the Foster Grandparents Program work in community and institutional settings with children who are labeled as handicapped. This category may include juvenile delinquents as well as individuals with physical or mental disabilities. The focus of this brief communication is the conflict that exists between the foster grandparents and the direct care workers in an institution for the mentally retarded, a conflict which the author argues grows out of opposing world views about care and service delivery.

Morris, Woodrow. 1961. Age Attitudes and Health.
    Adding Life to Years 8:3-6.

This article is the third in a series summarizing and discussing the findings in an interview survey conducted in thirteen Iowa counties as part of Iowa's preparation for the White House Conference on Aging held in Washington D.C. in January 1961. Iowans over sixty tend to think of themselves as middle-aged until the age of sixty-nine. After that they tend to think of themselves as being "old-man" or "old-woman." The tendency is to view "old" in other than chronological terms, the most important being state of health. They would consider themselves old only if they were unable to look after themselves.

Neugarten, Bernice L. and David C. Garron. 1959. Attitudes of Middle-Aged Persons toward Growing Older. **Geriatrics** 14 (1).

Random sample interviews with 625 women and men aged forty to seventy residing in a metropolitan area were analyzed for evaluations of the present and future. The attitudes of the subjects were found to be unrelated to age. Fear of aging consistently meant fear of dependency involving loss of income and loss of health.

Oltman, Andrew M. and Timothy J. Michals. 1980. Structure of Depression in Older Men and Women. **Journal of Clinical Psychology** 36:672–674.

The Wakefield Self-Assessment Depression Inventory was administered to 173 noninstitutionalized men and 329 noninstitutionalized women fifty-nine years of age and older. Members of both sexes shared common dimensions of anxious depression and general dissatisfaction. For women, a third factor toward depression was sleep impairment. Women, in general, were found to be more susceptible to depression than men.

Phillips, Bernard S. 1957. A Role Theory Approach to Adjustment in Old Age. **American Sociological Review** 22 (2):212–217.

This paper outlines a theoretical framework that can be utilized in predicting the degree of adjustment of the aged. Age identification in this approach would be considered an intervening variable between role change and adjustment.

Rawson, I.G., et al. 1978. Nutrition of Rural Elderly in Southwestern Pennsylvania. **The Gerontologist** 18 (1):24–29.

A nutritional study was conducted among elderly residents of rural southwestern Pennsylvania. Diet analysis showed deficiencies in calcium and calorie intakes, conditions not uncommmon in elderly people. Diet and nutrition for these elders, as well as program planning and suggestions for changes in nutrition programs for them are discussed.

Ridley, Jeanne Clare; Christine A. Bachrach and Deborah A. Dawson. 1979. Recall and Reliability of Interview Data from Older Women. **Journal of Gerontology** 34:99-105.

In order to test the recall reliability of older women, 211 white older women were questioned about their fertility histories. They were asked questions about events that occurred fifty or more years ago as well as more recent events. Fifty of the original respondents were reinterviewed by telephone. It was found that 90 percent of the responses were exact answers. Reliability ratios were judged to be comparable with those noted in studies of women of childbearing age.

Riesman, David. 1954. Some Clinical and Cultural Aspects of the Aging Process. In **Individualism Reconsidered**, Pp. 484-491. D. Riesman, ed. Glencoe, Ill.: The Free Press.

In search of a typology for the analysis of Kansas City data, Riesman suggests a tripartite divison: (1) autonomous aging--self-renewal, sustained from within; (2) "adjusted" aging--cultural preservation, sustained from without; and (3) anomic aging--decay, unsupported.

Rosen, Jacqueline L. and Bernice L. Neugarten. 1960. Ego Functions in the Middle and Later Years. **Journal of Gerontology** 15 (1):62-67.

This article reports on a study to determine if increased age coincides with less ego energy available for outside involvements.

Rosow, Irwin. 1973. The Social Context of the Aging Self. **The Gerontologist** 13 (1):82-87.

The loss of roles in old age excludes and devalues people, undermining their social identity. While response to such stress varies with personality factors, it invariably improves with strong group support. Nevertheless, the aged are not a viable group, and their membership and solidarity ties wither away. There is no compensation for the social losses of aging, although public policy and political activity could yield alternatives.

Tallmer, Marjot. 1977. Some Factors in the Education of Older Members of Minority Groups. **Journal of Psychiatry** 10:89–98.

The need exists for large-scale social action to alleviate some of the psychosocial and biomedical hazards of aging. Adult education is seen as one form of social action, and the elderly are urged to enroll in educational programs. The article discusses some of the problems as well as some of the benefits of educating the elderly.

Tobin, Sheldon S. and Bernice L. Neugarten. 1961. Life Satisfaction and Social Interaction in the Aging. **Journal of Gerontology** 16 (4):344–346.

This article reports on a study on disengagement theory and its relationship to psychological well-being.

Tuckman, Jacob and Irving Lorge. 1953–54. Old People's Appraisal of Adjustment over the Life Span. **Journal of Personality** 22:417–422.

A comparison is made between groups of graduate students and old people of their attitudes toward life experiences during various periods of their lives.

Tuckman, Jacob and Irving Lorge. 1954. Classification of the Self as Young, Middle-Aged or Old. **Geriatrics** 9 (11):534–536.

Four groups differing in age, education, and socioeconomic status were asked to classify themselves as young, middle-aged, or old. It was found that self-perception was influenced by health factors, environment, sex, marital status, occupation, productivity, loss of occupation, and other related variables.

Tuckman, Jacob; Irving Lorge and Frederic Zeman. 1961.
The Self-Image in Aging. **Journal of Genetic
Psychology** 99:317-321.

Drawings by old people are studied with respect to
how they relate to individuals' self-images.

Uhlenberg, Peter. 1979. Older Women: The Growing
Challenge to Design Constructive Roles. **The
Gerontologist** 19 (3):236-241.

The author thinks that just as the medical profession
has ignored preventive medicine in favor of curative medicine, social gerontology has been preoccupied with dealing
with the weak, frail, and underprivileged elderly rather
than the healthy aged. Over thirteen million American
women over the age of sixty-five are healthy and capable of
contributing positively to society. This population is an
untapped resource, and the discipline of gerontology needs
to reorient its focus in order to incorporate these women
and find constructive roles for them in society.

U.S. Superintendent of Documents. 1979. **Rape and Older
Women: A Guide to Prevention and Protection.**
Washington, D.C.: U.S. Government Printing Office.

Discussion is offered of the process of growing older
in our society, the special vulnerability of older women,
and the physical and psychological impact that fear of crime
and assault have on older women.

2. Marriage and the Family

Albrecht, Ruth. 1953. Relationships of Older People with
Their Own Parents. **Marriage and Family Living** 15
(4):296-298.

A sample of 100 persons over sixty-five were interviewed to determine the degree to which older adults care
for their parents. Three types of aged parent-adult child
relationships were found: no close contact (immigrants); no
need to care for parents (who either cared for themselves
or died young); and taking care of ailing parents (those
who did so were more often women, single or widowed).

Albrecht, Ruth. 1954. The Parental Responsibilities of
    Grandparents. **Marriage and Family Living** 16
    (3):201-204.

An examination of parental responsibilities assumed by
grandparents over sixty-five in a midwestern community.
In a sample of 100 persons, most preferred to maintain some
distance from their grandchildren, but gained stimulation,
new ideas, emotional responses, and enriched their lives
from short occasional visits.

Apple, Dorrian. 1956. The Social Structure of
    Grandparenthood. **American Anthropologist** 58
    (4):656-663.

This study confirms and expands Nadel's idea of
friendly equality between grandparents and grandchildren
appearing only when family social structure permits it. The
author's data support the hypothesis that formality between
grandparents and grandchildren is related to association of
grandparents with family authority while an indulgent,
close, and warm relationship is fostered by dissociation of
grandparents from family authority.

Barrett, Carol J. 1977. Review Essay: Women in
    Widowhood. **Signs** 2 (4):856-868.

Barrett, a psychologist, presents an overview of widowhood in the United States based upon a review of more
than forty sources published between 1950 and 1975. According to U.S. census data, there were about ten million
widows, with a median age of sixty-four, in the nation in
1970. Most of them "hate the word 'widow' ... [and] ...
people respond to them as if they had an infectious disease." The essay is divided into two parts: The Stresses
of Widowhood--which deals with grief, the economic burden,
and social factors such as isolation; and Social Policy

Implications--with subsections on education of the public about widowhood, proposed government support such as research funding, institutional support programs by community and other organizations, and directions for social change that would be beneficial for widows.

Bachrach, Christine A. 1980.   Childlessness and Social Isolation Among the Elderly. **Journal of Marriage and the Family** 42:627-36.

The data examined in the article suggest a strong association between childlessness and social isolation among the elderly.   Health and occupational class were the two major variables in measuring isolation.   Those persons who were in poor health and from working-class backgrounds had a higher probability of isolation.   The article does not address the issue of causality--if childlessness was self-selected.   The author suggests that if zero-population growth were to be achieved, there would be increasing isolation for older people.   Bachrach also thinks that the social world that future older cohorts will experience will differ from the present situation: expectations of self-fulfillment and the importance of grown-up children may decline.

Fenwick, Rudy and Charles M. Barresi. 1981.   Health Consequences of Marital Status Change Among the Elderly: A Comparison of Cross-sectional and Longitudinal Analyses. **Journal of Health and Social Behavior** 22:106-116.

This is an examination of the effects of marital status on change in health status of elderly respondents over a fourteen-month interval.   The data used came from 7696 respondents from the HEW 1973-74 Survey of the Low Income Aged and Disabled.   Findings suggest that it is change from married to unmarried status--not the unmarried status itself--that leads to a decline in perceived health.

Kirschner, Charlotte. 1979.   The Aging Family in Crisis: A Problem in Living. **Social Casework** 60:209-216.

When the family is unable to cope with the transitions associated with aging, the author suggests an ecological approach to the problem.   The ecological approach is defined as "the relations between organisms and their environments, and the adaptive process by which they achieve a good fit." Using this approach the author suggests studying the relationship between the individual and aging, family tensions, and an unresponsive environment, with emphasis on a total perspective leading to a healthy adaptive process to a problem of living.

Lipman, Aaron. 1961. Role Conceptions and Morale of Couples in Retirement. **Journal of Gerontology** 16 (3):267-271.

One hundred retired couples over the age of sixty living in the Miami, Florida, area were the subjects of this study. Prior to retirement, there was role differentiation on the basis of sex: the male role was occupational and the female, domestic. After retirement, husbands became more involved in domestic activities and were more supportive of their wives. Expressions of love, understanding, companionship, and compatibility became the most important aspects of marriage.

Lopata, Helena Z. 1970. The Social Involvement of American Widows. **American Behavioral Science** 14 (1):41-57.

Based on a sample of 301 widows in the metropolitan Chicago area, Lopata hypothesizes that societies increasingly remove ascribed roles and social relationships from widows without making others available. Independent residence indicates the changed relationship between mothers and children.

Lopata, Helena Z. 1971. Widows as a Minority Group. **The Gerontologist** XI (1, part 2):67-77.

Based on her work with widows in the Chicago area, Lopata sees women as facing discrimination and poverty upon their husbands' death. Factors influencing adaptation to new status fall into three basic categories: Social structure, family structure, and personality. Some cross-cultural data, particularly on levirate and filiation rights, are given.

Lopata, Helena Z. 1979. **Women as Widows: Support Systems.** New York: Elsevier North Holland.

This major study reaffirms Lopata's status as an authority on widowhood (see **Widowhood in an American City,** 1973). A cross-cultural and diachronic overview serves as an introduction and a means of placing widowhood in America into a broad perspective. The main body of the work is an analysis of the efforts of trained, middle-aged women interviewers who conducted two-hour interview with a random sample of 1,169 Chicago area widows. Special attention was given to the social support systems aiding reintegration of widows into the community and larger society and to an examination of the role--or the nonrole--status and daily life of widows. As might be predicted, Chicago area widows are heterogeneous; there is significant variation in their use of supports by race, education, and age.

Lopata, Helena Z. 1981. Widowhood and Husband Sanctification. **Journal of Marriage and the Family** 43 (2):439-450.

This study of urban Chicago widows observes their tendency to idealize a deceased spouse and, to a lesser extent, the previously shared married life. Several factors influenced the degree of sanctification: older women sanctified their spouses more than younger women; the more educated to a greater degree than the less educated; and whites more than nonwhites--although this may be a reflection of the younger age and lesser education of the nonwhites as much as a cultural variation. The need for further work in memory reconstruction is suggested by the author.

Messer, Mark. 1968. Age Grouping and the Family Status of the Elderly. **Sociology and Social Research** 52 (3):271-279.

Because of conjugal family structure in complex societies, the elderly parent has, in many ways, an "extra-familial" status. The last phase of the life cycle, however, is said to be characterized by consummatory needs, which are regarded as a corollary function of the family. The authors find some empirical evidence suggesting that age-concentrated living arrangements might serve as a functional alternative to the family for the satisfaction of those consummatory needs.

Nydegger, Corinne N. 1983. Family Ties of the Aged in Cross-Cultural Perspective. **The Gerontologist** 23 (1):26-31.

Three American myths are outlined: (1) The Golden Age--an ideal period in the past; (2) The Golden Isles--an ideal place "just out of reach"; and (3) The "natural" Rosy Family. The author then argues that our society has developed subsets of these myths specific to the elderly: they were once accorded respect; in other societies they have much better situations, and they are cared for in multigenerational households. The myths are examined from a cross-cultural perspective, with emphasis on their reverse aspects so as to illuminate the unpleasant features of family life. Nydegger is a persuasive advocate for reality.

Peterson, John L. and Constance Miller. 1980. Physical Attractiveness and Marriage Adjustment in Older American Couples. **Journal of Psychology** 105:247-252.

This study of thirty-two middle-class, aged couples in a small West Coast town examined the effect of attractiveness on marital adjustment. They were given photographs of each other, a self-evaluation of attractiveness and a five-point evaluation of the attractiveness of the spouse. The Locke-Wallace Short Form was selected to be used as a measure of marital adjustment. The result of the study was that among American older couples the attractiveness of females was less emphasized than that of males, and the attractiveness of the male was a major factor in marital adjustment. The wife's perception of the husband's attractiveness was related to his better adjustment, and also the husband's perception of his wife's attractiveness was related to his better adjustment.   It appears from this study that the men were more conscious of their attractiveness than the women, and the wife's perception of the husband's attractiveness enhanced the relationship. It is evident that physical attractiveness remains important after many years of marriage and that its importance is greater for men than women.

Skeen, Anita and Carol J. Barrett. 1979. Interdisciplinary Study of Widowhood: Convergence of Poetry and Psychology. **Signs** 5 (2):353-365.

A brief consideration is offered of the advantages of interdisciplinary cooperaton and what Skeen and Barrett hope to accomplish through their development of an anthology of poems on widowhood. They propose to incorporate material from diverse cultures.

Smith, Harold. 1965. Family Interaction Patterns of the
    Aged: A Review. In **Older People and Their Social
    World**. Arnold Rose and Warren Peterson, eds.
    Philadelphia: F.A. Davis.

A review article on the aged in the context of family interaction, family and kinship are viewed as a social institution, having numerous ties with other aspects of society such as governmental regulation of marriage, care of dependent children, family adoption of religious teachings in character building, etc. Kinship structure is viewed in nuclear and extended families, in relation to the aged married couple, the aged and their children, the three-generational family, and the aged and grandchildren. The lack of an adequate theoretical framework for the study of family interaction is pointed out, with suggestions for the use of conceptual framework and improved research design in order that empirical findings will lead to testing of hypotheses.

Streib, Gordon. 1958. Family Patterns in Retirement.
    Journal of Social Issues 14 (2):46-60.

This paper discusses attitudes of older people toward norms of achievement and familial assistance and the impact of retirement on these attitudes.

Troll, Lillian E. 1971. The Family of Later Life: A
    Decade Review. **Journal of Marriage and Family**
    33:263-290.

Surveys study the latter phase of the cycle of family life. The article summarizes gerontological concerns of the 1960s, such as the importance of extended kin relationships and contact between the aged and their children. Concerns for future work on the family of later life are suggested.

Uhlenberg, Peter and Mary Anne P. Myers. 1981.
Divorce and the Elderly. **The Gerontologist**
21:276-282.

While a small percentage of elderly women are divorced
today, it is projected that the dramatic increase in divorce
since 1964 will subsequently affect the elderly population,
particularly the women. This paper examines the rise in
the levels of divorce among older people and its implications. The authors suggest that even though divorce
among the elderly might give rise to economic and social
problems, it might benefit women in dealing with later widowhood. They also suggest that due to high divorce rates
there will be a greater availability of unattached males,
leading to more nonmarital sexual activity.

Ward, Russell A. 1979. The Never-Married in Later Life.
Journal of Gerontology 34:861-869.

Among the 162 never-married persons aged 50 and
over, highly educated women are most likely to remain single. Family background is not a predictor. The never-
married find life more exciting in the age group 25-49, but
reverses occur in later life. The never-married are less
happy than the married and slightly more happy than the
widowed or divorced. The problems considered include
changes accompanying aging that lessen the viability of
single life-styles and lowered support for single living by
cohort members.

3. Work and Retirement

Binstock, Robert H. 1983. The Aged as Scapegoat. **The
Gerontologist** 25(2):146-143.

Binstock explores the changing stereotypes concerning
older persons that have had an impact on policy issues in
America. He believes these demonstrate that the aged are

now bearing the blame for the economic and political frustrations of many and that this type of scapegoating has gained acceptance. He examines the axioms associated with the scapegoating, discusses the potential consequences of widespread popularity of these beliefs and possible strategies to counter them.

Campbell, Shirley. 1979. Delayed Mandatory Retirement and the Working Woman. **The Gerontologist** 19 (3):257-263.

Analysis of the effects of the mandatory retirement law has mainly focused on the male worker and retiree, whereas women have been largely overlooked. Women are already represented in larger numbers than men in the older population. With more women in the future years joining the work force, the mandatory retirement age will negatively affect women. Old women who are singe, divorced, or widowed have a different attitude toward retirement than men. The author suggests that longer employment for women will not only benefit older women economically and keep them actively involved, but will also alleviate the strain on the faltering social security system.

Carp, Frances, ed. 1966. **The Retirement Process.** Public Health Service Publication, No. 1778.

This is a monograph dealing with growth, maturation, retrogression and deterioration. It also deals with the biological, psychological, and cultural forces that influence the process of aging. The aim of this monograph is to focus on the developmental processes involved in preparation for, realization of, and reestablishment of life following retirement from the major life work of early adult years. Fifteen small chapters make up the book, presenting different perspectives by various authors.

Friedeman, Joyce S. 1979. Development of A Sexual Knowledge Inventory for Elderly Persons. **Nursing Research** 28:372-374.

The purpose of Friedeman's investigation was to develop an instrument to test the sexual knowledge of older persons. Her review of the existing literature points out that most professional analyses and opinions are based on sparse data. One consistent finding is the continuing interest in sexuality among the aged, but sexual expression is influenced by value systems, socioeconomic variables, physical and emotional health, earlier patterns of sexual behavior, and knowledge or ignorance about sexuality. After several pilot studies to test the validity of the twenty-five item questionnaire, 100 older women volunteers served as respondents. The basic conclusion is that the test instrument (SKE) is valid and reliable. Also, older persons are comfortable discussing sexual matters.

Goodstein, Leonard. 1962. Personal Adjustment Factors
and Retirement. **Geriatrics** 17:41-45.

Work is one of the important ways of satisfying many of man's psychological needs. While the economic needs are probably primary, work also represents a source of status and prestige, a way of achieving personal independence, a means of providing social contacts, and a way of taking up time. Many of the problems of retired workers are the consequence of not having had these needs met in retirement.

Havinghurst, Robert J. 1954. Flexibility and the Social
Roles of the Retired. **American Journal of Sociology**
59 (4):309-311.

Between the ages of fifty and seventy-five great changes occur in social roles. Roles of the homemaker and church member are usually intensified, while that of worker, parent, and spouse (after death of partner) are reduced. These age groups become more active as citizens, members of informal groups, and in other ways. The author suggests that exposure to a variety of roles in the middle years would allow for cultivation of flexibility and easier adaptation to these new roles.

Holahan, Carole Kovalic. 1981. Lifetime Achievement
Patterns, Retirement and Life Satisfaction of Gifted
Aged Women. **Journal of Gerontology** 35 (6):741-749.

Studying 352 women in Terman's 1977 study of the gifted, this investigation seeks to associate lifetime achievement patterns--homemaking, job, or career--with such dependent variables as health, happiness, life satisfaction, work attitudes, ambitions and aspirations, and participation in leisure activities. Results showed job holders as being generally less satisfied. Marital status and work patterns interact with respect to impact on life satisfaction. Activity involvement was differentially related to life satisfaction as a function of retirement status and career pattern.

McClure, Janet. 1983. Across the Generations: Research and Policy toward Intergenerational Harmony. **National Archive of Computerized Data on Aging Newsletter**: 2-3.

This is a brief article about the fiscal conflict between working taxpayers and the growing number of retirees. The author suggests the possibility that intergenerational conflict is an artificial condition created by policymakers who address the needs of particular interest groups. She stresses the need for better understanding of generational relations.

Morgan, Leslie A. 1980. Work in Widowhood: A Viable Option. **The Gerontologist** 20:581-587.

Working outside the home is most often suggested as an option for older and middle-aged widows. The author suggests that though labor force participation is a useful outlet for energies and also means economic independence, other options for reinvolvement should be examined for the postretirement period of widowed women's lives.

Prasad, Benjamin S. 1964. The Retirement Postulate of the Disengagement Theory. **The Gerontologist** 4 (1).

Data and tests revealed that there was not empirical evidence to support the Cumming and Henry disengagement theory among industrial workers in a modern-day situation. It was found that neither older male workers who retired at sixty-five nor those who retired later, were ready to disengage upon retirement.

Sheppard, Harold L. 1971. **New Perspectives on Older Workers.** Kalamazoo, Mich.: Upjohn Institute.

A short but excellent study, this book deals with the elderly in the work force. Offering a statistical and analytical approach to gerontology, the book is a compilation of four short studies. First the status of the elderly in the job market is reviewed, including the question of the handicapped, age discrimination, and the fact that participation of the elderly in the work force is underestimated. The second part deals with how age and migration are important variables in the socioeconomic condition of black and white urban women. The third part deals with an emerging pattern of second careers for people over forty and the discontent that leads this group of people to look for new options after forty. The final part deals with older worker problems and focuses on sociopsychological dimensions of older workers' lives.

Streib, Gordon F. 1956. Morale of the Retired. **Social Problems** 3 (4):270:276.

In this article, based on a nationwide survey, the author rejects the broad generalization that retirement adversely affects morale and adjustment in the elderly. Instead he suggests that in a multigroup society such as the United States, multiple factors should be taken into account in which retirement could be viewed as a prime causal variable along with socioeconomic status, health, variations of interests, activities, and values.

4.   General

Abu-Laban, Sharon M. 1981. Women and Aging: A Futurist Perspective. **Psychology of Women Quarterly** 6 (1).

With the focus on feminism, the situation of older women seems to be improving. Reproductive freedom, freedom of sexual expression, and labor force participation, may give the aged woman of the future enhanced personal status, and socioeconomic emotional security. The author also discusses the possible negative impact of antifeminism and religious conservatism, antiabortionists, and opposition to the ERA amendment on older women of the future.

Albrecht, Ruth. 1951. The Social Roles of Old People.
Journal of Gerontology 6 (2):138-45.

The intent of the study was to identify activities and
social roles of people over sixty-five in a midwestern town
(population 6,000), and to find out how these related to
personal adjustment. Using nondirective focused interviews
with a sample of 100 subjects, Albrecht found that the majority of older people were still active. Active social participation when younger seemed to lead to better adjustment
to aging.

Barberis, Mary. 1981. America's Elderly: Policy
Implications. **Population Bulletin Policy Supplement**
35 (4).

America's elderly, their problems and the policy implications of those problems are briefly surveyed. The problems include poverty, retirement, employment, housing, and
health. Policy implications concern social security and other retirement income systems and the United States health
care system.

Barg, S.K. and C. Hirsch. 1972. A Successor Model for
Community Support of Low-Income Minority Group
Aged. **Aging and Human Development** 3 (3):243-252.

This article describes the model cities Senior Wheels
East Program in Philadelphia. The emphasis is on community activities and endeavors to achieve "senior power." The
author discusses the development of cross-generational ties
between worker and client and the use of indigenous community workers in social welfare agencies working with the
aged. The purpose of the program is to achieve political
power by the elderly in order to obtain the necessary supportive services on a permanent rather than demonstration
basis in all neighborhoods of the urban community.

Becker, Gaylene. 1980. **Growing Old in Silence.**
Berkeley, Calif.: University of California Press.

Asking herself questions such as "How are deaf individuals different from other aged persons?" and "How are
they the same?" the author began an anthropological study
of the deaf elderly. Becker's primary purpose is to
present information for practitioners who provide services

to the aged deaf population. Initially she explains the effect of deafness on old age and outlines the characteristics
of the aged deaf. She discusses the importance of early
life experiences in community formation among the deaf.
Deaf identity and its implications for the development of
specific coping mechanisms are examined.

The latter portion of the text investigates family life
and other social relationships and processes. Adaptation to
old age and death are discussed at length, and, finally, the
author turns to the problems of aging in America in relation
to their implications for studying the aged deaf.

Blau, Zena Smith. 1956. Changes in Status and Age
    Identification. **American Sociological Review**
    21 (2):198–203.

The sociopsychological and physical aging processes
can be analytically distinguished. Age identification rather
than actual age constrains older people to recognize changes
in themselves and changed perception of others toward
them. Two hypotheses, related to retirement and widowhood, were tested; it was found that cultural evaluation
through retirement, but not widowhood, tended to force a
person to perceive being socially defined as old.

Blau, Zena Smith. 1961. Structural Constraints on
    Friendship in Old Age. **American Sociological Review**
    26 (3):429–439.

The effects that widowhood or retirement have on
friendships of older people of Elmira, New York, were
found to vary with the age, sex, and class structure of the
individuals. In those groups in which widowhood and retirement are relatively rare, the change in status places the
individual in a deviant position among his peers, thereby
exerting a detrimental effect on friendships. In those
structural contexts, where these changes are prevalent, it
is those still married or employed who are deviant to their
peers and whose social life seems more restricted.

Crittenden, John A. 1962. Aging and Party Affiliation.
    Opinion Quarterly 26:648–657.

Data gathered over twelve years showed that aging
and generational theories complement each other in explaining why older people are often Republicans.

Cutler, S.J., et al. 1980. Aging and Conservatism: Cohort Changes and Attitudes about Legalized Abortion. **Journal of Gerontology** 35:115-123.

This article examines whether aging is accompanied by conservative attitudes, with particular reference to abortion. The study was conducted over a twelve-year period, and data from seven national surveys were used. It was found that between the years 1965 and 1973, there was an increasingly favorable attitude toward abortion; after that there was a general stability of attitude. Contrary to the aging-conservatism hypothesis there was no evidence of attitudinal rigidity, or change at a slower rate among older cohorts.

Drake, Joseph T. 1957. Some Factors Influencing Students' Attitudes Towards Older People. **Social Forces** 35 (3):266-271.

Studies of attitudes toward racial and ethnic groups indicate that significant differences occur between individuals who have close contact with minority group members and those who do not. In this article the author uses the same hypothesis to study attitudes of students toward the aged "social minority." It was found that those students who had no intimate contact with the aged held stereotypical attitudes about them, while those who had such contacts had an overall favorable attitude. However, the author cautions against the idea that intimate contact is the only variable in the stereotypical attitude.

Eisdorfer, Carl. 1983. Conceptual Models of a New Frontier. **American Psychologist** 27:197-202.

Several models are briefly explored vis-a-vis their potential impact on scientific and professional approaches to the aging. The author believes that some narrow models have perpetuated a detrimental mythology of aging. He suggests that a biopsychosocial model may best recognize the complexity of the subject.

Fry, Christine L. 1976. The Ages of Adulthood: A Question of Numbers. **Journal of Gerontology** 31 (20):170-177.

To examine the number of subjective age categories in the post-high-school portion of the American life cycle, adult respondents, selected on a probability basis in Lafayette-West Lafayette, Indiana, sorted cards describing people in terms of major life events and classified them according to age. A nonlinear decrease in the number of age distinctions occurred in the late portion of middle age (46-65 years). The decrease was explained in terms of the developmental cycle of domestic units and age homogeneity of the kinship network.

Ginzberg, Raphael. 1952. The Negative Attitude toward the Elderly. **Geriatrics** 7 (5):297-302.

Contrary to most beliefs, negative attitudes toward the elderly have existed throughout the ages, all over the world, the attitude being that the elderly are lost causes and are placed outside of any active social organizations. However, these attitudes are not always apparent and are expressed as part of inner motivation. It has been suggested by the author that understanding of the inner mechanism is instrumental for paving a new way to better social and personal adjustment of the elderly.

Golde, Peggy and Nathan Kogan. 1959. A Sentence Completion Procedure for Assessing Attitudes toward Old People. **Journal of Gerontology** 14 (3):355-63.

Studies of attitude toward old people have focused on the aged as a unique group. In this article an instrument was devised to test the hypothesis that beliefs and attitudes regarding old people are qualitatively different from those concerning the larger class of people in general. A sentence completion instrument was chosen in order to elicit spontaneous responses. One hundred students whose ages ranged from seventeen to twenty-three were tested. The results confirmed the hypothesis of differences in beliefs and attitudes toward the two groups.

Kalish, Richard A. 1975. **Late Adulthood: Perspectives on Human Development**. Monterey, Calif.: Brooks/Cole Publishing.

Kalish focuses on the psychology of later maturity and old age. Areas discussed include cognitive factors, personality, social relationships, and physical and social environments. The book is intended to be useful to students in many fields, including psychology, social work, nursing, psychiatry, sociology, urban studies, education, public health, and recreation.

Keith, Pat M. 1978. Sex Differences in Correlates of Political Activity Among the Aged. **Journal of Voluntary Action Research** 7 (3-4):55-64.

The contrasting factors that foster political involvement among older men and women are examined through consideration of the differential effects of life changes in late adulthood, demographic characteristics, and earlier political participation of the two sexes. For women, it was found that aside from health changes affecting voting, their political involvement was less influenced by loss of roles or other negative aspects of old age. Work outside the home was found to encourage political involvement. However, if withdrawal from work was associated with negative effectiveness, then political involvement was less for women. The profile of the older politically active woman was one who viewed retirement as a time to do what she wanted to do.

Kimmel, Douglass C. 1978. Adult Development and Aging: A Gay Perspective. **Journal of Social Issues** 34 (3):113-130.

To provide a model for understanding adult development and aging among gays, Levinson's developmental periods are applied to existing data on older gay males. The lack of data about older lesbians and nonadvantaged male homosexuals is noted. Stereotypes of lonely, depressed, sexually frustrated, aging gay men are clearly invalid for the majority of respondents studied. Needs of older gays include reduction of stigmatization, assistance if physically disabled, and support during bereavement.

Kogan, Nathan and Michael A. Wallach. 1961. Age Changes in Values and Attitudes. **Journal of Gerontology** 16 (3):272-280.

This is a study of value differences between young and old adults. Values studied include work and leisure; self-concept; attitudes toward minorities; and family-interpersonal values.

Liang, Jersey. 1982. Sex Differences in Life Satisfaction among the Elderly. **Journal of Gerontology** 37 (1):100-108.

This study seeks to investigate the relationship between causal mechanisms in life satisfaction and assignment to different gender groups. A causal model of life satisfaction uses four sets of data, with sample sizes ranging from 961 to 3996. The results suggest that the same causal mechanism operates for both males and females with respect to satisfaction in later years.

Martel, Martin U. 1961. A Report on the Iowa Survey of Life After Sixty: Family and Friendship Patterns of Older Iowans. **Adding Life to Years** 8 (7):3-6.

This article is the seventh in a series summarizing the interview survey conducted in five metropolitan and eight nonmetropolitan counties in Iowa. It deals with the importance of familial ties. In the past such ties had many advantages for older persons, including companionship, financial support, and support during illness. However, in the past century intergenerational reciprocity has diminished. With the breakdown in family and increased mobility of people, older people have lost the commanding position in the family and subsequently there is a loss of help and care in later years. The family has been replaced by friends; however most persons in the survey complained of significant loneliness and expressed a need for more friends and greater degrees of socializing.

Matthew, Sarah H. 1979. **The Social World of Old Women: Management of Self-Identity.** Beverly Hills, Calif.: Sage Publications.

The author argues that the stereotype of the aged as poor, isolated, and physically incapacitated results from social arrangements which in turn perpetuate the marginal position of the old. She challenges the accuracy of the stereotype, especially the view of the aged as physically disabled and in poor health. Matthews used archival research, participant observation, and interviews in her focus on how her informants--white widows, over seventy years of age, who are mothers and live alone--avoid self-identification as worthless.

Orbach, Harold L. 1961. Aging and Religion: A Study of Church Attendance in the Detroit Metropolitan Area. **Geriatrics** 18 (10):530-540.

There is no adequate proof to substantiate the view that people become more religious with age. Studies of the relationship between age and religion do not support this common view and suggest that older people's religious behavior is a function of more direct social and cultural factors.

Orbach, Harold L. and David M. Shaw. 1957. Social Participation and the Role of Aging. **Geriatrics** 12 (April):241-246.

American elderly are left in a functionally deficient role after retirement because they are cut off from interests and activities that gave them status within the community. This study examines the inability of certain segments among the elderly to maintain roles that will confer status. The authors suggest that the socialization and preparation for such roles begin at an early age.

Pollak, Otto. 1943. Conservatism in Later Maturity and Old Age. **American Sociological Review** 8 (2):175-179.

The author suggests that there is no generation gap between the old and the young. A comparison of attitudes of people below and above forty shows that there are more conservative older people. However the numerical differences were negligent--the majority of both old and young rejected change. This article suggests that as far as change is concerned, there is no social conflict between old conservatives and young progressives in terms of large population groups opposing each other.

Richards, Mary Lynne. 1981. The Clothing Preferences and Problems of Elderly Female Consumers. **The Gerontologist** 21:263-267.

Eighty-three older women between the ages of 55-84, with 70 percent between 65-74, were given questionnaires regarding their preferences for day wear. The questionnaire consisted of black and white drawings of different styles of dresses, with distinctions of necklines and sleeves to distinguish summer and winter dress. The response indicated that the majority of women preferred dresses to be waistless, A-line, front zipped, darted with fullness around; having set-in sleeves, shirt collars and long bishop sleeves for winter dresses, and a collarless V with short sleeves for the summer. Sixty-one percent of the respondents felt the need for special "elderly-sized" clothing.

Riley, Matilda White; Anne Foner; Beth Hess and Marcia L. Toby. Socialization for the Middle and Later Years. 1969. In **Handbook of Socialization Theory and Research.** D. Goslin, ed. Pp. 951-982. Chicago, Ill.: Rand McNally.

In contemporary society the individual is always learning new social roles. As a person ages he or she has to learn to adapt: to face the loss of dependent children, a job, or the life of a loved one. This learning process during the life cycle is contradictory to the widely held view that adults are unteachable. The authors suggest a more positive aspect of adult socialization through social support and valued roles in order to aid this learning process in the face of an increasingly complex environment of a highly industrial society.

van Willigen, John; Thomas A. Arcury, and Rober G. Cromley. 1985. Tobacco Men and Factory Hands: The Effects of Migration Turn-Around and Decentralized Industrialization on the Social Lives of Older People in a Rural Kentucky County. **Human Organization** 44 (1):50-57.

A number of social changes in rural central Kentucky appear to have led to migration turnaround, i.e., the influx of a young, nonnative population, which decreased economic cooperation among neighbors and increased age segregation in the communities of the county studied.

Zola, Irving K. 1962. Feelings about Age among Older People. **Journal of Gerontology** 17 (1):65-68.

This is a study of perception of individual aging by sex and in relation to the view held of one's parents' aging.

D. <u>AMERICAN CULTURE</u>

Anderson, Barbara Gallatin. 1972. The Process of
    Deculturation--Its Dynamics Among United States
    Aged. **Anthropological Quarterly** 45 (4):209-216.

Through a process of conscious as well as unconscious
conditioning, the older American is gradually groomed for
total cultural withdrawal. The dynamics of this process in
many ways replicate--in reverse--the enculturation process
of early childhood. Cultural lag in adaptation to a changing life cycle has facilitated the cultureless position of the
old.

Arth, Malcolm. 1961. American Culture and the
    Phenomenon of Friendship in the Aged. **The
    Gerontologist** 1 (4):168-170.

Friendship among Bostonians ranging in age from sixty
to ninety is discussed.

Butler, Robert N. 1978. How to Grow Old and Poor in an
    Affluent Society. In **Issues in American Society**.
    Joseph Boskin, ed. Encino, Calif.: Glencoe
    Publishing Company.

Poverty in America is usually associated with black
ghettos or white rural communities. Because the elderly
are invisible, due to timidity, illness, lack of money and
transportation, fear of crime, etc., they are usually ex-
cluded from the poverty picture. It is often assumed that
older people need less money, have no needs other than
food and a few feet of space; and the elderly are often
blamed for not saving enough for their old age. It is these
myths that the author deals with in his article. He suggests that some of the hurdles can be overcome by focusing
on the problems, providing visible forms of work for the elderly, and providing safer places for them to live in. It is
also suggested that since the social security system has
failed to eliminate poverty, the state should find alternatives to adequately meet the changing needs of the elderly.

Fischer, David Hackett. 1977. **Growing Old in America**.
The Bland-Lee Lectures. New York: Oxford
University Press.

Fischer, a social historian who sees society as "a system of age relations which embraces everyone according to
his chronological condition," examines the history of old
age. His intent is to understand the logical relationship
between the past and present and the changes that have
occurred.
Beginning with early America, Fischer looks at age and
old age from the time of the Puritans, through the Revolution, and into modern-day society. In the final chapters he
analyzes old age as a social problem and expresses his
views on old age in the future.

Hunter, Woodrow W. and Helen Maurice. 1953. **Older
People Tell Their Story: Report of a Survey of the
Needs of Older People.** Ann Arbor, Mich.:
University of Michigan, Institute for Human
Adjustment.

This book contains a report of a survey to determine
the needs of people over sixty-five years of age that was
undertaken in Grand Rapids, Michigan, and the recommendations for community action developed by a local forum on
aging. It is the third phase of the educational program entitled the Grand Rapids Survey. The volume explores how
a community may proceed to study and to identify the
needs, describe the steps taken to achieve maximum community participation in conducting a survey, and the methods
used to identify the subjects. It discusses the techniques
employed to develop the questionnaire, to train volunteers
and to conduct interviews.
The report is noteworthy because the work was accomplished with the assistance of a group of older students
(average age sixty-one years) who were enrolled in the
"Living in Later Years" courses. It demonstrates that adult
education for the aging becomes meaningful when it employs
methods that allow older people to understand the problems
and to share with others the task of finding solutions.

Kutner, Bernard; David Ganshel; Alice M. Togo and
Thomas S. Langner. 1956. **Five Hundred Over Sixty**.
New York: Russell Sage.

A comprehensive report is made on the needs of old

people in the Kips Bay-Yorkville area of New York City. The study was carried out by the health center for that major urban area when it was recognized that little or nothing was being done for the older population in a total population of 250,000. The principle questions asked in this study were: (1) What are the sociocultural factors facilitating adjustment to old age? (2) Which people can successfully adjust? (3) What programs should be designed to serve the needs of the aged in this particular area? The study is offered not as a model but rather as a prototype, suggesting approaches to problems of aging in social and cultural contexts.

Manny, James D., Jr. 1974. **Aging in American Society: An Examination of Concepts and Issues.** Ann Arbor, Mich.: The Institute of Gerontology, the University of Michigan, Wayne State University.

How people view aging and aged people affects how they vote, how they treat the elderly, and even how they approach personal goals in life. Ultimately every individual's aging process is affected by their perspective on the process itself. The book is written taking this view into consideration, with the aim of providing guidelines to people who go into the field of gerontology. It provides an overview of the skills and training required in the field, that is, public relations, technical planning, administrative aspects, fund raising, organizing the community, etc. The book contains an excellent bibliography and sources of information for persons interested in the field of social gerontology.

Monk, Abraham. 1977. Education and the Rural Aged. **Educational Gerontology** 2:147-156.

This paper proposes an ecological-consultative continuum of education centered around the outreach functions by a multi-disciplinary team. It is felt that the rural population has a negative attitude toward publicly sponsored social programs. The health teams and social advisors should therefore go to the people, not the other way around, so that the elderly may receive the help they need, the help to which they are entitled, in circumstances palatable to them.

National Council on Aging Incorporated. 1976. **Arts and the Aging--An Agenda for Action.** Washington, D.C.

This report includes summary statements by representatives of more than forty agencies. The statements and the subsequent discussion are divided into chapters that focus on music, visual and theater arts, an agenda for action accessibility, vulnerable and institutionalized aged, and factors of intergenerational programs. Only two of the statements contain references to material on different cultures, and there is no discussion of different needs of varying cultural groups.

Porcino, Jane. 1983. **Growing Older, Getting Better--A Handbook for Women in the Second Half of Life.** Menlo Park, Calif.: Addison-Wesley.

This volume is certainly useful as a handbook, especially regarding health matters to which slightly more than half of the 364 pages are devoted. It also has a feature which makes it useful as a research tool: at the end of each chapter there is a list of organizations as well as recent publications relevant to the particular chapter topic. Other topics pertain to family matters and marital statuses, aging parents, traditional and nontraditional housing options, work and income, and going back to school.

Rosow, Irving. 1974. **Socialization to Old Age.** Berkeley, Calif.: University of California Press.

Rosow analyzes the socialization of elderly Americans into old age, a transition that the author believes is not as effectively accomplished as earlier status changes in American life. He discusses: the institutional position of the aged, the life cycle and related status situations, and the prospects for change. Rosow also offers a theoretical perspective on alternatives.

Schramm, Wilbur. 1969. Aging and Mass Communication. In **Aging and Society. Vol. II Aging and the Professions.** Matilda White Riley et al. eds. Pp. 352-750. New York: Russell Sage Foundation.

This excellent article takes to task the fact that mass communication has not been active in focusing attention on the elderly. Mass communication helps in policymaking, planning, and counseling and should be used as a source for reintegrating the older person into the ongoing social order. The author gives a sophisticated analysis of mass media audiences, emphasizing their importance to the aged. He suggests that the media has a very special function by way of information and entertainment for older people and that for the elderly it could become one of the main means of maintaining the process of engagement with society.

Todd, Harry F., Jr; Gail Venti and J.L. Ruffini. 1983. Neighborhood Grievances in Old Age. **Human Organization** 42 (1):59-63.

The study examines the legal problems of middle-class, white residents of a San Francisco neighborhood who are sixty-five or older. Most own their homes and live in two-person households. The survey found that legal problems pertaining to residential area were most common; they included other people's improper parking or dangerous driving, noise, property damage, garbage and litter. The authors suggest that those delivering free or low-cost legal services to the elderly should be aware of their problems and not assume that dealing with social security entitlements, Medicare/Medicaid eligibility, age discrimination, and the writing of wills would be sufficient.

Zborowski, Mark 1962. Aging and Recreation. **Journal of Gerontology** 17 (3):302-309.

Contrary to the implications of the disengagement theory, this paper concludes that aging has an insignificant influence upon people's recreational patterns and preferences. There may be some necessity to give up certain activities due to social or physical pressure, but the preference is in favor of maintaining and retaining patterns of living that have developed in the past.

II. STUDIES OF AGING OR THE AGED IN SINGLE ETHNIC, NATIONAL, RACIAL, REGIONAL OR OTHER CATEGORIES

A. U.S.A.

1. Asian Americans

Carp, Frances M. and Eunice Kataoka. 1976. Health Care Problems of the Elderly of San Francisco's Chinatown. **The Gerontologist** 16 (1):30-38.

This article reports on the health care problems of elderly Chinese living in San Franciso's Chinatown. An important inclusion is the description of Chinatown and its older residents.

Fujii, Sharon. 1976. Older Asian Americans: Victims of Multiple Jeopardy. **Civil Rights Digest** 9:27-29.

The plight of Asian American elderly is exacerbated by linguistic and cultural differences. The paper also points out that the lack of information about existing social services impedes their use by the Asian elderly.

Fujii, Sharon M. 1976. Elderly Asian Americans and Use of Public Services. **Social Casework** 57 (3):202-207.

The elderly Asian American has some special problems, including stereotypical poverty, distrust, and fear as well as the reality of racial discrimination. Those who offer services do not comprehend the context of Asian-American life. Changes in service and understanding must be made.

Kalish, Richard A. and S. Moriwaks. 1973. The World of the Elderly Asian American. **Journal of Social Issues** 29 (2):187-209.

The stereotype that the Asian American aged do not have any problems and therefore need no help is a myth. This article outlines these problems and asks for more funds for communities with elderly Asian Americans.

Kiefer, Christie W. 1974. Lessons from the Issei. In **Late Life: Communities and Environmental Policy**. Jaber F. Gubrium, ed. Pp. 167-187. Springfield, Ill.: Charles C. Thomas.

The Issei in San Francisco feel that successful aging depends on carefully developed communication skills. Since their numbers are small in most cities, they know each other, at least by reputation, and this guarantees some understanding, if not friendship, from other elderly Issei. However, technology has made the life of the aged more difficult in society.

Masuda, Minoru. 1975. Aging among Japanese-Americans. Paper presented at the Tenth International Congress of Gerontology, Jerusalem, Israel.

This paper reports on living arrangements and family support. The adaptive patterns of these elderly and their use of public services are discussed.

Mizokava, Donald T. 1977. Some Issues in the Educational Gerontology of Japanese-American Elders. **Educational Gerontology** 2:123-129.

A presentation is made to heighten awareness of a few of the variables involved in assessing and meeting the needs of elderly Japanese Americans.

Osako, Massako Murakami. 1976. Intergenerational Relations as an Aspect of Assimilation: The Case of Japanese- Americans. **Sociological Inquiry** 46 (1):67-72.

The intergenerational living arrangements and interactions of Japanese Americans are investigated. Their ideas of kinship relationships differ greatly from those of non-Japanese Americans; for example, family solidarity takes precedence over individual achievement, and dependence is emphasized. The sample was drawn from two groups in the Chicago area; forty-two Issei and forty-six Nisei responded. The authors concluded that while Japanese Americans are emotionally dependent on their children, the belief in economic self-sufficiency is highly developed.

Wu, Frances Y-Tsing. 1974. **Mandarin-Speaking Aged Chinese in the Los Angeles Area: Needs and Services**. Los Angeles, Calif.: University of Southern California.

The main problem of immigrant Mandarin-speaking, Chinese elderly is the inability to speak or understand English. The second concern is the lack of transportation; the third is the lack of leisure activity. Health and income are not considered major problems. The children of these elderly Chinese were often unable to be of much assistance because of cultural and social differences found in America.

2.   Black Americans

Beard, Virginia Harrison.   1976.   **A Study of Aging Among a Successful, Urban Population.**   Ph.D. Dissertation, St. Louis University.

Investigated were the areas of life satisfaction, adjustment, and self-perception of being black in a predominantly white society, in order to identify distinguishing characteristics held in common by successful black aged persons. The subjects were members of black organizations in St. Louis City and County. It was found that the population of successful elderly black people is heterogeneous even if uniform in some socioeconomic aspects. The black elderly experience life satisfaction and self-perception as individuals, not as a group.

Blake, J. Herman.   1979.   Doctor Can't Do Me No Good. **The Black Sociologist** 8 (1-4):6-13.

An analysis of the world views of elderly Sea Islanders as these relate to health and use of standard versus traditional medicine. The elderly blacks believe in a balance between health and nature, which is reflected in their reliance on traditional, that is "natural," remedies. The total sociohistoric context, including world view and the degree of literacy, must be considered in any attempt to extend the benefits of modern health care in this area.

Chunn, J.   1978.   The Black Aged and Social Policy. **Aging** 287-288:10-14.

Public policy often ignores many of the needs of the black elderly and in some cases works against their interest and well-being, in the view of this author. It is his opinion that what is needed is a National Policy on Aging that will be comprehensive and assure adequate and just services and income to all, instead of punishing the black elderly for being a minority.

Daly, F.Y. 1976. To Be Black, Poor, Female, and Old.
Freedomways 16 (4):222-229.

The author suggests that black women who have
experienced racism and sexism encounter the additional
prejudice of agism, making them special victims of discrimination. Elderly black women undergo a passage from
"nigger" to "broad" to "old bag," with their unacceptability
increasing in direct ratio to the decline of their strength as
they grow old. In the author's opinion, not only do black
women face this stereotype in the media, but care and
service from health facilities and the welfare department
also reflect the triple prejudice. The author discusses the
dilemma of being too old to work and too poor to qualify for
benefits of better paying jobs (including retirement and
health benefits). She suggests that these women lose their
self-image and self-esteem through discrimination. They
may seem to lose all importance except as the scapegoats of
people who may hold them responsible for society's problems.

Dancy, Joseph. 1977. **The Black Elderly: A Guide for
Practitioners.** University of Michigan--Wayne State
University, Institute of Gerontology.

This is a manual for those who provide services for
the black elderly in the community. A general discussion
of the black elderly--their food preferences, employment,
language, access to power, and institutional support, among
other things, are followed by four appendices. These
appendices include an outline of a training program for
practitioners, a list of films and videotapes, and lists of
institutions concerned with the elderly. A comprehensive
bibliography is also provided.

Ehrlich, Ira F. 1975. The Aged Black in America: The
Forgotten Person. **Journal of Negro Education**
44:12-23.

The author discusses the multiple jeopardy of being
old, black, poor, and/or sick, disabled, and handicapped.
He suggests that educational institutions meet their responsibilities to elderly blacks in two ways. First, by increasing educational opportunities, especially in such vital areas
as tenant-landlord laws and relations, health, personal
care, wills, and death and dying, as well as in leisure or
hobby areas. Second, he suggests the training of more

gerontologists, with an emphasis on recruiting more black students to the field.

Faulkner, Audrey O. 1975. Black Aged as Good
    Neighbors: An Experiment in Volunteer Service. **The
    Gerontologist** 15 (5):554-559.

This paper reports on unsuccessful efforts to carry out a program of one-to-one volunteer activity by urban low-income black elderly in Newark, New Jersey. Fears for personal safety and other problems prevented the success of the program. An alternative program of volunteering for group activities emerged and was positively received.

Faulkner, Audrey et. al. 1975. Life Strengths and Life
    Stresses: Exploration in the Measurement of the
    Mental Health of the Black Aged. **American Journal of
    Orthopsychiatry** 45:102-110.

In order to provide pertinent mental health and social work services to older black men and women, an attempt to comprehend the social characteristics, personal strengths, and weaknesses of a group of elderly blacks was made and is described in this paper. The results show that in spite of a life full of stress and difficulties, the majority of the elderly in this group have a highly positive self-concept. They compare themselves favorably with other people their own age and express relatively high satisfaction with life and themselves. In the author's opinion, this showed their strengths and was highly relevant to mental health.

Gillespie, Bonnie J. 1975. Elderly Blacks and the
    Economy. **Journal of Afro-American Issues** 3:324-335.

This is a general survey of the literature on the situation of elderly blacks in the economy. Gillespie draws some conclusions about the impact of a downturned economy upon elderly blacks in the areas of health, income, housing and poverty.

Golden, H.M. 1976. Black Ageism. **Social Policy**
    7 (3):40-42.

In the absence of reliable data on older blacks there is an increasing tendency on the part of planners to rely on research findings more appropriate to middle-class white elderly for the design of programs intended for blacks. The black aged are not a homogeneous group, although racism is an important factor and has adversely affected their preparation for old age. The author's opinion is that black elderly will receive the attention they deserve only if their unmet needs are separated from the problems of other groups and independent action for meeting them is taken.

Hicks, Nancy. May 1977. Life After 65: It's Already a Stigma to Be Old and to Place on Top of That the Stigma of Being Black and Poor Is a Triple Negative. **Black Enterprise** 7:18-22.

The author's concern is with the poor black elderly, who get less of a fair share than their white counterparts. Some leading black authorities on the black elderly are quoted. There are no references or bibliography.

Hill, R. 1978. A Demographic Profile of the Black Elderly. **Aging** 287-288:2-9.

The social and economic status of elderly blacks today is significantly better than it was a decade ago. Life expectancy has increased by almost three years. Although the economic gap between elderly blacks and whites has narrowed since 1970, the incomes of elderly blacks are only two-thirds of the incomes of elderly whites. Because of inflation, elderly blacks pay disproportionate shares of their incomes for food, shelter and other basic necessities. Consequently, although elderly blacks have made significant strides, they will have a long way to go in obtaining an equitable and adequate quality of life.

Huling, William E. 1978. Evolving Family Roles for the Black Elderly. **Aging** 287-288:21-27.

Historically, older blacks have provided a cohesiveness for the family by offering both material and spiritual sup- port to their children and grandchildren. As more blacks become urbanized, it appears that the persistence of tradi- tional roles for the black aged is highly uncertain. A breaking down of the black family system because of move- ment into the middle class may well be emerging.

Huling, William E. 1978. **Aging Blacks in Suburbia:**
Patterns of Culture Reflected in the Social
Organization of a California Community. Ph.D.
Dissertation, University of Southern California.

The effect of culture on the social organization of a
black, suburban southern California community is investigated. Culturally generated survival skills that have been
used by the residents through their lifetime and which are
to see them through old age, are researched. The
dynamics of this community are examined from a black
perspective. Migration and church were found to be of
prime importance. It was concluded that the residents were
culturally similar; external pressures influence survival
skills; and intergenerational differences are a problem for
the community. Self-segregation helps to preserve a life-
style.

Jacklen, Cary . 1971. Aged, Black, and Poor: Three
Case Studies. **Aging and Human Development.**
2 (3):202-207.

The case studies feature open-ended discussion of the
lives of three urban, lower-class blacks living in an age-
segregated, new high rise apartment complex in a southern
urban area.

Jackson, Jacquelyne Johnson. 1971. Negro Aged: Toward
Needed Research in Social Gerontology. **The**
Gerontologist 11 (1, part 2):52-57.

This paper provides good background material and
references about research done on the subject of the black
aged up to 1970. It discusses areas in need of further
study.

Jackson, Jacquelyne Johnson. 1971. Sex and Social Class
Variations in Black Aged Parent-Adult Child
Relationships. **Aging and Human Development**
2 (2):96-107.

This study considers the relationships of aged black
parents and their adult children. The author studied
thirty-two aged black parents and their eighty-three children and discovered significant sex and social class differences with respect to patterns of instrumental aid (money,

errands) between parents and children, and with respect to affectional relationships (giving, receiving, moral support and advice: degree of emotional closeness).

Jackson, Jacquelyne Johnson. 1976. Plight of Older Black Women in the U.S. **Black Scholar** 7:47-55.

This is an assessment of economics, loneliness, mortality, and isolationism confronting black women when they are young and continuing--and worsening--into old age. It stresses the importance of improved and preventive health care and suggests that the needs of elderly black women are better met through the efforts of one major organization, such as the National Association for the Advancement of Colored People (NAACP), than through a variety of smaller efforts by organizations representing separate characteristics such as sex or age. It is suggested that these specialized organizations may serve black elderly women poorly and may add to their isolation by fragmentation and separation form larger efforts.

Jackson, Jacqueline Johnson. 1976. Menopausal Attitudes and Behaviors Among Senescent Black Women and Descriptors of Changing Attitudes and Activities Among Aged Blacks. **Black Aging** 1:8-18.

The author outlines some hypotheses about psychological and sociocultural events related to the menopause. These are drawn from an exploratory study of a sample of fifty-one postmenopausal black women. Jackson deals with relationships between demographic variables and menopausal symptoms, with expected and occurring symptoms, with attitudes about reproductive loss, with symptomatic clustering, and with the women's use and evaluation of medical treatment.

Jackson, Jacquelyne Johnson. 1978. Special Health Problems of Aged Blacks. **Aging** 287-288:15-20.

This article focuses on health perceptions, age changes, prevalent diseases, functional health, and the use of health resources as they relate to aged blacks. Contemporary aged blacks do have some special health problems, but few, if any, are racially unique.

Jackson, Jacquelyne Johnson. 1977-78. Life Satisfaction
    Among Black Urban Elderly. **Aging and Human
    Development.** 9 (2):169-179.

One hundred and two nonindustrialized retired men
and women residing in a large urban area were interviewed
in this study of life satisfaction among black elderly.
Important factors in determining life satisfaction were:
education, perceived health, religious attitudes, need affiliation, self-esteem, and attitudes toward employment of
the aged.

Jackson, Jacquelyne Johnson. 1982. The Black Elderly:
    Reassessing the Plight of Older Black Women. **The
    Black Scholar** 13:2-4.

This article introduces a special issue devoted to the
black elderly. Jackson points out that despite economic
improvement many aged black women are still poor and not
living with their spouses. Lack of concern about the
socioeconomic conditions of black women before they become
aged and the high proportion of black women bearing
illegitimate children is still a basic problem. Jackson also
suggests the need for more longitudinal studies, for more
gerontological data on aging black women, and the social
conditions that influence their plight.

Jenkins, Albert H. 1972. The Aged Black: Some
    Reflections on the Literature. **Afro-American Studies**
    (3):217-221.

A review of the literature indicates that while the
black aged are at a special risk for the effects of social
stress, they do not represent a homogeneous population.
The role of the aged in extended family settings is delineated and directions for future research are discussed.

Johnson, R. 1978. Barriers to Adequate Housing for
    Elderly Blacks. **Aging** 287-288:33-39.

For elderly blacks there are many barriers to adequate
housing, including cultural, social, bureaucratic, economic,
and political factors. The author's opinion is that housing
legislation is based on policy research which does not
separate the black elderly from the elderly in general, and
the black elderly are then underrepresented when research

is done and when legislative decisions are made.

Lambing, Mary L. 1972. Leisure-Time Pursuits Among
    Retired Blacks by Social Status. **The Gerontologist**
    12 (4):363-367.

The leisure-time activities of 101 Florida blacks, representing upper-middle, upper-lower, and lower-lower
classes, were studied and the basis for their choices examined. The researchers found a great interest in self-im-
provement and new leisure-time activities among their
subjects.

Lambing, Mary L. 1972. Social Class Living Patterns of
    Retired Negroes. **The Gerontologist** 12 (3):285-289.

This paper discusses the differences in living arrangements and family contacts between blacks with different
class backgrounds: professionals, and blue-collar workers,
and those on public assistance.

Lee, Irene Kathy. 1977. **Intergenerational Interaction
    Among Black Limited Resource Middlescent Couples,
    Adult Children, Aging Parents.** Ph.D. Dissertation,
    Kansas State University.

This investigation approaches intergeneratonal family
interaction among blacks along three dimensions: the
patterns of interaction between aging parents and their
adult children; what factors influence varying support
patterns; and how the intergenerational network articulates
with the neighborhood network and other support systems.

McCummings, Betty Lou Hall. 1977. **The Incrementalist
    Nature of Public Policy Service Utilization
    Implications for the Black Elderly Under the Older
    Americans Act.** Ph.D. Dissertation, Syracuse
    University.

Selected performance measures were analyzed in order
to establish the effect of incrementalism inherent in the
public policy of the Older Americans Act of 1965. It was
concluded that a more responsive and sensitive manner for
delivering human services is needed if the elderly black are
to benefit greatly.

McPherson, Judith, et al. 1978. Stature Change With
    Aging in Black Americans. **Gerontology** 33 (1):20-25.

According to a sample of 500 black Americans 50 to 104
years old, black people have a greater decrease in stature
with aging than do white people. A comparison of arm-span
measurement and height was used.

Meyers, Leana Wright. 1979. Elderly Black Women and
    Stress Resolution: An Exploratory Study. **The Black
    Sociologist** 8 (1-4):29-37.

Focusing on the older woman in Mississippi, Meyers
examines the role of church, family, and marital support
systems in resolving stress. The data from a sample of 200
married, separated, divorced, and widowed women under-
scores the importance of religious and kinship ties in stress
resolution.

Moland, John, Jr. 1979. The Quality of Life Among Older
    Blacks. **The Black Sociologist** 8 (1-4):14-28.

A study of life satisfaction among 380 elderly black
respondents in three counties of rural Louisiana. The
significance of social participation and lower anomie levels of
the respondents is discussed. The implications of these
findings for designing programs for the elderly are considered.

Morse, D. W. Aging in the Ghetto: Themes Expressed by
    Older Black Men and Women Living in a Northern
    Industrial City. **Industrial Gerontology** 3 (1):1-10.

Approximately 100 older black Americans in a large
northeastern city participated in an oral history project to
record recollections and experiences, thoughts, and feelings
from their early days up to the recent past. Self-pride
and self-reliance were important themes. A sense of worth
seemed closely related to the meaning of work and activity
in the minds of older blacks. Work was not pleasurable; it
was a necessity. Although older southern blacks often
expressed a longing to return to the South, retirement
realistically meant remaining in the city. For those covered
by social security, the monthly check is a difference between a life of dependence or independence.

Quarterly Contact

This is a publication of the National Center on Black Aged, Inc., funded by a grant from the Administration on Aging. It includes brief articles on current research on black elderly and other minority elderly. It also offers reports on relevant programs and services for these groups. Topics covered in issues have included: rural blacks, senior centers for the black elderly, attitudes of Navajo youth, the economic position of the nonwhite elderly, and migration behavior of elderly adults.

Rubenstein, D. 1971. An Examination of Social
   Participation Found Among National Sample of Black
   and White Elderly. **Aging and Human Development**
   2 (3):172–188.

This article compares the social participation with family and kin of black and white elderly. A sample of 3,827 black and white elderly living in the United States was surveyed. It was found that black elderly are not alone more than white elderly. The authors caution against neglecting the black elderly or treating them like another segment of the population.

Sheppard, N. Alan. 1978. A Federal Perspective on the
   Black Aged: From Concern to Action. **Aging**
   287–288:28–32.

This article profiles the needs and concerns of elderly blacks. The author discusses how the federal government can increase the delivery of services to aged blacks and protect their rights. He suggests the following actions: a guaranteed annual income for the elderly; a comprehensive policy that will increase the supply of housing for the elderly; an affirmative action policy that will guarantee social justice for elderly minorities; reform of the welfare system to reduce the poverty gap to one half of what it is; and a fight against age discrimination as well as racial discrimination and sexism.

Smith, Alicia Deneise. 1978. **Life Satisfaction and
   Activity Preferences Among Black Inner City Senior
   Center Participants.** Ph.D. Dissertation, University of
   Massachusetts.

A possible relationship between individual preferences for particular learning activities and living conditions that account for life satisfaction was investigated through black senior center participants who live in a northeastern urban community. Perceptions of survival, or coping, needs were also studied. Results showed (1) diversity among the participants is equal to that of the general population; (2) health and length of residency influence life satisfaction; (3) activities that are personal and health related are preferred; (4) social activities are considered important.

Stretch, John J. 1976. Are Aged Black who Manifest Differences in Community Security Also Different in Coping Reactions? **Aging and Human Development** 7 (2):171-184.

The level of community security and individual coping reactions were tested among seventy-two aged blacks who were residing in public housing or waiting to be admitted to a public housing project. Differences in community security accounted for differences in coping ability. The findings are important to planners of communities for the elderly.

Swanson, W.C. and C.L. Harten. 1971. How Do Elderly Blacks Cope in New Orleans? **Aging and Human Development** 2 (3):210-216.

Twenty elderly blacks in New Orleans were interviewed as part of a study of attitudes toward and experience with suicidal behavior. These older black people discussed the difficulties of daily life and their efforts to resolve them. Despite old age, poverty, and poor health, they do not consider that life might not be worth living; nor can they conceive of problems with which they cannot cope by themselves or "with the help of the Lord." Their one common characteristic is a dogged desire to survive.

U.S. Senate Special Committee on Aging. 1971. **The Multiple Hazards of Age and Race: The Situation of Aged Blacks in the United States.** Senate Report on Public Bills, 92nd Congress. Rep. 450, Abs. 1517. Washington, D.C.: U.S. Government Printing Office.

This sixty-three page report consists of three chapters and four appendices. Some of the major topics covered are problems related to the life-style of elderly blacks, to

poverty, employment and unemployment, health and housing, social and emotional factors, and urbanization. The
appendices cover issues such as social security benefits,
growing old black, work and educational attainments and
constraints.

Wylie, Floyd M. 1971. Attitudes Toward Aging: The
    Aged Among Black Americans: Some Historical
    Perspectives. **Aging and Human Development**
    2 (1):66-70.

This article discusses the behavior of black Americans
toward their older folk and the attitudes of the older folks
toward themselves and their senior citizenship. The author
suggests that the cultural heritage of West African values
and attitudes toward aging and the aged is an important
factor in considering black American respect for aging and
the aged. In the author's opinion many of the cultural
values and attitudes regarding the elderly have changed
little since the Africans left their home' continent. He
suggests that issues of "belongingness" rather than of
productivity appear important in the role of the aged.

Yelder, Josephine E. 1975. **Generational Relationships in
    Black Families: Some Perceptions of Grandparental
    Role.** Ph.D. Dissertation, University of Southern
    California.

The different aspects of the role of grandparent were
examined among 41 black grandparents. The participants
were interviewed in their homes. The age range was
forty-three to seventy-five years; there were 107 children,
248 grandchildren, and 52 great-grandchildren. A greater
generation gap was found between parents and children
than between grandparents and grandchildren. Differing
attitudes between formal and caretaker grandparents were
evident.

3. Underline: European Americans

Guttman, David. 1974. **Social Indicators, Jewish Identity and Morale of the Age.** Ph.D. Dissertation, Catholic University of America.

Social indicators, Jewish identity, and morale of the aged are interrelated. A sample of subjects was drawn from a Jewish community center's senior adult members in order to test this hypothesis. Some of the findings were: the majority of the Jewish aged lived in or near poverty; country of origin and cultural background were influential factors on morale; Jewish identity was significantly associated with morale.

Lozier, John and Ronald Althouse. 1975. Retirement to the Porch in Rural Appalachia. **Aging and Human Development** 6 (1):7-15.

Old men who have retired to the porch in Laurel Creek, West Virginia, are the focus of this study. They furnish an example of many small town, rural, and sometimes urban old men who use the front porch for their social interactions, their claim to a presence in the community, and as last places of communication with friends and neighbors before death.

Lozier, John and Ronald Althouse. 1974. Social Enforcement of Behavior Toward Elders in an Appalachian Mountain Settlement. **The Gerontologist** 1 (1):69-80.

This is a study of the attitudes and behavior of younger people toward the elderly in Laurel Creek, West Virginia. It is suggested that Laurel Creek society controls the behavior of its younger people, which has consequences for the elderly. Larger scale societies do not control individual behavior and thus cannot enforce sanctions of inadequate behavior toward the elderly.

Meyerhoff, Barbara. 1980. **Number Our Days.** New York: Simon and Schuster.

A highly acclaimed account of the lives of elderly Jews in Venice, California, this sensitive study is full of insights, wisdom, wit, and the shining courage of elders in facing poverty, poor health, and other problems. The section of chapter one dealing with the author's entry into the community, her approach, and feelings about her work should be required reading for every anthropologist planning to do field research.

Rubin, Barbara. 1977-78. The Role of the Community Center in Meeting the Health Needs of the Aged: An Overview. **Journal of Jewish Communal Service** 54:32-38.

New directions in health maintenance for the aged may be useful in preventing or delaying their submissions to custodial care. A description of present and projected prevention/health programs in community centers is presented.

Siegel, Martha Kaufer. 1976. **The Aging Experience: A Description of the Role of Religion in Response to Physical Dysfunction in a Sample of Jewish Women 65 to 83 Years of Age.** Ph.D. Dissertation, Harvard University.

Aging in the context of Jewish history and tradition is explored. Only Jewish women were interviewed since physical aging affects them more than men in Western culture. Attitudes toward health and religion were studied. Time's passing is an issue of concern, indicating the finite and limited earthly future. The author feels that educators should inquire into aging because it is an evolutionary process and mechanism for self-realization.

4.   Native Americans

Ford, Clellan. 1941. **Smoke From Their Fires, The Life of a Kwakiutl Chief**. New Haven, Conn.: Yale University Press.

The last chapter, "Later Years," depicts a chief's old age.

James, Harry. 1956. **The Hopi Indians**. Caldwell, Idaho: The Carton Printers.

There is a short description of old age and death. Economic and emotional security is granted elderly clan members.

Lange, Charles. 1959. **Cochiti--A New Mexico Pueblo, Past and Present**. Austin, Tex.: University of Texas Press.

The chapter about "Life Cycle" covers the subject of death.

Leighton, D. and A. Leighton. 1944. **The Navajo Door**. Cambridge, Mass.: Harvard University Press.

The main focus of the book is Navajo religion and curing practices. The chapter, "Navajo Lives," has autobiographies of a man, aged fifty, and a woman, aged fifty-five, and conveys some sense of grandparent-grandchild relations.

Lowie, Robert H. 1935. **The Crow Indians**. New York: Farrar and Rinehart.

Field work was done in 1907 and again in 1931 to study the religion, social organization, kinship structure, and folklore of the Crow tribe now in North Dakota.

References to the elderly are scattered throughout the book.

Lowie, Robert H. 1963. **Indians of the Plains.** Garden City, N.Y.: The Natural History Press.

This is a cross-cultural and historical study of many Indian tribes who lived between the Mississippi River and the Rocky Mountains. The elderly are included in discussions of age societies, family life, social organization, and the supernatural.

Murdock, S.H. and D.F. Schwartz. 1978. Family Structure and the Use of Agency Services: An Examination of Patterns Among Elderly Native Americans. **The Gerontologist** 18:475-481.

The need for and use of social services by elderly Native Americans are the subjects of this paper. One hundred and sixty elderly living on a reservation were interviewed. Those living in extended families were more aware of and made more use of services provided by agencies than those living alone. Family structure is of great importance to elderly Native Americans.

O'Kane, Walter. 1953. **The Hopis: Portrait of a Desert People**, Norman, Okla.: University of Oklahoma Press.

The author gives many examples of older Hopis who are productively employed. The status and continued participation of old people in the community is one of the main themes.

Radin, Paul. 1970. **The Winnebago Tribe.** Lincoln, Neb.: University of Nebraska Press.

This investigation of the Winnebago, based on field-work done between 1908 and 1913, focuses on social organization, material culture, and religion. There is some material on the elderly throughout the book.

Reichard, Gladys. 1939. **Dezba, Woman of the Desert.** New York: J.J. Augustin.

Dezba is a grandmother. The book deals with older people and grandparent-grandchildren relationships as part of a portrait of a family and its community.

Shaw, Anna Moore. 1974. **Pima Past.** Tucson, Ariz.: University of Arizona Press.

The autobiography of a seventy-six-year-old Pima Indian who is a great-grandmother. The author brings together her own knowledge and historical sources to recreate the past. A major theme in the book is concern for the negative changes that acculturation has caused for Pima old people.

Smithson, Carna Lee. 1959. **The Havasupai Woman.** Anthropological papers of the Department of Anthropology, University of Utah. No. 38.

A short section on old age indicates that the healthy elderly (often in their eighties) are respected if they are knowledgeable. Impatience and distaste is sometimes shown the helpless aged by their immediate families.

Spier, Leslie. 1928. **Havasupai Ethnography.** Anthropological papers of the American Museum of Natural History. Vol. 29.

The principal informant is an energetic well-informed seventy-one-year-old man. Much of the material is autobiographical so that the book is as much an account of the old man's life as it is an ethnography.

5. Spanish-speaking Peoples

Abad, F. et al. 1974. Model for Delivery of Mental Health
     Services to Spanish-speaking Minorities. **American
     Journal of Orthopsychiatry** 44:584-595.

     Special mental health services for Spanish-speaking
people are needed, services that will recognize their unique
linguistic and cultural traits. The authors discuss some
common cultural characteristics of Puerto Ricans and the
role of women, which can often be in conflict with American
values. Folk healing and spiritism are described. It is
suggested that understanding why the Puerto Rican patient
finds a faith healer helpful will be beneficial to the clinician
in offering treatment geared to the patient's needs and
expectations.

Bastida, Elena. 1979. Family Integration in Later Life
     Among Hispanic Americans. **Journal of Minority Aging**
     4:42-9.

     Data were collected from 160 noninstitutionalized Ameri-
cans of Mexican, Puerto Rican, and Cuban origins who were
sixty-two years of age or older. The investigation focused
on the impact of ethnic and sociodemographic variables on
family integration. Ethnic factors, particularly intra-group
marriage, were found to be the stronger indications of
family integration.

Carp, Frances M. 1970. Communicating with Elderly
     Mexican-Americans. **The Gerontologist**
     10 (2):127-134.

     The means by which older Mexican-Americans keep in-
formed and a comparison of their communication capabilities
with those of the non-Mexican-American elderly, are the
subjects of this report. Avenues of improved communication
between the whole community and the elderly are explored.

Coles, Robert. 1973. **The Old Ones of New Mexico.** Albu-
    querque, N. Mex.: University of New Mexico Press.

Included are stories about individual Chicano elderly
whom the author visited and interviewed and who expressed
to the author "those qualities of mind, heart, and spirit
which distinguishes them from some of the rest of us."
The importance of marital and family relationships is made
clear.

Crouch, B.M. 1972. Age and Institutional Support:
    Perceptions of Older Mexican Americans. **Gerontology**
    27 (4):524-529.

Interview   data   were   obtained   on   how   older
Mexican-Americans view old age and how they perceive the
family, church, and Anglo government as sources of support in old age. Implications of the findings for program
planning are presented.

Cuellar, Jose Bernardo. 1977. **El Oro de Maravilla: An
    Ethnographic Study of Aging and Age Stratification in
    an Urban Chicano Community.** Ph.D. Dissertation,
    University of California.

Chicanos over forty-five years of age were the subjects of this study carried out in Los Angeles. The problems and needs of older Chicanos are outlined from the
Chicano point of view. The study was conducted under the
direction of Chicano community representatives. It helped
to identify factors associated with the low status of
Chicanos in Los Angeles. The present Chicano communmity
is described, and implications are drawn for Chicano community service providers and agencies.

Maldonado, D., Jr. 1975. The Chicano Aged. **Social Work**
    20:213-216.

The traditional roles and personal security provided to
the elderly under the extended family structure are seriously threatened by the increased mobility and urbanization
of the younger Chicano generations. Often, Chicanos do
not receive the services provided to the aged of other
cultures.

Mizio, E. 1977. Commentary (On Ghali: "Culture Sensitivity and the Puerto Rican Client"). **Social Casework** 58:469-474.

The need for knowledge of and sensitivity to cultural factors in working with Puerto Rican clients is discussed. The author suggests that the therapist will probably need to be seen, in some way, as part of the extended family in order to be successful. This partially friendly and social approach is needed to establish trust and confidence in the client-therapist relationship. The importance of adapting the Anglo attitudes of the therapist to Puerto Rican cultural patterns in order to make the client comfortable and to make therapy relevant in the eyes of the client is suggested.

Torres-Gil, Fernando M. 1976. **Political Behavior: A Study of Political Attitudes and Political Participation Among Older Mexican-Americans.** Ph.D. Dissertation, Brandeis University.

Political activity, particularly electoral processes, are of particular interest in this study of Mexican-American elderly people living in San Jose, California. The elderly are politically very interested and aware, but do not participate much. The main interests were Chicano and age-related issues. United States birth influenced the degree of political activity of the elderly.

B.   OTHER: BY CONTINENT
OR OTHER GEOGRAPHICAL AREA

1.   Africa

Alland, Alexander, Jr. 1975. **When the Spider Danced.** Anchor Press.

This ethnography places emphasis on nutrition and the health practices of the Abron of the Ivory Coast. Brief discussion of the elderly is included, and some emphasis is given to the role of the Queen Mother and her functions as a leader.

Arth, Malcolm, J.   1968.   An Interdisciplinary View of the Aged in Ibo Culture.   **Journal of Geriatric Psychiatry** 2 (1):33-39.

Young-old relationships among village Ibo in Nigeria are described. Traditional values and changes associated with modernization are discussed.

Arth, Malcolm.   1968.   Ideals and Behavior: A Comment on Ibo Respect Patterns.   **The Gerontologist** 9 (4):242-244.

Aged Ibo in Nigeria are respected. They maintain high status and continued relevance to the culture. Psychosenility and disengagement are rare or nonexistent.

Arth, Malcolm M. 1972.   Aging: A Cross-Cultural Perspective.   In **Research Planning and Action for the Elderly**.   D. Kent, R. Kastenbaum, S. Sherwood, eds. Pp. 352-364.   New York: Behavioral Publications.

This article is based on the author's work in the village of Nsukka, Nigeria, where he lived from 1964 to 1966. It deals with aging from a cross-cultural perspective, focusing on the Ibo of southeastern Nigeria. The data presented negates the stereotypical view that the aged occupy a venerated position in tribal cultures. Ibo values and customs contribute a certain amount of stress in adjusting to old age while facilitating the aging process in other ways. Acculturation adds another dimension to the problem. It is suggested that gerontological studies should use a model other than the dysfunctional one when studying value changes in nonwestern cultures, since no culture totally operates on a functional-rational model.

Bloch, Maurice.   1971.   **Placing the Dead**.   New York: Academic Press.

The Merina of central Madagascar are the subjects. The study deals with the reverence for ancestors and "the old ways," as well as with burial and the building of tombs.

Childs, Gladwyn Murray. 1949. **Umbundu Kinship and Character.** Oxford: Oxford University Press.

Age categories are fundamental to the social organization of the Ovimbundu of northern Angola. The elderly age set's relationship to the socialization of children and child development is discussed.

Goldschmidt, Walter. 1976. **Culture and Behavior of the Sebei.** Berkeley, Calif.: University of California Press.

An ethnographic study of the adaptive processes of culture, society, and individual behavior of the Sebei, a people of southern Uganda. it compares two life-styles, one pastoral and the other agricultural. In both Sebei groups authority and deference are based on age and seniority. The elderly pass cultural traditions to their grandchildren. When an old person dies, the death is called a "sweet death" and is celebrated like a wedding.

Hamer, John. 1976. Myth, Ritual and the Authority of the Elderly in an Ethiopian Society. **Africa** 46 (4):327–339.

A description of mythological and ritual sequences honoring dead elders among two peoples of Ethiopia is followed by comments on gerontocratic authority of the Holo-Garbico people. There is noticeable pressure from proselytizing efforts of Christian missionaries, with the new converts denouncing non-Christian practices. The number of Islamic converts has also increased tremendously. The rituals and myths still provide a sense of security and continuity despite a changing way of life.

Little, Kenneth. 1965. **West African Urbanization: A Study of Voluntary Association in Social Change.** London: Cambridge University Press.

In this study of migration in West Africa, Little indicates the roles of the elderly in precipitating the migratory process. There is relatively limited information on the elderly.

Nahemow, Nina and Bert N. Adams. 1974. Old Age Among the Baganda. In **Late Life: Communities and Environmental Policy**. Jaber F. Gubrium, ed. Pp. 147-166. Springfield, Ill.: Charles C. Thomas.

The Baganda, who comprise roughly 25 percent of the population of Uganda, traditionally grant no political or economic authority to their aged. The elders' main contributions are in the context of their role of grandparents.

Ottenberg, Simon. 1968. **Double Descent in an African Society**. Seattle, Wash.: University of Washington.

The study compares two types of descent groups of the Afikpo Ibo in Nigeria: one is matrilineal and the other, patrilineal. In both groups, the elders have ultimate authority and control conflicting forces, but age is a secondary consideration to leadership and decision-making abilities. Ranking by age is followed at all ceremonial and cultural events.

Shelton, Austin J. 1965. Ibo Aging and Eldership: Notes for Gerontologists and Others. **The Gerontologist** 5 (1):20-23, 48.

The process of disengagement is nonexistent in Ibo society in Nigeria. The physical inability to farm and perform manual labor is replaced by broader responsibilities of preservation of law and order within the clan and in teaching the young what the aged have learned through experience. Being old in Ibo country is to be stress-free and also command respect.

Townsend, Norman. 1977. Age, Descent and Elders Among the Pokomo. **Africa** 47 (4):386-397.

This paper considers the part played by notions of age and descent of the Pokomo of Kenya, East Africa. The older men dominate the day-to-day lives of the villagers--access to land, age at marriage, choice of spouse, and access to God and to ancestors. Violent conflict between younger and older men has resulted from this domination.

Wilson, Monica. 1951. **Good Company: A Study of Nyskyusa Age-Villages.** Boston: Beacon Press.

Research was done from 1934 to 1938 among Nuakyusa along the Tanganyika-Nyasaland border. Age villages are formed by males, who attain power at about age thirty-five from reluctant elders. There is some indication that young men formerly killed the old. Problems result from an incomplete transfer of power.

2. <u>Asia</u>

Benedict, Ruth. 1946. **The Chrysanthemum and the Sword.** Boston: Houghton Mifflin.

Information about the elderly is found in the discussions on family life, ancestor worship, and age stratification. The data were obtained from Japanese-American informants and published sources.

Delaney, William Phillip. 1977. **Socio-Cultural Aspects of Aging in Buddhist Northern Thailand.** Ph.D. Dissertation, University of Illinois.

Elderly people living in a lower-class Chiangmai neighborhood were investigated. The factors accompanying rapid change in social organization, city life, religious circumstances of growing old in Thailand are the subjects of this thesis. Special beliefs concerning death and rebirth are discussed. These beliefs and rituals help Thais of all ages to adjust to modern changes.

de Young, John E. 1955. **Village Life in Modern Thailand.** Berkeley, Calif.:   University of California Press.

In general, there are few references to the elderly. Elderly persons are treated and spoken of with respect.

They are subject to fewer taboos. After retirement, they become more religious and learn to resign themselves to death.

Dore, R.P. 1963. **City Life in Japan**. Los Angeles, Calif.: University of California Press.

Through the use of an elaborate interview schedule, Dore describes a small neighborhood near the center of Tokyo. The aged are discussed in terms of ancestor worship, family relations, and the role of the family in the social structure. Demographics cover morbidity, mortality, and composition of the population.

Dozier, Edward P. 1967. **The Kalinga of Northern Luzon, Philippines**. New York: Holt, Rinehart and Winston.

One section on the kinship system is devoted to consideration of the close, affectionate relationship between grandparents and grandchildren, and there are a scattering of brief references to the aged in other sections of the book. Death, mourning, and the power of a deceased grandparent "to make a child ill in order that the child may join him in the afterworld" are also dealt with. Dozier notes the importance of old men as informants about headhunting activities of the past.

Embree, John F. 1939. **Suye Mura: A Japanese Village**. Chicago: University of Chicago Press.

This ethnography presents data from field work done in 1936 in a remote rural community in southern Japan. It describes the network of social relations in one neighborhood group. Topics such as ancestor worship, age stratification, behavior patterns, household management, and political activities include material on the aged.

Fei, Hsiao-Tung. 1939. **Peasant Life in China**. London: George Routledge and Sons.

Rural life in the Yangtze Valley of China in 1935 is presented with emphasis on the relationship of the economic system to a geographical setting in a period of change. Some details on the elderly are found in connection with ancestor worship, household arrangements, and land inheritance.

Firth, Rosemary. 1966. **Housekeeping Among Malay Peasants**. New York: Humanities Press.

This study of a community of fishermen and peasants on the east coast of Malaya focuses on family structure and household economy. Research was done in 1939-40, with a return visit in 1963. Maintenance of independence and autonomy by the elderly are briefly discussed.

Freedman, Maurice. 1966. **Chinese Lineage and Society: Fukien and Kwangtung**. New York: Humanities Press.

This is an addition to a previous study of kinship and social organization in a number of villages in two provinces of southeast China. The author discusses the elderly mainly in the context of ancestor worship.

Geddes, W.R. 1961. **Nine Dayak Nights**. London: Oxford University Press.

The aged are referred to in terms of their position in the family stucture.

Geertz, Hildred. 1961. **The Javanese Family**. New York: The Free Press.

Through interviews and observations made during a field trip in 1954 the author presents a study of kinship and socialization in a Javanese town of 20,000 people. Material on the aged, interspersed throughout the book, suggests that the elderly are respected and cared for by their children and their society.

Goldstein, Melvyn C. and Cynthia M. Beall. 1981. Modernization and Aging in the Third and Fourth World: Views from the Rural Hinterland in Nepal. **Human Organization** 40 (1):48-55.

A study of Sherpas in highland villages of Nepal, the research focuses on the status of the elderly, their work and other activities, and the indirect impact on their lives of changes in Darjeeling, India, that have encouraged out-migration of young Sherpas. The authors question: (1) the assumption of aging-and-modernization theory that traditional patterns will accommodate the elderly, and (2) ideas from longevity studies that productive work and physical activities in mountain environments produce physically fit elderly who are psychologically well-adjusted to the process of aging.

Harlan, William H. 1964. Social Status of the Aged in
    Three Indian Villages. **Vita Humana**
    7 (3-4):239-252.

The problematic status of the aged in industrial societies is often contrasted with the aged holding positions of power, prestige, and authority in preindustrial societies. The article refutes such a comparison. Three Indian villages were studied. It was found that the head of the household is not usually the oldest man or woman but rather a son who wields power within the family. The older members are usually relegated to a peripheral role upon the marriage of the oldest son or upon the loss of a spouse. Another variable is loss of socioeconomic status.

Hsu, Frances L.K. 1967. **Under the Ancestor's Shadow.**
    Garden City, N.Y.: Anchor.

This ethnography, based on field research done in 1941-42, describes a semirural community in southwestern China. The main emphases of the work are family and religion. Ancestor worship, cooperative economic arrangements, and the residence patterns of the extended family furnish much data on the aged.

Kii, Toshimasa. 1976. **Aging in Japan: Policy Implications
    of the Aging Population.** Ph.D. Dissertation,
    University of Minnesota.

The economic aspects of life of the Japanese elderly are examined. The relationships between actual living arrangements and the financial status of the elderly are analyzed. In describing the Japanese retirement system, it is shown that the lack of welfare programs has forced the elderly to rely on the family almost exclusively.

Ko Shioya. 1981. The Graying of Japan: A Hidden
    Crisis. **Asia**: 38-42, 52.

The author discusses the illusion of lifetime employment
for the Japanese, except for the 13.5 percent who work for
leading businesses. The majority must retire at age fifty-five and they find that other job opportunities are rare.
Suicides among the elderly have increased since World War
II, at a faster rate than the increase of the number of aged
in the population. There has been erosion of traditional
values and family structure. At the same time, effective
government programs to assist the elderly are lacking.
Poignant examples are combined with facts and figures.

Leach, Edmund R. 1965 (orig. 1954). **Political Systems of
    Highland Burma**. Boston: Beacon Press.

Although the study of Kachin social structure has few
references to the aged, there are indications that the aged
are respected because of their experience and knowledge of
custom.

Lebra, Takie Sugiyama. 1979. The Dilemma and Strategies
    of Aging Among Contemporary Japanese Women.
    Ethnology 18 (4):337-354.

Postwar education and changes in cultural values,
economic growth and industrialization, geographical mobility
and the weakened solidarity of the neighborhood, and increasing life expectancy are all discussed as they relate to
the aging Japanese woman and her traditional expectation of
dependency on her children for care in her old age. The
author's informants desire self-sufficiency economically,
physically, and in their inner lives. Ancestral worship is
seen by the author as a form of preparation by the elderly
for their own enshrinement. It seems that Japanese elderly
women are in a state of transition from the old ways to the
new.

Lewis, Oscar. 1958. **Village Life in North India**. New
    York: Random House.

The purpose of the study was to evaluate a construction project in a peasant community in India. Field work in
1952 included interviews, questionnaires, census data, and

participant-observation. References to the aged are in the context of development, caste, land tenure, and family patterns. Some comparisons are made with data from Tepoztlan, Mexico.

Maduro, Renaldo. 1974. Artistic Creativity and Aging in India. **Aging and Human Development** 5 (4):303-329.

This paper examines artistic creativity in relation to different phases of the Hindu life cycle. Life histories and psychological test data were collected from 110 male Brahmin folk painters at an orthodox sacred pilgrimage center in western India. It is argued that artistic creativity does not necessarily decline with chronological age.

Maeda, Daisaku and Hitoshi Asano. 1979. Public Policies for the Aged in Japan. **Aging** 301-302:36-45.

In contrast to other nations, 74 percent of all old people in Japan live with their children. This is due chiefly to the Japanese tradition of sharing family life. About 30 percent of the aged live on their own earnings, and 70 percent are supported by their children. The mandatory retirement age is very low (fifty-five to fifty-nine years old) and public programs to support the elderly are still in their infancy. Public pension programs are not yet adequate to support retired workers. Health and medical services are also inadequate for the needs of the elderly.

Osgood, Cornelius. 1951. **The Koreans and their Culture.** New York: Ronald Press.

An ethnographic study of rice farmers on a Korean island done in 1947, this book has comparative data from the culture as a whole. The initial section on the village has detailed descriptions of the lives of the elderly covering extended family residence and economic groups, ancestor worship, and clan organization.

Plath, David W. 1973. Ecstasy Years--Old Age in Japan. **Pacific Affairs** 46 (3):421-430.

Ancient law and custom provide for the support of aging parents in Japan, but few ever expect it. The dilemma of the ever increasing number of old people in Japan is reviewed and many of their problems are outlined.

Prybyla, Jan S. 1976. Growing Old in China. **Current History** 71:56-69.

This article focuses on the rural and urban cooperative self-help system in operation in China. The old people are urged to work productively, and to avoid a free hand-out mentality. Religion is not encouraged, but "correct" political thought is encouraged. The family is no longer the main support of the elderly: the great majority of Chinese elderly live within the rural cooperate self-help system, with the family aiding as much as possible and the production team of the commune supplementing what is considered necessary. The system is infused with class hatred.

Smith, Arthur H. 1970. **Village Life in China.** Boston: Little, Brown and Company.

Smith's book deals mainly with the problems that the aged are facing due to the breakdown of the traditional Chinese system of caring for the elder members of the family.

Vogel, Ezra F. 1971. **Japan's New Middle Class.** Los Angeles, Calif.: University of California Press.

This study describes the lives of "salary men" working in Tokyo businesses and living with their families in a suburban neighborhood. The focus is on the changing family, and social and economic relationships stimulated by industrialization. Material on the elderly is dispersed throughout the book. Participant-observation techniques were utilized.

Von Furer-Haimendorf, Christoph. 1964. **The Sherpas of Nepal.** Los Angeles, Calif.: University of California Press.

During 1958 and subsequent years, the author studied Sherpa settlement in several areas of Nepal as a participant observer. The book emphasizes kinship, social organization, and religion with references to the elderly in terms of the   cultural   tendency   toward   individuality   and self-management.

3.   Canada

Ewanchyna, C., et al. 1979. A Ten Point Model for Home
     Care Delivery. **Aging** 301-302:29-35.

     This article describes the Home Care Program in the
Province of Manitoba, Canada, which provides a range of
services to those who need assistance at home. This free
service is funded through general tax revenues. The
continuum of care for the elderly moving from home to
hospital or nursing home is coordinated. Integrated services, according to a person's needs at the time, are emphasized.

Konzak, Burt. 1977. **Retirement and Aging in Canadian
     Society.** Ph.D. Dissertation, University of Toronto.

     This study is based on data collected from question-
naires administered to retired persons in the Toronto area.
The transition from work to retirement was generally viewed
favorably; many people retired because of health reasons.
Retirement income and health were the prime concerns of
respondents; for most, income was sufficient for a comfortable life.

Reiner, Annette. 1979. Ethnic Music in Music Therapy:
     A Program for Jewish Geriatric Residents.
     Administration Quarterly 3 (4):301-306.

     A music therapy program was started at a Jewish
Hospital and home for the Aged in Montreal, Canada, to
help improve the quality of life for geriatric residents.
The objective was to discover the kinds of response that
could be evoked through music therapy with the residents

and to see how their responsiveness could be used to meet their needs for emotional release, improved self-esteem, stimulation, and involvement. The music therapy helped residents to relive memories, express emotions, share feelings and concerns, and overcome loneliness and isolation.

4. Caribbean

Beckwith, Martha W. 1969 (orig. 1929). **Black Roadways: A Study of Jamaican Folk Life**. New York: Negro University Press.

This study of rural Jamaican life-styles in the 1920s has some information about the aged: respect for the aged; financial responsibilities of the young to the elderly; and the role of some old men and women as religious practitioners.

Clarke, Edith. 1957. **My Mother Who Fathered Me: A Study of the Family in Three Selected Communities in Jamaica**. London: G. Allen & Unwin.

A comparative study of three rural Jamaican communities, the position of the elderly is examined in relation to family organization and land tenure. The elderly assume a variety of roles; in particular, the grandmother-headed household is stressed in certain villages.

Foner, Nancy. 1973. **Status and Power in Rural Jamaica: A Study of Educational and Political Change**. New York: Teachers College Press.

In rural Jamaica, older persons are treated with some deference by the young. However, the economic status of a person is considered of most importance, i.e., an older man who cannot support himself is not fulfilling the expect-

ed role of the Jamaican male. Age allows persons an opportunity to accumulate material goods. The process of aging
rather than age per se is a basis of prestige.

Greenfield, Sidney M. 1966. **English Rustics in Black
    Skin: A Study of Modern Family Forms in a
    Pre-industrialized Society.** New Haven: College and
    University Press.

A small rural community in Barbados is the site of this
study in modernization and social change. The elderly are
discussed in reference to the extended family and to the
ownership of houses and property. These are important
subjects because property ownership is a life-long goal and
confers prestige. Of the female house owners, 76.5 percent
were over fifty years old.

Henriques, Fernando. 1953. **Family and Colour in Jamaica.**
    Bristol: Western Printing Services Ltd.

This book deals with the role of grandmother in families in which there is a daughter with a child and with the
economic interdependence between the elderly and their
older married children.

Herskovits, Melville. 1937. **Life in a Haitian Village or
    Valley.** New York: Alfred Knopf.

Elders in this community give their approval to marriages, support family values, and carry out economic
functions. The elderly receive deference and the duties
and attitudes toward them show African influence.

Kerns, Virginia B. 1977. **Daughters Bring In: Ceremonial
    and Social Organization of the the Black Carib of
    Belize.** Ph.d. Dissertation, University of Illinois.

The dissertation describes the very important role
elderly Black Carib women play in the cultural and ceremonial life of the people of Belize.

Kerns, Virginia. 1983. **Women and the Ancestors: Black
    Carib Kinship and Ritual.** Urbana, Ill.: University of
    Illinois Press.

This study of the Black Carib of Belize focuses on women: including life cycle changes and the contrast in roles, obligations, and rights between younger and older women. Older Black Carib women enjoy more freedom and have fewer constraints on their behavior than younger women. Rituals center on death and mourning. Women are the "core participants" in the ritual activities and assume the major responsibilities for them. A woman's involvement in these rituals really begins when her mother ceases to be active because of old age or death.

Mintz, Sidney, W. 1960. **Worker in the Cane: A Puerto Rican Life History.** New Haven: Yale University Press.

The socioeconomic changes that have occurred in Puerto Rico over the past sixty years are examined in relation to the life history of one middle-aged man and his family. It is descriptive of the initial process of growing old.

Smith, M.G. 1962. **West Indian Family Structure.** Seattle: University of Washington Press.

The aged are referred to in their roles as members of a family structure. The book contains age/sex distribution charts for West Indian locales.

5. Europe

Arensberg, Conrad. 1968. **The Irish Countryman.** New York: The Natural History Press.

This ethnography describes the Irish countryside's inhabitants including the aged--in relation to traditional beliefs, folklore, kinship, residence patterns, and community attitudes.

Benet, Sula. 1974. **Abkhasians: The Long-living People of the Caucasus.** New York: Holt, Rinehart, and Winston.

This book is based on eight months of field research and a year's study of the records and literature. It is not an in-depth anthropological monograph, but gives the main outlines of Abkhasian culture and social organization in an easily readable form.

Bott, Elizabeth. 1957. **Family and Social Network.** London: Tavistock   Publications.

The purpose of this study is to understand the social and psychological organization of urban families. Various configurations of conjugal roles and social networks are described. The study was done in London in 1950-1953 using interviews conducted in the home.

Chapman, Charlotte Gower. 1971. **Milocca: A Sicilian Village.** Cambridge: Schenkman Publishing Co.

A detailed study is made of a community in which the aged occupy a prominent role. Participant-observation was the method of data collection.

Cochrane, A.L., et al. 1980. Mortality in Two Random Samples of Women Aged 55-64 Followed Up for Twenty Years. **British Medical Journal** 280:1131-33.

This longitudinal study on mortality uses two random samples of women in Scotland. Height, weight, and cholesterol concentration were considered. There was a strong positive association between a height/weight index and mortality from ischaemic heart disease. There was no significant association between cholesterol concentration and mortality from ischaemic heart disease. The results showed that the height/weight index is more significant in mortality prognoses than cholesterol concentration.

Cool, Linda Evers. 1976. **Outsiders in Their Own Land: Ethnicity and the Dilemma of Aging Corsicans.** Ph.D. Dissertation, Duke University.

This investigation concerned ethnic consciousness and

its possible relation to the aging process. Elderly Corsicans were studied in their own land and in Paris, where and emigrant community of Niolans live. The reasons for leaving Corsica as well as their reactions to the necessary adaptation to modern industrial society were determined. The disengagement of the elderly was viewed as a result of modernization and industrialization rather than any personal factors. Ethnic group membership is seen as important to happiness and adjustment.

Dunn, Stephen P. and Ethel Dunn. 1967. **The Peasants of Central Russia.** New York: Holt, Rinehart and Winston.

This ethnographic study is based on secondary sources. It has minimal mention of the elderly, apart from a brief statement on the economic relationships between old parents and children and the residence patterns of older persons.

Elder, Gladys. 1977. **The Alienated.** London: Writers and Readers Publishing Cooperative.

Moving accounts are given of the feelings and experiences of a number of old people in London. Photographs are included.

Figa-Talamanca. 1976. The Health Status and the Health Care Problems of the Aged in an Italian Community. **Aging and Human Development** 8 (1):39-48.

The purpose of this study was to identify the health needs of the elderly population of a small urban Italian community in order to plan medical services. The sample consisted of 1,291 individuals over sixty years of age. About one-third reported poor health. Health complaints were especially common among those in disadvantaged social and economic conditions. The great majority were found to be self-sufficient and ambulatory. Results indicate that present health needs of the elderly include new health services, such as home care, that will help them avoid future hospitalization.

Friedl, Ernestine. 1962. **Vasilika: A Village in Modern Greece.** New York: Holt, Rinehart and Winston.

The aged are referred to in terms of their relationship to younger members of the community. Friedl deals with deference and reciprocal nondeference.

Gris, Henry. 1978. **May You Live to be 200!** South Brunswick, N.J.: A.S. Barnes.

Entertaining and enlightening description of a trip to the Transcaucasian Republics of the Soviet Union where the author observed the life-style and culture of several centenarians. In addition to description, the book contains a discussion of longevity projects of some professors from the University of Kiev.

Karsten, Anitra. 1961. Social Integration of the Aged in Finland. **Vita Humana** 4 (3):143-147.

The integration of the aged in society depends upon four factors: (1) degree of contact with society; (2) socioeconomic status; (3) psychophysical state; and (4) work and outside interests. Activity, replacement of lost elements of social units, encouragement to accept national pensions are some means for integrating the aged in society.

Keur, John Y. And Dorothy L. Keur. 1955. **The Deeply Rooted, a Study of a Drents Community in the Netherlands.** Seattle, Wash.: University of Washington Press.

Life after retirement is examined in terms of recreational activities and family relations. The book also deals with attitudes towards death, and contains many photographs.

Mishara, Brian L. 1975. Changes for Bicetre and Its Elderly Residents: The Paradox of Progress. **Aging and Human Development** 6 (2):81-84.

This study considers the effect of relocation on a group of elderly women living in Bicetre, a historic French rest home which was due for restoration and revitalization. The relocation proved traumatic for the 104 residents, and the question of "progress vs. home" became important.

Novosti Press Agency. 1970. Very Old People in the U.S.S.R. **The Gerontologist** 10 (2):151–152.

This very short paper deals with the elderly in the Soviet Union who, it is claimed, are between 100 and 165 years old.

Rosenmayr, Leopold, and Eva Kockeis. 1966. Housing Conditions and Family Relations of the Elderly: Report on the Evaluative Study in the City of Vienna, Austria. In **Pattern of Living and Housing of Middle-Aged and Older People.** F. Carp, ed. Pp. 29–46.

Survey data is based on (1) a stratified sample of 661 Viennese aged 65 and over; (2) a stratified sample of 190 residents in old-age homes; (3) 200 residents of new old-age settlements; (4) an in-depth study of 92 residents in four old-age settlements; (5) a microcensus (1 percent) including 6,877 Viennese households. Types of housing, furnishings, family relations, and living companions are examined. The authors support independent living and gradations to institutional care by encouraging a great diversity of housing types within local communities.

Skogland, John 1979–1980. Attitudes Toward the Elderly in Sweden; Correlates and Age Group Comparisons. **Aging and Human Development** 10 (1):47–62.

Swedish retired people and younger adults were interviewed about their perceptions of old age and old people. Social interaction was viewed positively, although older people feared involvement in new activities. Predictors of attitudes were age, education, gender, residence, occupation, and social class.

Steshenko, Valentina S. and Vladimir P. Piskunov. 1974. Evaluating Population Aging. **International Social Service Journal** 26 (2):235–243.

Observing the principal trends shown by the changing age structure of the population in the Ukraine USSR, and analyzing factors determining these trends may indicate a number of approaches to the interpretation of the process of population aging as an "objective reality." There is much that can be done to prolong life and postpone the onset of old age. Socialism is interpreted as providing the foundations for "harmonious demographic development" and scientifically valid population policies.

Townsend, Peter. 1963. (Revised from the 1957 edition, with a new postscript.) **The Family Life of Old People: An Inquiry in East London.** London: Penguin Books.

The home and family, marital status and children, household economy, extended kinship networks, articulation of family with community, and the problems of the East London aged are studied. Methodology and a tentative theory of family structure are discussed and three interview reports and examples of diaries kept by old people are included.

Van Houtte, Jan and Jef Breda. 1978. Maintenance of the Aged by Their Adult Children. **Law and Society Review** 12:645-664.

The authors discuss the family as a residual agency in the solution of poverty among the elderly in Belgium.

Williams, W.M. 1969. **The Sociology of an English Village: Gosforth.** London: Routledge and Kegan Paul.

A study of community life in a remote farming village in northwestern England in 1950-52. The elderly are treated in terms of the life cycle, residence patterns, and economic arrangements where their authority derives from control over land and capital.

Willmott, Peter and Michael Young. 1960. **Family and Class in a London Surburb.** London: Routledge and Kegan Paul.

The purpose of this study is to trace the influence of social class on family. Two neighborhoods in London

1957–59 are compared in terms of such factors as kinship, residence, and recreation. One neighborhood is working class and the other, middle class.

Zonneveid, Robert Jacques van, M.D. 1961. **The Health of the Aged: An Investigation Into the Health and a Number of Social and Psychological Factors Concerning 3149 Aged Persons in the Netherlands, Carried Out by 374 General Practitioners Under the Direction of the organization for Health Research T.N.O.** Assen: Van Gorcum and Co.

This two-year study of patients over sixty-five concentrated on gathering health data. The compilation of data is not directed toward a hypothesis. The text is in English; the tables and appendices are in Dutch.

6. Meso-America

Beals, Ralph L. 1946. **Cheran: A Sierra Tarascan Village.** Washington, D.C.: U.S. Government Printing Office.

The ethnographic study of the largest Indian village in the Tarascan section of Mexico contains a brief but comprehensive section devoted to old age.

Foster, George M. 1948. **Empire's Children: The People of Tzintzuntzan.** Mexico: Imprenta Nuevo Mundo.

A study of an Indian village in the Tarascan area of Mexico was done in 1945–46 using paid informants, census data, and observation. Material on household arrangements, economic patterns, and family life suggests that the elderly remain an integral part of the community.

Foster, George M. 1967. **Tzintzuntzan: Mexican Peasant in a Changing World.** Boston: Little, Brown and Company.

A sequel to Foster's work, **Empire's Children: The People of Tzintzuntzan,** this cognitive study links behavior and belief systems to underlying cultural patterns. There are some references to the aged in the discussion of family relationships.

La Farge, Oliver. 1947. **Santa Eulalia.** Chicago: University of Chicago Press.

This study of a Guatemala Indian village in 1932 examines native religion and ceremonies for evidence of Mayan survivals. The status of the aged in terms of their control over property, capital, and magic and medical knowledge is presented.

Lewis, Oscar. 1960. **Tepoztlan.** New York: Holt, Rinehart and Winston.

A study of the peasantry in one area of Mexico in 1943, this ethnography describes the aged in terms of family relationships, fictive kin relations (<u>compadrazgo</u>), and practices related to death.

Lewis, Oscar. 1969. **Life in a Mexican Village: Tepoztlan Restudied.** Urbana, Ill.: University of Illinois Press.

This volume covers much of the same material as the earlier work but with further elaboration and with the addition of some brief ethnographic sketches of the life styles of the aged. Field work done in 1947–48.

Lewis, Oscar. 1964. **Pedro Martinez: A Mexican Peasant and His Family.** New York: Vintage Books.

This extended case study of a Mexican family, which links personal with historical data, is based on field research done between 1943 and 1963. A lengthy section in narrative form covers the old age of the main character.

Parsons, Elsie Clews. 1936. **Mitla, Town of Souls.**
    Chicago: University of Chicago Press.

    A study of a town in southern Mexico was conducted
in 1929-33. The process of assimilation is explored in terms
of the Spanish and Indian cultures present, with an effort
to further an understanding of social change. Some references to the elderly are made under such topics as civic
responsibilities and the status of women.

Press, I. and M. McKool, Jr. 1972. Social Structure and
    Status of the Aged: Toward Some Valid
    Cross-Cultural Generalizations. **Aging and Human
    Development** 3 (4):297-307.

    The authors found that four determinants decide the
level of prestige accorded to people in Meso-American
peasant communities: (1) advisory, (2) contributory, (3)
control of family or community resources, and (4) residual,
the continuation of useful and valued activities. These
determinants can be applied cross-culturally, with minor,
culturally necessitated variations, but one or more must be
present for the elderly to be accorded respect.

Redfield, Robert. 1941. **The Folk Culture of Yucatan.**
    Chicago: The University of Chicago Press.

    A comparative study was made of four Mayan communi-
ties in the Yucatan. The aged are mentioned in material on
the family.

Redfield, Robert and Alfonso Villa Rojas. 1962. **Chan
    Kom: A Maya Village.** Chicago: University of
    Chicago Press.

    Mayan Indian life in a village in Yucatan is described
on the basis of field work done in 1930. Practices related
to death are described in detail.

Reina, Ruben. 1966. **The Law of the Saints.** New York:
    Bobbs-Merrill.

    This study of Mayan Indians in Guatemala has a sec-
tion on old age.

7. Middle East

Ghurayyib, Rose. 1982. Women and old Age. **Al-Raida.**
    5 (20):1. (Published by the Institute for Women's
    Studies in the Arab World, Beirut University College,
    Beirut, Lebanon.)

The brief editorial draws attention to the problems of
old women in the Middle East in relation to the family
system and traditions. Directions for research are suggested.

Ghurayyib, Rose. 1982. The Status and Role of the Aged
    in Lebanon. **Al-Raida** 5 (20):12-13. (See
    publication information above.)

This is a condensation of a study made by Dr. Mounir
Khoury and submitted to the United Nations in 1973, a critique of the study, and policy update. Data were collected
from 600 students at four universities in Lebanon, mostly
from persons who are middle and upper class and come from
urban areas. Any general conclusions about Lebanese aged
through the eyes of these young is challenged because of
factors of class and urban residence.

Guttman, David. 1974. Alternatives to Disengagement:
    The Old Men of the Highland Druze. In **Culture and
    Personality** R. LeVine, ed. Pp. 232-245.
    Chicago: Aldine.

This is a report based on data from the middle aged
and older men of the Druze sect of the Golan, Galilee, and
Carmel regions of Syria and Israel. The aim of the study
was to develop, through a comparative method, some basis
for a developmental psychology of aging. Intensive interviews were carried out among the age groups of thirty-five
to fifty-four and fifty-five and over in three societies: the
lowland and highland Maya of Mexico, the traditional or
western Navajo, and the Druze of Israel. There was a
predicted age shift from the mode of active mastery (striv-
ing to achieve magical power) in younger men to passive

mastery in older men who have achieved magical mastery. The Druze case shows that the movement toward passive mastery is not a move toward disengagement; rather the older person becomes an interpreter and administrator of the moral sector of society. The disengagement process is only a first step in the transition toward an emerging disposition. The psychic development of later life in Druze and other cases studied show that this development is valued and older people have a new role articulation, a new social rebirth.

Sakdur, Handan. 1976. Social Security, Social Services, and Social Assistance for the Elderly in Turkey. **International Social Security Review** 29:355-359.

Because of increasing population size--generally and among the elderly--difficulties persist in finding a solution to the problems of the elderly. The article discusses these problems in terms of social security and social services and assistance.

Wershow, Harold L. 1973. Aging in the Israeli Kibbutz: Growing Old in a Mini-Socialist Society. **Jewish Social Studies** 35 (2):141-148.

These aged are concerned about loneliness, quarreling, and ill-health; but they enjoy the security and physical activity provided in the kibbutz. Technological and ideological changes are also of concern to them.

Wershow, Harold L. 1973. Aging in Israeli Kibbutz: Some Further Investigation. **Aging and Human Development** 4 (3):211-227.

Residents over sixty-five years of age of five long-established kibbutzim were interviewed via a questionnaire, as to their education, health, occupation, social activi- ties, and self-image. The majority of the elderly work in the kibbutz, seem healthy and vigorous, and feel that they are useful and important members of their community.

8.   Oceania

Elkins, A.P.   1948.   **The Australian Aborigines.**   Sydney,
    Australia: Angus and Robertson.

Based on field work done in 1926 and 1946 in many
parts of Australia, this description of aboriginal life includes perspectives of social and physical anthropology,
linguistics, and psychology.   Seniority is respected; there
is a division between the healthy elderly and those close to
death.   The political role of elderly women is discussed.

Geddes, W.R.   1945.   **Denba, A Study of a Fijian Village.**
    Polynesian Society.

This is a community study of a district of four villages
in the Denba district of Fiji in 1942.   Its primary concern
is the effects of the Pacific campaign of World War II on
traditional life-styles.   Community responsibility from the
elderly, ancestor worship as an important function of clan
solidarity, and the elaborate funerals of high-ranking
villagers are discussed.

Hart, C.W.M. and Arnold Pilling.   1960.   **The Tiwi of
    Northern Australia.**   New York: Holt, Rinehart and
    Winston.

This is a brief report about a gerontocratic society
located on Melville and Bathurst Islands, Australia.
Intergenerational conflict among men, resulting from unequal
access to women as wives, is a basic theme.

Maxwell, Robert J.   1970.   The Changing Status of Elders
    in a Polynesian Society.   **Aging and Human
    Development**   1 (2):137-146.

The influence of Western culture on Samoans since
World War II has had a negative effect on the traditional
status of the elderly.   The elders are found to be irrelevant, without economic power, and their moral influence is

decreasing. However, respect is still shown the aged, and young people often give gifts to the chiefs.

Nurge, Ethel. 1965. **Life in a Leyte Village.** Seattle, Wash.: University of Washington Press.

The aged are mentioned in relation to religion, political structure, and cultural continuity.

Powdermaker, Hortense. 1933. **Life in Lesu.** New York: Norton.

This study of a village in New Ireland examines the elderly in relation to the socialization of grandchildren. The real governing force rests with important old men, but status is derived not only from age but from strength of personality, oratorical ability, and knowledge of magic. Special funerals are held for the elderly with high status and prestige.

Rappaport, Roy. 1968. **Pigs for the Ancestors.** New Haven, Conn.: Yale University Press.

This ecological study analyzes the complex ritual functions in the social organization of the Tsembaga Maring, horticulturalists of the New Guinea Highlands. The major divisions within the group are according to gender and kinship. There is very little reference to the elderly except to those who have died and are now ancestors.

Ritchie, James. E. 1963. **The Making of a Maori.** London: A.H. and A. W. Reed.

North Island of New Zealand is the setting for this culture and personality study of a Maori community in the process of acculturation. According to tradition, male elders represented Maori opinion; however, by the late 1950s, the younger generation was unhappy with elders speaking on their behalf and with the elders' inability to handle government officials. Changing leadership roles and a shift from gerontocracy to democracy are discussed.

9.   South America

de Jesus, Carolina Maria. 1962. **Child of the Dark: The Diary of Carolina Maria de Jesus.** New York: New American Library.

This is the diary from 1955 to 1960 of a poor woman who lived in a shantytown in Sao Paulo. She recorded the impact of poverty on her neighbors. Older people, usually being less employable, are suggested to have an even more difficult time than their younger neighbors unless sustained by kinship or patron-client relations.

Mazess, Richard B. and Sylvia H. Forma. 1979. Longevity and Age Exaggeration in Vilcabamba, Ecuador. **Journal of Gerontology** 34 (1):94-98.

Birth records of informants (when available) and their children, marriage certificates, genealogies, death records of relatives, and other church and civil records were used to assess the accuracy of age-reporting. It was found that age exaggeration began at the average age of 70 and that at the stated age of 100 the informants were approximately 84 years old. All the reported centenarians in Vilcabamba were determined to be in their eighties and nineties.

Peattie, Lisa Redfield. 1968. **The View from the Barrio.** Ann Arbor: University of Michigan Press.

Life in one neighborhood in a Venezuelan city is described in terms of the problems inherent in a rapidly developing country. Little specific material on the elderly is offered except in reference to fictive kin relations and urban nuclear family patterns.

Simos, Bertha. G. 1975. Migration Relocation and Intergenerational Relations: Jews of Quito, Ecuador. **The Gerontologist** 15:206-211.

This paper focuses on the intergenerational problems

and relations of Jews in one of the small, dying Jewish communities of the diaspora. It supports the thesis that traditional Eastern European modes persevere despite dislocation and political interruptions of life.

Steward, Julian H., ed. 1946-48. **The Handbook of South American Indians. Bureau of American Ethnology Bulletin** 143 (Vols. I-IV).

References to the aged are few. They occur in the following selections: "The Patagonian and Pampean Hunters," "The Ona," and "The Yaghan" by John M. Cooper in volume I; "The Caingaing" and "Ethnography of the Chace" by Alfred Metraux in volume I; and "The Tupinamba" by Alfred Metraux in volume III.

Wagley, Charles. 1968. **Amazon Town: A Study of Man in the Tropics.** New York: Alfred A. Knopf.

The ethnography presents "the richness of Amazon culture" in Ita, Brazil, in 1948. The aged are mentioned in connection with residence patterns, ritual coparenthood, sex roles, and health problems.

Willems, Emilio. 1952. **Buzios Island: A Coicora Community in Southern Brazil.** Seattle, Wash.: University of Washington Press.

Willems deals with the position of the elderly within the household and various methods of determining inheritance.

III. STUDIES COMPARING TWO OR MORE ETHNIC, NATIONAL, RACIAL OR OTHER CATEGORIES

A. U.S.A.

Abbott, Julian. 1977. Socioeconomic Characteristics of the
Elderly: Some Black-White Differences. **Social
Security Bulletin** 40 (7):16-42.

This article compares several characteristics of the
black and white population aged sixty and older in March
1972. There are tables on social security beneficiary status, income, education, work experience, occupation, and
income sources.

Abrahams, Ruby, and Robert D. Patterson. 1978-79.
Psychological Distress Among the Community Elderly:
Prevalence Characteristics, and Implications for
Service. **Aging and Human Development** 9 (1):1-18.

This paper reports the results of a survey of elderly
persons in a predominantly blue-collar, New England town.
Investigated were the extent and nature of the psychological
problems in coping with aging and the characteristics of the
elderly who are most vulnerable. These elderly were stud-

ied along ethnic lines--Italian, Canadian, Yankee, Irish, and other European backgrounds. Mental health services were not reaching the needy elderly, and there was minimal use of other helping services.

Aging. September-October 1976. Nos. 264-264.

This issue is devoted to elderly Native American Indians. It includes discussions of the Papago of Arizona, the Navajos of New Mexico, the Inter-Tribal Council in California, the Pima Indians of Arizona, and the Inter-Tribal Council of Nevada.

Arling, Greg. 1976. Resistance to Isolation Among Elderly Widows. **Aging and Human Development** 7 (1):67-86.

The ability of widows to resist isolation in old age was studied. Observations and conclusions were based on the study of 409 widows, black and white, from the Piedmont region of South Carolina. Good health and economic viability were of prime importance in a widow's relationship to family and friends and in participation in social activities.

Auerbach, Marilyn, et al. 1977. Health Care in a Selected Urban Elderly Population: Utilization Patterns and Perceived Needs. **The Gerontologist** 17:341-346.

Using the data from interviews, the utilization of medical care and the health needs of 251 ambulatory elderly at the Lenox Hill Senior Center and New York Hospital clinics are compared using data from interviews. Two-thirds of the elderly were generally satisfied with their health care and opposed to a specialized geriatrics facility. They expressed a need for more information about medical care, particularly services in emergency situations.

Benitez, Rosalyn. 1977. Ethnicity, Social Policy, and Aging. In **Aging: Prospects and Issues.** Richard H. Davis, ed. Pp. 164-177. Los Angeles, Calif.: Ethel Percy Andrus Gerontology Center, U.S.C.

Problems of the elderly--such as income, transportation, housing, and health in the perspective of the black, Mexican-American, Indian, Asian-American, and Jewish minority groups--are discussed. The author feels that lower-class minority elderly, unlike the middle and upper class, cannot advocate for themselves because of language differences, lack of education, or feelings of fear. Current social policies do not alleviate the unique problems of the minority elderly.

Bourg, Carroll. 1972. **The Motility of the Elderly in a Southern Metropolitan Area.** Nashville, Tenn.: Center for Community Studies, Fisk University.

A statistical study of the elderly in the Nashville area, comparisons are made between the local black elderly (56 percent), the local white elderly (44 percent), and those in the southwest. Family composition, life-style, the means and extent of moves, destinations, and the latent needs of the elderly are all discussed.

Bastida, Elena. 1979. Family Integration in Later Life Among Hispanic Americans. **Journal of Minority Aging** 4:42-49.

The relative impact of both ethnic and sociodemographic factors upon family integration are examined, using data from a sample of Mexicans, Puerto Ricans, and Cubans in the United States who are sixty-two or more years of age. Ethnic factors are shown to be stronger indicators of family integration than more general sociodemographic variables such as income, education, and occupation.

Bell, Duran, et al. 1976. **Delivering Services to Elderly Members of Minority Groups--A Critical Review of the Literature.** Santa Monica, Calif.: Rand Corporation.

Literature relevant to the delivery of social services to elderly members of selected minorities in the United States was reviewed with a view toward identifying existing inadequacies. The minority groups were: Chinese, Japanese, Filipinos, Samoans, American Indians, Mexican-Americans, and black Americans.

Cantor, Marjorie H. 1973. The Elderly in the Inner-City: Some Implications of the Effect of Culture on Life

Styles.   (Conference Paper.)   New York: New York Office for the Aging.

Ethnicity, culture, and aging in twenty-six New York City neighborhoods characterized by poverty, decay, and high risk, are the topics of this paper.

Cantor, Marjorie and M. Mayer.   1976.   Health and Inner City Elderly.   **The Gerontologist**   16 (1):17-24.

The inner-city elderly have poorer health and higher levels of incapacity than elderly on a citywide or national level.   Ethnicity and income affect use of health services. Barriers to health care are: lack of money, fragmentation of medical services, and the depersonalization of health care services systems.   The study was undertaken in selected inner-city areas of New York City.

Davis, Dolores Jean Anderson.   1974.   **Guide for Minority Aging Program at the Institute of Gerontology.**   Ann Arbor, Mich.:   University of Michigan.

The results of a twenty-five-item questionnaire, given to 120 gerontology students at the University of Michigan in 1974, were used as a guide for the development of a minority aging program at the University of Michigan.   Significant differences in the perception of needs were found between black and white respondents.

Dowd, James J. and Vern L. Bengtson.   1978.   Aging in Minority Populations: An Examination of the Double Jeopardy Hypothesis.   **Journal of Gerontology** 33 (3):427-36.

As the title suggests, "double jeopardy" is being old and a member of a minority group.   The authors introduce their study with a fairly extensive review of the double jeopardy literature as well as research suggesting that disparities between white and nonwhite persons tend to decline among the aged.   Using a sample of 1,269 middle-aged and older whites, blacks, and Mexican Americans in Los Angeles County, the authors found that double jeopardy exists for some variables (e.g., income and health), but support for the "age as leveler" hypothesis was found for the variables of life satisfaction and frequency of contact with relatives.

Fandetti, Donald V. and Donald E. Gelfand. 1976. Care of the Aged: Attitudes of White Ethnic Families. **The Gerontologist** 16 (6):544-549.

In order to ascertain the attitudes of Polish and Italian Baltimore-area ethnic persons concerning care of their elderly family members, a random sample of 100 residents was interviewed. The results show that intergenerational living arrangements for ambulatory elderly, and church-regulated and church-operated services were preferred. The sample also indicated that the ethnic background of professional caretakers was not viewed as important.

Gatz, Margaret et al. 1982. Psychosocial Competence Characteristics of Black and White Women: the Constraining Effect of 'Triple Jeopardy.' **Black Scholar** 13:5-12.

A model based on the work of Brewster, Smith, and Tyler was used to examine the patterns of competence of 114 black and white, older and adolescent women. An important component of competence is a sense of personal control which correlates with active coping skills and distinguishes more effective from less effective criterion groups. Patterns of competence vary within the age and race subgroups, thus supporting the ideas that social conditions that restrict opportunity also contstrain the development of competence. Older black women scored especially high on the measure of active coping.

Gelfand, Donald E. and Alfred J. Kutzik, eds. 1979. **Ethnicity and Aging: Theory, Research and Policy.** New York: Springer Publishing Company.

This book focuses on both minority and white ethnic aged, with a strong emphasis on the role of the family in the life of the elderly. It is volume five of the Adulthood and Aging Series.

German, P.S. et al. December 1978. Health Care of the Elderly in Medically Disadvantaged Populations. **The Gerontologist** 18 (6):547-555.

This study examines how health care is used by people sixty-five and over, and the factors influencing their use, in two white communities and one black one. Very high proportions of older individuals with serious health conditions were less likely to be treated in all three communities. The exception to this was a group of elderly people receiving care at a new inner-city health maintenance organization, who sought care for less serious conditions, such as arthritis, as well as for serious ones.

Gitelman, Paul J. 1976. **Morale, Self-concept and Social Integration: A Comparative Study of Black and Jewish Aged, Urban Poor.** Ph.D. Dissertation, Rutgers, the State University of New Jersey.

More complete data were sought than were previously available concerning black elderly in the poverty areas of New York City. These data are necessary for a better and more reliable understanding of the unique problems of aging minorities. Data collected concern health, income, family, friendship, neighborhood networks, physical environment, work history, life satisfaction, functional ability, happiness, and worry. It was found that place of birth is an essential variable regarding life-styles and coping patterns, and that the elderly are a heterogeneous group. The insights provided are intended to aid policymakers and practitioners.

Harper, Dee Wood, Jr. 1967. **Socialization for the Aged Status Among the Negro, French and Non-French Subcultures of Louisiana**. Ph.D. Dissertation, Louisiana State University.

The objectives of the research were to examine variations in aging within the specific subcultures in one area of Louisiana, to test the relationship of attitudes toward aging and the willingness to assume the status of the aged. Random samples of 577 individuals of Negro, French, and non-French subcultures were used. The attitudes toward aging, learning the requirements of the aged status, and the assumption of the aged status were found to be interrelated.

Hunter, Kathleen et al. 1979. Living Arrangements and Well Being in Elderly Women. **Experimental Aging Research** 5 (6):523-535.

This is a psychosocial and health study of fifty black and forty-seven white females aged sixty-five and over. They were divided according to whether they lived alone, with spouse only, or with persons other than (or in addition to) the spouse. There was significant interaction between the variables of race and living arrangement with respect to anxiety; no differences were found with respect to depression, diet, or activity level.

Hunter, Kathleen. 1979. Minority Women±s Attitudes About Aging. **Experimental Aging Research** 5 (2):93-108.

To examine the effects of culture, background, and familial characteristics on attitudes toward age, 304 middle-aged women from black, Cuban, American Indian, Chicano, and white cultures were studied. Attitudes about death, family, and church affiliation were found to be important.

Jackson, Jacquelyne Johnson. 1974. NCBA, Black Aged, and Politics. **Annals of the American Academy of Political and Social Science** 415:138-159.

Black aged people often suffer from racism in addition to age and poverty; thus they are different from other minority aged. The National Caucus on the Black Aged (NCBA) feels that these specific problems can and must be solved with NCBA's assistance and political action involving the aged and other black people. NCBA background material is provided, comparisons between aged black, Spanish, and white people are drawn in many tables and figures. A good bibliography on aged blacks is included.

Jackson, Jacquelyne Johnson. 1979. Aged Negroes: Their Cultural Departures from Statistical Stereotypes and Rural-Urban Differences. **The Gerontologist** 10:140-145.

Commonly held stereotypes of aged Negroes as opposed to aged whites are described and discussed. The author stresses the differences between rural and urban Negroes, and the importance of planning programs for aged Negroes as heterogeneous groups. The samples were people living in Georgia.

Jackson, Jacquelyne Johnson. 1980. **Minorities and Aging**. Belmont, Calif.: Wadsworth Publishing Co.

The author examines issues pertaining to the study of aging in American minority groups, by gender. Information about black Americans, Hispanic Americans, and Anglo-American women covers such topics as life expectancy, support systems, and interaction patterns. Models for training professionals to serve these populations are included.

Johnson, Lois Mary. 1978. **Religious Pattern, Coping Mechanisms and Life Satisfaction of the Black and White Aged.** Ph.D. Dissertation, St. Louis University.

This study examines religious involvement and life satisfaction. Black aged were more religious and used religion more to cope with aging; blacks' and whites' life satisfaction scales were similar, but high religiosity did not mean high life satisfaction.

Kalish, Richard A. and Sam Yuen. 1971. Americans of East Asian Ancestry: Aging and the Aged. **The Gerontologist** 11:36-47.

This article discusses the problems and cultural differences of the aging Chinese, Japanese, and Filipinos who have immigrated to the United States at various ages and have suffered discrimination and cultural barriers. Directions for further research are suggested.

Kalish, Richard A. 1976. **Death and Ethnicity: A Psychocultural Study.** Los Angeles, Calif.: Ethel Percy Andrus Gerontology Center.

This is a study of death acceptance, practices and beliefs, of black, Japanese, and Mexican Americans.

Kandel, R.F. and M. Heiden. 1979. Friendship and Factionalism in a Tri-ethnic Housing Complex for the Elderly in North Miami. **Anthropological Quarterly** 52 (1):49-59.

A HUD-subsidized development for black, Cuban, and white elderly in North Miami was the setting for this study of the impact of architectural design, internal politics, and ethnicity. Community participation, culture brokers, the tenants council's relationship to the external political structure, and the conditions of the elderly are discussed, and suggestions are made for utilizing the results of this research in future housing designs.

Kart, C.S. and B.L. Beckham. 1976. Black-White Differentials in the Institutionalization of the Elderly: A Temporal Analysis. **Social Forces** 54 (94):901-910.

Census data for 1950, 1960, and 1970 provide the background information for this study of the differential distribution of elderly blacks and whites in seventeen categories of institutions that provide institutional care for the elderly. Substantial differences according to type of institution were observed, although these differences decreased over time. Some explanations are given for the findings.

Kasschau, Patricia L. 1977. Age and Race Discrimination Reported by Middle-Aged and Older Persons. **Social Forces** 55 (3):728-742.

Black, white, and Mexican American residents, totaling 1144, of Los Angeles County, forty-five to seventy-four years old, were surveyed regarding race and age discrimination in the job market. Overwhelming numbers reported both types of discrimination--especially blacks, followed by Mexican Americans. Age discrimination was reported less often than race discrimination, although blacks reported more encounters in both categories.

Kent, Donald P. 1971. The Elderly in Minority Groups: Variant Patterns of Aging. **The Gerontologist** XI (1, part 2):26-29.

This is the introduction to an issue on minority aging. Differences in aging are based on social, cultural, and personality patterns that are not static and do not develop in vacue.

Koenig, R. et al. 1971. Ideas About Illness of Elderly Blacks and Whites in an Urban Hospital. **Aging and Human Development** 2 (3):217-225.

The purpose of this study was to examine black and white patients' perceptions of their illness experiences at a Detroit public hospital. The sample of fifty-nine patients reflected the compositon of the aged population of the hospital (70 percent black). The issues discussed with the patients were: how they defined illness for themselves and their assessment of their health problems; their opinions about the causes of illness; their beliefs in the importance of voodoo or reliance on God's help in their sickness; what factors they consider responsible for longevity; and whether suicide or "giving up" were ever justified. Illness was seen not as a natural part of physical deterioration but as part of aging.

Krause, Corinne A. Summer 1977. Italian, Jewish, and Slavic Grandmothers in Pittsburgh: Their Economic Roles. **Frontiers** 2 (2):18-27.

Krause describes the contribution of immigrant women of different backgrounds to their families' economic growth.

Lacayo, Carmela G. and Isabel Lindsay. 1975. Black and Latino Women. **National Policy Concerns for Older Women: Commitment to a Better Life.** Washington, D.C.: Federal Council on Aging.

This article discusses the poverty and financial insecurity of black and Latino elderly women that results from many forms of long-term discrimination. The existence of outmoded stereotypes and the lack of enforcement of antidiscrimination laws contribute to further discrimination.

Lieberman, Morton A. 1978-79. Social and Psychological Determinants of Adaption. **International Journal of Aging and Human Development** 9 (2):115-126.

This article strives to elucidate the interrelationships between culture and aging as factors influencing adaptation in middle and late life. Major indices to successful adaptation were: personality traits and processes, and social surroundings. The subjects of the study were 360 foreign born people aged forty to eighty living in the Chicago area and belonging to Irish, Italian, and Polish ethnic groups.

Linn, Magraret W.; Kathleen I. Hunter and Priscilla R.
    Perry. 1979. Differences by Sex and Ethnicity in
    Psychosocial Adjustment of the Elderly. **Journal of
    Health and Social Welfare** 20:273-81.

A study of white, black, and Cuban elderly persons
suggests the effect of sex and culture on psychosocial adjustment. The variables used were social participation, depression, social function, life-satisfaction, and self-esteem.
Research was conducted in Miami, Florida, during 1976-78
and all participants were sixty-five or older. There was
basically no sex difference in overall adjustment. However,
strong cultural differences were found--blacks showing the
most adjustment, then white, and then the Cubans--when
social class and levels of disability were held constant.
The Cubans were the least adjusted, due to their displace-
ment from Cuba; the whites also rated low on adjustment
because they had migrated to Miami after retirement; the
blacks, who were mainly natives of the area, were best adjusted.

Markides, Kyriakos S. et al. 1977. Psychological Distress
    Among Elderly Mexican-Americans and Anglos. Paper
    presented at the Conference of the Gerontological
    Society, New York.

Psychological distress is investigated in a sample of elderly Mexican Americans and Anglos living in Texas. Comparisons of the two ethnic groups are drawn. A critical
evaluation of the applicability of the social selection and social stress hypotheses to psychological distress among minority cultural groups is given.

Marquis Academic Media. 1967. **Source Book on Aging.**
    Chicago: Marquis Who's Who Inc.

The chapter "Special Concerns/Problems" presents
charts on economic status, social security, and other benefits. Federal programs and policies in 1976 affecting problems of black, Hispanic, Native American, and Asian American elderly are discussed. The census data of 1976 show
that elderly persons in minority groups were hard hit by
the 1974-75 recession. This article discusses the economic
situation of minority elderly in the mid-1970s and suggests
the possible beneficial effect of the 1980 census in updating
the basic data about minority elderly. It should help the
development of bigger and better programs and services for

the minority elderly that more appropriately suit their needs.

McCaslin, Rosemary and Calvert Welton. 1976. Social Indicators in Black and White: Some Ethnic Considerations in Delivery of Services to the Elderly. **Gerontology** 30 (1):60-66.

This paper stresses the need for considering ethnic differences when developing and designing delivery of services for the aged--whether the elderly are members of minority or majority groups. The subjects for this study were a sample of older persons who contacted the Central Intake Referral and Information Service in a Houston Model Project.

McCoy, John L. and David L. Brown. 1978. Health Status Among Low-Income Elderly Persons. **Social Security Bulletin** 41:14-26.

Text and tables illustrate the difference in health between rural and urban elderly people. The study demonstrates, through data from a national survey, that the rural aged enjoy less good health than their urban counterparts. The authors attempt to identify some general factors that affect the health status of the elderly. Many detailed tables categorizing the elderly by ethnic origin are provided.

Morgan, Leslie A. 1976. A Re-examination of Widowhood and Morale. **Gerontology** 31 (6):687-695.

In order to compare the morale of widowed women and married women, 232 widowed and 353 married women, forty-five to seventy-four years old, were evaluated in Los Angeles County. The samples consisted of white, Mexican-American and black women so that specific ethnic patterns could be examined. Health, income, age, family interaction, and employment status were analyzed. Most ethnic differences were less important than family interaction and health; Mexican Americans particularly seemed to need family interaction. Lower morale scores of the widowed could be attributed to secondary factors rather than to widowhood itself.

Myers, Beverlee A. 1977. Paying for Health Care: The
    Unequal Burdens. **Civil Rights Digest** 10:12-17.

    This article analyzes the operation of Medicare and
Medicaid, pointing out the differences in benefits received
by whites and nonwhites.

Neusome, Barbara L. ed. 1977. **Insights on the Minority
    Elderly**. Washington, D.C.: National Center on Black
    Aged.

    Two symposia for training faculty on aging are tran-
scribed.   Contents include: conversation among noted
black gerontologists, issues related to working with the minority elderly, working with the Asian elderly, major concerns of the elderly Native American, the Spanish-speaking
elderly, etc.

Pierce, R.C. et al. 1978-79. Generation and Ethnic
    Identity: A Typological Analysis. **Aging and Human
    Development**. 9 (1):19-20.

    Mexican-American and Japanese-American elderly in
San Francisco were examined for their cognitive, behavioral, and philosophical acculturation.   It was found that age
and generation are not the sole determinants of adaptation
to a host country.

Rogers, C.J. and T.E. Gallion. 1978. Characteristics of
    Elderly Pueblo Indians in New Mexico. **The
    Gerontologist** 18 (5):482-487.

    Demographic differences are explored between a sample
of elderly Pueblo Indians in New Mexico and the general
population of non-Indian elderly, particularly with respect
to living arrangements and life-style.   The results suggest
a need for follow-up research on values and adjustment to
aging among the Indian elderly, and the design of culturally appropriate services.   Obstacles to service delivery discussed are: unreliability of data on age, which means that
elderly Indians are unable to prove that they meet eligibility requirements based on age; insufficient data leading to
insufficient funding of programs; lack of knowledge of English; lack of transportation; and lack of fit between services and the culturally-based needs of the Indian elderly.

Sauer, William John. 1975. **Morale of the Urban Aged: A Regression Analysis by Race.** Ph.D. Dissertation, University of Minnesota.

The variables of age, sex, race, education, occupation, income, marital status, health, participation in solitary and voluntary activities, and social interaction were studied and tabulated. Random samples of 936 low-income aged blacks and whites living in the Philadelphia area were collected. The results showed that health and voluntary participation in solitary activities were of prime importance for blacks. White elderly also needed interaction with family and a sex life.

Stillman, S.M. 1976. Increasing Black Client Participation in an Agency. **Social Work** 21:325-326.

At a rehabilitation center for adults who have had psychiatric hospitalization, black clients participated less in social group work sessions than white clients, until an Afro-American group was formed. Black clients who joined this group participated more than those in the mixed black/white groups.

Stojanovic, Elizabeth J. 1970. **Morale and Its Correlates Among Aged Black and White Rural Women in Mississippi.** Ph.D. Dissertation, Mississippi State University.

An assessment is made of the morale of black and white, low-income elderly women with a determination of the relationship between morale and activities, selected demographic, economic, social, and attitudinal characteristics. Black women's morale was relatively higher than white women's. They liked outdoor activities and desired better housing and recreational possibilities. White women were most concerned about their health and were more sedentary.

Teski, Marea; Robert Helsabeck; Franklin Smith and Charles Yeager. 1983. **A City Revitalized: The Elderly Lose at Monopoly.** Lanham, Md.: University Press of America.

The impact of rapid urban change upon Atlantic City elderly is the subject of this book with separate chapters devoted to black, Hispanic, Italian, and retirement neighborhoods. A loosely structured ecological model is used to explain why the elderly "lose at monopoly" as property values rise in the wake of the introduction of casino gambling. The authors offer suggestions for the development of urban policy.

Urban Resources Consultants, Inc. 1978. **Issue Paper of the Minority Aging.** Washington, D.C. Urban Resources Consultants, Inc.

This paper was prepared under a contract from the Administration on Aging, Department of Health, Education and Welfare. Its purposes are to pinpoint (1) the special needs and problems of low-income and minority older persons, as understood through a review of the literature, (2) needs and problems in service delivery; and (3) the involvement of older persons in service programs. The main categories of elderly are: blacks, American Indians, Oriental Americans, Spanish Americans, low-income older persons, "poor," and "near-poor."

U.S. Congress, House Select Committee on Aging. 1977. Subcommittee on Housing and Consumer Interests. **Older Americans Act: Impact on the Minority Elderly: Hearing Before the Subcommittee on Housing and Consumer Interests of the Select Committee on Aging, 95th Congress, First Session, August 23, 1977, Los Angeles, California.** Washington, D.C.: U.S. Government Printing Office.

This report discusses the effect of the older American Act on minority elderly.

Wellin, E. And Eunice Boyer. 1979. Adjustments of Black and White Elderly to the Same Adaptive Niche. **Anthropological Quarterly** 52 (1):39-48.

Within the adaptive niche of public housing for the elderly, black and white residents make different adjustments. A comparison is made between the adjustments of black residents in a building in which the population is mixed and white residents when they are the majority group. The adaptive niche has six primary characteristics --three concerned with the population within the project and three with the setting. The research was carried out in Milwaukee, Wisconsin; it shows differences in social participation and satisfaction, but the authors suggest that racial integration has been beneficial.

B. <u>OTHER.</u>

Davies, David. 1975. **The Centenarians of the Andes.**
London: Barris and Jenkins.

Based on research carried out during four visits be-tween 1971 and 1973, this popularly written work examines life in Vilcabamba, Ecuador, and nearby villages, including the centenarians of the area, their health and diet. Com-parisons are made with the Hunzukuts (Hunza) of Pakistan and China and the Abkhasians of Russia. The genetic, en-vironmental, and cultural aspects of longevity are examined, and general conclusions are drawn. Davies also reaches specific conclusions about the effects on longevity of alti-tude, aridity, the equator, diet, alcohol consumption, eth-nic origins, genetic factors, sex linkage, sleep, use of plants and herbs, and the lack of stress.

European Social Research Committee. 1972. **Elderly People Living in Europe.** Paris: International Center of Social Gerontology.

This book offers a contemporary view of the work of European social gerontologists; it focuses on the aged gen-erally, and the aged worker. Trends of work and retire-ment as well as some necessary innovations in health care are discussed.

Great Britain. Central Office of Information. Reference Division. 1977. **Care of the Elderly in Britain.**

The finances, health and social services, housing, employment, and leisure activities of elderly Britons are discussed.

Kozlov, Victor. 1982. The Fires of Winter: A Joint
    U.S.-Soviet Enquiry into Extreme Old Age. **UNESCO
    Courier** :10-14.

Kozlov focuses on shared attributes and experiences of very old people in different cultures. He discusses cooperative efforts by United States and Soviet scientists to study societies with a large number of centenarians. He also discusses the effect on longevity of factors such as diet.

Leaf, Alexander. 1973. Every Day is a Gift When You Are
    Over 100. **National Geographic** 143 (1):93-119.

An M.D. reports his observations of centenarians in Ecuador (Vilcabamba), Kashmir (the Hunza), and Russia (the Abkhazians). There is discussion of trying to determine chronological ages by probing people's memories as well as official records. Diet and physical activity, marital status and sexual behavior, and expectations and beliefs about longevity are briefly considered. The article concludes with a comment about the Ninth International Congress of Gerontology held in Kiev, some questions about the physiological aspects of aging, and recent theories about rejuvenation.

Leaf, Alexander. 1973. Getting Old. **Scientific American**
    229 (3): 45-53.

The article reports on Leaf's visit to three areas purportedly exhibiting longevity: Vilcabamba in Ecuador; Hunza in Pakistan; and the Soviet Caucasus. The purpose of the visits was to assess longevity among healthy old people and to identify the factors that appear to be associated with good health in late life. Leaf characterizes longevity as the outcome of a "multifactorial" process, including genetic inheritance, regular physical exercise, and psychological and sociocultural factors.

Lipman, Aaron. 1970. Prestige of the Aged in Portugal:
    Realistic Appraisal and Ritualistic Deference. **Aging
    and Human Develpment** 1 (2):127-136.

This paper assesses the differences in prestige rankings of the aged in contemporary Portugal. The author attempts to test the generalization that the high social prestige of the elderly decreases as urbanization increases. He compared the attitudes about the aged of respondents from Tislon, a highly urbanized and industrialized area, with respondents from three less urban Northwest districts. Results showed that "degree of prestige of the aged" was at least a two-dimensional concept involving ritual deference and realistic appraisal. This paper includes cross-cultural references to India and Ireland, and to attitudes toward the aged of the ancient Greeks, Hebrews, and Romans.

Little, Virginia. 1979. Open Care of the Aging: Alternate Approaches. **Aging** 301-302:10-23.

This article discusses open care in the community encompassing all of the programs aiming to support living in one's own home and forestalling premature or unnecessary institutionalization. The author discusses open care for the elderly in Western Samoa, Hong Kong, Sweden, and Eastern Europe (Poland, Yugoslavia, Czechoslovakia, and Hungary).

McRae, John M. 1979. Elderly Housing in Northern Europe. **Aging** 301-302:24-28.

This article discusses housing for the elderly in Sweden, Denmark, Norway, Finland, and Holland. The author finds that there is an emphasis on independence and self-sufficiency balanced with government insurance, pensions, housing subsidies, and home service programs. There is also an increased diversity of services and choices for the elderly through centers that offer many housing, recreational, health, and cultural services. Primary social service reponsibility is at the level of the municipality--the most responsive level of government to meet the needs of the community.

Medvedev, Zhores A. 1974. Caucasus and Altay Longevity: A Biological or Social Problem? **The Gerontologist** 14 (1):381-387.

Various regions of the USSR have residents who enjoy exceptional longevity, and no scientific explanation as yet has been found for this circumstance. This longevity is examined as a social problem growing out of many social, cultural, traditional, and local situations.

Reckman, Will. 1973. Old Age in the Old World. **European Community** 15-16.

This article concerns the economics of old age in the European economic community. It describes the social service provisions of European countries and how much reliance is placed on the individual family for aid to elderly family members.

Slater, Philip E. 1963. Cultural Attitudes Toward the Aged. **Geriatrics** 18 (4):308-314.

This article suggests that a close examinaton of data from age-oriented and youth-oriented societies shows that differences in attitudes toward the aged are often exaggerated. Using the classical Greek attitude model of "age of misfortune" and the Middle Eastern view that age is the "summit of life" the author proposes an interesting hypothesis. He suggests that the aged in most "civilized" societies are isolated because of a malevolent power often attributed to them, consciously in authoritarian societies and unconsciously in democratic and highly mobile societies.

Weihl, Hanna. 1970. Jewish Aged of Different Cultural Origin in Israel. **The Gerontologist** 10 (2):146-150.

This paper represents a study of urban Jewish aged in Israel in 1966. The data indicate that the aged of Oriental origin are more family-oriented than the others. Therefore services provided for them should be primarily family directed.

Yakushev, Lev P. 1976. Old People's Rights in the USSR and other European Socialist Countries. **International Labor Review** 113:243-256.

This article presents the official view of the Soviet government regarding social services, retirement and pension rights, medical care, homes for the elderly, and in particular the right to continue working beyond a pensionable age. Comparisons are drawn from Bulgaria, Czechoslovakia, East Germany, Hungary, Poland, and Romania.

C. U.S.A. AND OTHER

Arnhoff, Franklyn N., Henry V. Leon and Irving Lorge.
1964. Cross Cultural Acceptance of Stereotypes
Towards Aging. **The Journal of Social Psychology**
63:41-58.

An extensive sociological study was conducted in six
countries using questionnaires administered to college students. Acceptance of stereotypes toward the aged was less
likely in the United States than in some other countries.
The aging process and the aged were found to be a problem
in "primitive," preindustrial, and industrial societies and
was found to be related to economics, politics, population
growth, and unemployment. It was not determined how the
acceptance of stereotypes about aging was related to these
variables.

Burgess, Ernest W., ed. 1960. **Aging in Western
Societies**. Chicago: University of Chicago Press.

Cross-national studies of demographic, economic, housing, insurance, and community service needs in addition to
physical and mental health and family relationships are presented. While essentially comparing the United States,
Sweden, the United Kingdom, Denmark, France, Germany,
and the Netherlands, the tables include data on smaller European countries, some socialist, and on Brazil, Mexico,
Egypt, and India.

Chandler, Albert R. 1949. The Traditional Chinese
Attitude Towards Old Age. **Journal of Gerontology**
4 (3):239-244.

This article compares United States and traditional
Chinese attitudes toward old age and the reasons for the
differences between them.

Chang, Rosanna Hwei-Chen. 1977. **Reference Group and
   Aging: A Cross-National Study.** Ph.D. Dissertation,
   Oklahoma State University.

American and Taiwanese elderly were compared in order to study activity indices and several other variables.

Clark, Margaret. 1972. An Anthropologist View of
   Retirement. In **Retirement**, F.M. Carp, ed. Pp.
   117-155. New York: Behavioral Publications.

Clark discusses (1) cross-cultural definitions of work
and retirement and their varying characteristics; (2) differences between social and psychological anthropology, suggesting the uses of these approaches; and (3) a behavioral
model developed in psychological anthropology. She demonstrates the use of the model.

Cowgill, Donald O. 1986. **Aging Around the World.**
   Belmont, Calif.: Wadsworth.

The basic theoretical perspective is modernization theory. The author compares this approach with several others and reevaluates all of them in the light of evidence presented in the book. The evidence covers comparative
demography--including a close look at the societies with a
reputation for long-lived people; aging and value systems,
such as filial piety, the cult of youth, and the work ethic,
kinship systems and family roles; economic systems and economic roles of the aged; and political, educational, and religious roles. A summary is provided at the end of each
chapter.

Cowgill, Donald O. and Lowell D. Holmes, eds. 1972.
   Aging and Modernization. New York:
   Appleton-Century-Crofts.

The opening chapter, A Theory of Aging in
Cross-Cultural Perspective, is followed by short studies of
the aged among the Sidamo of Ethiopia, the Igbo of Nigeria,
the Southern African Bantu, the Samoans, the Salt River
Pima, and the Zapotecs of Santo Thomas Mazaltepec village
in Oaxaca, Mexico. Other chapters focus on the aged in
Thailand, Japan, the USSR, Ireland, Australia, Israel, Norway, and the United States. Margaret Clark discusses dependency and cultural values; Helena Lopata examines

widowhood from a world perspective. The concluding chapter by Cowgill and Holmes reviews the theory presented in the first chapter and ends with a restatement in the form of eight universals and twenty-two variations pertaining to modernization, aging, and the aged.

Firth, Raymond; Jane Hubert and Anthony Foreg. 1970.
Families and Their Relatives. New York: Humanities Press.

To study the structure and meaning of kinship in modern Western society Firth, in 1968, examined a middle-class sector of London as part of an Anglo-American project that also included a study being done in Chicago by David M. Schneider. (See **American Kinship: A Cultural Account.** 1968. Englewood Cliffs: Prentice-Hall.) Data on the elderly and their relationships appear throughout the book.

Foner, Anne and David Kertzer. 1978. Transitions over the Life Course: Lessons from Age-Set Societies.
American Journal of Sociology 83 (5):1081-1104.

A cross-cultural comparison is made of the transition process of twenty-one African age-set societies and the United States. The article challenges long held views of smooth transitions in "simple" societies and troubled transitions in highly technological societies. Despite the contrast between societies, similarities appear regarding anxieties and conflicts of transitional roles. Both types of societies have adaptive mechanisms in order to deal with change.

Foner, Nancy. 1984. **Ages in Conflict: A Cross-Cultural Perspective on Inequality Between Old and Young.**
New York: Columbia University Press.

The age stratification model, as developed by Matilda White Riley and her collaborators, shows how age systems have inequality as a central aspect. The model was originally developed with Western industrialized societies in mind. Foner proposes its usefulness for cross-cultural analysis--"a new way to look at relations between old and young in different societies." She examines the nature of inequality, whether age inequalities lead to conflict between members of different generations, factors that prevent age conflicts, the possibility that the disadvantaged age status (whether the young or the old) develops a consciousness and cohesiveness, and the ways in which far-reaching changes during the past century have affected relationships among cohorts. As part of the conclusion, age inequality is compared with other forms of stratification.

Francis, Doris. 1984. **Will You Still Need Me, Will You Still Feed Me, When I'm 84?** Bloomington, Ind.: Indiana University Press.

This is a study of Jewish elders in Cleveland, Ohio, and Leeds, England, who have an Eastern European heritage in common. Both groups now live in planned neighborhoods, having been displaced from their old, established Jewish neighborhoods by other immigrants and as a result of urban planning. Francis utilizes role and network theory in analyzing the adaptation of her informants to change.

Holden, Karen C. 1978. Comparability of the Measured Labor Force of Older Women in Japan and the United States. **Journal of Gerontology** 33:422-426.

This study was undertaken after it had been reported that there was greater particpation of older women in the work force in Japan than in the United States. The author reports that the data has been misconstrued by not taking into account sociocultural factors. People in Japan value and accept participation of older women in the work force more than do people in the United States. Also, in Japan unpaid household work, farm work of fifteen hours or more per week or in the family business is reported as being work. The author feels that more accurate enumeration by the Japanese leads to a higher statistical count of aged women being in the work force. She believes that older American females have been misrepresented in the data.

Kagan, Mary Dianne. 1976. **Being Old in Bojaca: A Study of Aging in a Colombian Peasant Village.** Ph.D. Dissertation, University of California, Riverside.

Older Americans and elders in the village of Bojaca, Colombia, are compared in an attempt to see if some of the problems of growing old in complex societies are intrinsic to aging or are a culturally determined phenomenon. There exists no identity flux among aging Bojaquenos. Continued integration and activity in village and family life provide a continuity in life activities and prevent loss of identity.

Kamerman, Sheila B. 1976. Community Services for the Aged: The View from Eight Countries. **The Gerontologist** 16 (6):529-537.

This article reports on a recently completed study of the social service systems of eight countries: Canada, West Germany, France, Israel, Poland, the United Kingdom, the United States, and Yugoslavia. Many figures and tables are provided.

Malina, Alexandra Swaney. 1975. **Ya Cumpli: A Profile of the Aged in Saltillo, Coahuila, Mexico.** Ph.D. Dissertation, University of Colorado.

Different value systems have a positive or negative effect on the capacity of people to adjust to old age. It is suggested that Mexicans may have a relatively less traumatic adjustment to growing old than North Americans. This is because of their tightly-knit, large families and a cultural style of passivity in the face of stress. Thirty-one respondents were interviewed.

Maxwell, Robert J. and P. Silverman. 1970. Information and Esteem: Cultural Considerations in the Treatment of the Aged. **Aging and Human Development** 1 (4):361-392.

This is an examination of the problems of the aged in cross-cultural perspective. The authors suggest that the amount of useful information controlled by the aged is reflected in the participation of the aged in community affairs. In turn, their participation will determine the degree of esteem in which they are held by other members of the community. They suggest that this information control, and consequently social participation, will decline with industrialization and rapid sociocultural change. For this study, twenty-six societies, including Navaho, Bali, Aleut, Micmac, and Ifugao, were sampled.

Maxwell, Robert J. and P. Silverman. 1978. The Nature of Deference. **Current Anthropology** 19 (1):151.

The authors studied data from ninety-five societies in an attempt to assess the treatment of old people by members of their communities. The main thrust of the investigation was the relationship between the control of useful information by old people and the deference shown them. The authors feel that three major ways exist to show respect to elderly people: (1) victual and service, (2) ceremonial, and (3) linguistic.

Murphy, Peter. 1979. A Migration of the Elderly: A Review. **Town Planning Review** 50:84-93.

A review is given of the migration patterns of elderly peoples of Europe, Australia, and the United States.

Neugarten, Bernice and R.J. Havinghurst. 1969. Disengagement Reconsidered in a Cross-National Context. In **Adjustment to Retirement: A Cross-National Study**. R.J. Havinghurst et al., eds. Pp. 138-146. Van Corcum and Company.

The aging process is to a large extent dependent on sociocultural setting. Among their sample of retired male steelworkers and teachers in Chicago and Milan, the authors found that life satisfaction has a positive relationship with the level of social interaction. This contradicts disengagement theory. Individual variation is assumed possible, which means interactions between biological, social, and psychological factors must be considered.

Palmore, Erdman. 1975. **The Honorable Elders: A Cross-Cultural Analysis of Aging in Japan**. Durham, N.C.: Duke University Press.

Theories about the aged are discussed in the introduction and reconsidered, in the light of data, in the conclusion. Comparisons are made between Japan and other nations, particularly highly industrialized ones such as the United States, Great Britain, and Denmark. Palmore's findings support some and contradict other propositions about modernization and aging found in Cowgill and Holmes (1972). There is also a section titled "suggestions" in the last chapter, in which Palmore notes ways in which the West could improve the situation of its elders by borrowing some Japanese patterns and practices.

Seedsman, Terence Anthony. 1979. **A Cross-National Focus on Contemporary Attitudes Toward Old Age and its Association with Leisure-Related Concepts as Shown**

**by American and Australian Elementary School
Teachers and Sixth Grade Children.** Ph.D.
Dissertation, University of Oregon.

This study compares the attitudes of 600 American and
Australian elementary school teachers and sixth-grade children toward the concept of old age, leisure time, recreation, retirement, and work in old age. It concludes that
there is pervasive uncertainty about old age and that more
education in this area is of major importance.

Shanas, Ethel; Peter Townsend; Dorothy Wedderburn;
Henning Friis; Poul Milhoj and Jan Stehouwer, eds.
1968. **Old People in Three Industrial Societies.** New
York: Atherton Press.

This book is the result of a cross-national survey of
living conditions and behavior of elderly people in Denmark,
Britain, and the United States. The topics dealt with are
health and incapacity in later life; the psychology of
health; welfare services and the family; the structure of
the family; the household; family attitudes toward the elderly; isolation, desolation, and loneliness of the elderly;
work and retirement; financial resources for the aged; and
the role of the government. In the conclusion, Peter
Townsend deals with important issues such as integration,
health differences between men and women, and social policy. Appendices deal with sample designs and methodological approaches to financial resources and the role of the
state in dealing with older people.

Simic, Andrei. 1977. Aging in the United States and
Yugoslavia: Contrasting Models of Intergenerational
Relationships. **Anthropological Quarterly**
50 (2):53-64.

The author thinks that life-style and life satisfaction
of the Yugoslav and American elderly can be directly related to the overall difference in social and personal values
found in these two countries. While America's excessive
emphasis on independence and aloofness might cause loneliness in the elderly, the Yugoslavian elderly experience
great levels of intergenerational continuity and reciprocity.
In Yugoslavia, relationships among family and kin are the
most compelling of all.

Simmons, Leo. 1970. **The Role of the Age in Primitive Society.** Hamden, Conn.: Archon Books.

An unaltered and unabridged edition of Simmon's 1945 classic, this cross-cultural work incorporates data about seventy-one societies, representing several forms of social organization, subsistence type, and other variables. The populations studied were geographically distributed over six continents and in Oceania and lived under very different climatic conditions. Simmons selected 109 physical and cultural characteristics pertaining to habitat, economy, political and social organization, religious beliefs, and so on; he tested correlations between these traits, looking for general trends; then he drew correlations between them and characteristics associated with the status and treatment of the aged. Eventually, 112 items were found to be related to the treatment and status of the aged and were analyzed separately for old men and old women. Concrete examples are given, but generalizations are based upon statistical analyses. The book suggests numerous hypotheses to be tested in the field.

Soodan, Kirpal Singh. 1975. **Aging in India.** Calcutta: Minerva Associates.

Chapter IX "Welfare of the Aged in India" and comparisons with social security programs in other countries are notable. Welfare of the aged in the United States, USSR, Britain, and Denmark is discussed. Included are demographic analysis, social and economic status of the aged, occupation and employment, health, roles and status in the family, recreation, and religiosity of the aged.

Sussman, Marvin B. and James C. Romeis. 1982. Willingness to Assist One's Elderly Parents: Responses from United States and Japanese Families. **Human Organization** 41 (3):256-9.

This article compares American and Japanese willingness to help and care for aged parents, other family members, and close friends--in different temporal, social, and health contexts. An examination is made of the effects on filial duty, of the age of household heads and the presence of children in the household. Members of both societies express strong commitments to parents; major differences are expressed regarding other family members and close friends.

U.S. Superintendent of Documents. 1977-78. **Social
Security Programs Throughout the World.** Washington,
D.C.: Government Printing Office.

This report highlights the principal features of the social security systems of 129 countries. Tabular summariza-
tions are included. Charts show the major features of each
system and are arranged to facilitate intercountry comparisons.

Werston, Harold J. 1979-80. The Outer Limits of the
Welfare State: Discrimination, Racism, and Their
Effect on Human Services. **Aging and Human
Development** 10 (1):63-75.

Provisions for the elderly in the United States are
compared with data from the Netherlands. Various types of
housing and care provided in the Netherlands are described. Problems exist in the United States as well as in
the Netherlands and other Western industrialized nations.
Adequate social planning and solutions for the care of the
aged are discussed.

IV. SINGLE AND CROSS-CULTURAL STUDIES

A. RESIDENTIAL SELECTION AND RESIDENTIAL TYPES

Aldridge, Gordon J. 1959. Informal Social Relationships in a Retirement Community. **Marriage and Family Living** 21 (1):70-72.

A brief summary is made of research in a small retirement community of 3,000 (almost 50 percent of whom were sixty or older) in central Florida. Aldridge discusses informal social relationships--leisure activities, cliques, mail call, shopping, bench-sitting, and eating out.

Beckman, R.O. 1969. Acceptance of Congregate Life in a Retirement Village. **The Gerontologist** 9 (4):281-285.

Observations are based on a one-month visit of an elderly man to a retirement village with several hundred occupants. The village administrator had wanted the author to evaluate the social and psychological adjustment of the residents. Beckman discusses the attitudes of the tenants and possible reasons for their satisfaction.

Bennett, Ruth. 1973. Living Conditions and Everyday
Needs of the Elderly with Particular References to
Social Isolation. **Aging and Human Development**
4 (3):179-198.

Social isolation is defined as "the absence of meaningful social roles or rolelessness," not in terms of housing
type. Fearing the negative effects of isolation, Bennett
calls for resocialization programs, such as friendly visiting.

Brand, Frederick N. and Richard T. Smith. 1974. Life
Adjustment and Relocation of the Elderly. **Journal of
Gerontology** 29 (3):336-340.

Sixty-eight tenants sixty-five years or older were relocated in a new housing project for the elderly because of
urban renewal. They were compared with sixty-nine
unrelocated elderly in the same community. On the basis of
the Life Satisfaction Index, the relocated showed higher
scores of maladjustment. Males adjusted better than females, and blacks adjusted better than whites. Relocation
may have disrupted social networks.

Brody, Elaine M. and Bernard Liebowitz. 1981. Some
Recent Innovations in Community Living Arrangements
for Older People. In **Community Housing Choices for
Older Americans**. M. Powell Lawton and Sally L.
Hoover, eds. Pp. 245-258. New York: Springer.

This article explores possible types of living arrangements for the elderly. It includes such specialized housing
for older people as apartment buildings, retirement communities, and boarding facilities. The focus is on an evaluation of a noninstitutional, service supported, communal
housing arrangement. It appears that age segregation
works well, and a high percentage of the tenants are con-
tented. Similar personality types and backgrounds are
suggested to be important factors to consider when planning
an age-homogeneous community.

Bultena, Gordon L. and Vivian Wood. 1969. The
American Retirement Community: Bane or Blessing?
Journal of Gerontology 24 (2):209-217.

Retired males who had migrated from the Midwest to
Arizona--521 subjects--were interviewed. Of these, 322 had

settled in retirement communites; 199 had settled in regular, age-graded communities. Those in age-homogeneous settings were found to have higher morale, although this might have been due to their somewhat higher socioeconomic status. Other factors included greater insulation from work-oriented norms in retirement communities.

Burgess, Ernest W. 1954. Social Relations, Activities, and Personal Adjustment. **American Journal of Sociology** 59 (4):352-360.

Sixty-four residents of Moosehaven were interviewed and classified as isolates, intimates, or leaders. These statuses were compared with recreational participation and happiness scores. The happiest men were nine times more active in group recreation than those with the lowest happiness scores.

Byrne, Susan W. 1974. Arden, An Adult Community. In **Anthropologists in Cities**. G. Foster and R. Kemper, eds. Pp. 123-152. Boston: Little, Brown.

Research was conducted in an affluent, cooperatively-owned development of 5,011 aged residents in California. The author spent nine months in 1968 visiting Arden, interviewing residents, and attending meetings and group activities. The residents were white, fairly affluent, at least forty-five years old, and politically conservative. There were mostly married couples (plus about 700 single women, most of them widows). Problems of doing research in such a setting are explored.

Cantor, Marjorie H. 1975. Life Space and the Social Support System of the Inner City Elderly of New York. **The Gerontologist** 15:23-27.

This article explores the issue of New York City as a place of residence for older people. It deals with the life space of the inner-city elderly, the extent to which functioning social support systems can be found, and the perceptions of the elderly of city life.

Carp, Francis M.   1966.   **A Future for the Aged: Victoria Plaza and Its Residents.** Austin, Texas: University of Texas Press.

A study of residents was conducted before and after they entered Victoria Plaza, a new apartment complex run by the San Antonio Housing Authority.   Three hundred and fifty-two applicants were interviewed and given psychological tests;   240 were later selected to live in Victoria Plaza. Carp elucidates a population profile, housing desire, reasons for moving, reactions to the complex and social behavior within it.   Carp emphasizes tenant morale and adjustments.

Carp, Frances M. and Wanda M. Burnett, eds.   1966. **Patterns of Living and Housing of Middle Aged and Older People.**   Bethesda, Md.:   Public Health Service Publication No. 1496.

A collection of articles deals with the importance of the effects of housing on old people.   A clear pattern emerges--environmental factors have a tremendous impact on aging, and there is a need for a variety of housing forms to meet the physical and social needs of older people.

Cohen, C.I. and J. Sokolovsky.   1978.   Isolation of the Inner City Aged: Ending an Old Myth with a New Method.   **Black Aging**   3:132-142.

The authors believe that the notion of isolation among inner-city elderly is largely a myth, and that myth is perpetuated in part by the use of inadequate research strategies.   They review and critically discuss previous methods. Using anthropological and sociological approaches to social network theory, they derive a new research instrument to explore the problem.

Donahue, Wilma.   1966.   Impact of Living Arrangements on Ego Development in the Elderly.   In **Patterns of Living and Housing of Middle-Aged and Older People.**   F. Carp, ed.   Pp. 1-9.   Bethesda, Md.:   Department of Health, Education and Welfare.

Donahue reviews a demonstration program in Ann Arbor in a nonprofit apartment house for the aged, Lurie Terrace.   Out of 125 tenants, 20 were given rent supplements.   Others are either financially independent or they receive help from relatives.   There are 16 married people, 98 single women, and 11 single men.   The author believes that the environment can be therapeutic for some people, but that it can also place added demands on those unaccustomed to sociability and the maintenance of community standards.

Eckert, J. Kevin.   1980.   **The Unseen Elderly: A Study of Marginally Subsistent Hotel Dwellers.**   San Diego, Calif.:   Campanile Press.

The marginal social and economic milieu of the elderly living in American, inner-city single room occupancy (SRO) hotels are studied.   Eckert used personal observations, interviews, life histories, and daily diaries to create a picture of the life styles, problems, life trajectories, interactions, values, and norms of elderly residents.

Eckert, J. Kevin.   1983.   Dislocation and Relocation of the Urban Elderly: Social Networks as Mediators of Relocation Stress.   **Human Organization**   42 (1):39-45.

A central hypothesis of Eckert's study was that aged residents of SRO hotels would be especially vulnerable to forced relocation resulting from urban renewal.   The hypothesis was not supported.   Several factors are noted in explanation, primarily that people could stay in the downtown area and move to similar SRO hotels.   The author also discusses the adaptability of the social networks of those relocated.

Erickson, Rosemary and J. Kevin Eckert.   1977.   The Elderly Poor in Downtown San Diego Hotels.   **The Gerontologist**   17 (5):440-446.

This is a study of nonwelfare elderly living independently in urban hotels (skid row, working class, and middle class).   The social patterns and support systems through which they maintain their independence are examined.

Fry, Christine. L.   1977.   The Community as a Commodity: The Age Graded Cases.   **Human Organization** 6 (2):115-123.

The author asserts that with the advent of the planned

retirement residence, the construction of "community" becomes part of the package that private developers can manipulate to make their properties more attractive to buyers. Foremost among the attractive qualities of a commodity community is the ability of the developer to protect against uncertainties and "undesirable" elements. Two trailer parks near Tucson are briefly examined in terms of their amenities.

German, P.S. et al. 1976. Ambulatory Care for Chronic Conditions in an Inner-City Elderly Population. **American Journal of Public Health** 66:660-666.

This article discusses factors which affect the inner-city elderly in receiving health care for the following three chronic conditions: high blood pressure, heart trouble, and arthritis. These factors are age, sex, living arrangements, and the presence of more than one condition. Findings indicate that many of the elderly who report these conditions also report receiving care for them.

Golant, Stephen M. 1984. **A Place to Grow Old: The Meaning of Environment in Old Age.** New York: Columbia University Press.

In interviews, a cross-section of Americans over sixty assessed their own living arrangements. The author communicates their feelings on several environmental contexts including neighborhood, community, and city.

Hampe, Gary D. and Audie L. Blevins, Jr. 1975. Primary Group Interaction of Residents in a Retirement Hotel. **Aging and Human Development** 6 (4):309-320.

Data were gathered in 1972 and 1973 concerning the interaction patterns of sixty-three retirees aged fifty-five and over living in an apartment hotel. People had to be poor in order to be admitted; most were white women. Their high housing satisfaction seemed to be due to improved living conditions and involvement in primary groups. The hotel provided a setting for social interaction and insulated the retirees from outsiders' attitudes about their uselessness.

Hazan, Haim. 1982. Beyond Disengagement: A Case
    Study of Segregation of the Aged. **Human
    Organization** 41 (4):355-359.

Hazan discusses a day-care center in a multiracial,
working-class neighborhood in London where a majority of
the members were first- or second-generation Eastern Jewish immigrants. Evacuations to nearby areas during World
War II resulted in the breakdown of family associations and
lack of mutual regard between today's affluent younger
generation and their old, "culturally deprived" parents.
The complex analysis of the old peoples' disengagement,
their construction of an alternative reality of egalitarianism
at the center, and reengagement contrasting to the earlier
situation in both form and content is concise and clear.
The author challenges the empirical validity of the disengagement theory and proposes another phase, beyond disengagement, in the aging process.

Hochschild, Arlie Russell. 1973. **The Unexpected
    Community.** Englewood CLiffs, N.J.: Prentice-Hall.

The author worked in and visited a senior citizens'
apartment building as a case study to disprove the theory
of disengagement. Merrill Court, a public housing project,
housed thirty-five widows, three couples, and two single
men in a town north of San Francisco. The author emphasizes interaction (peers versus kin ties), and sees Merrill
Court as an exception to the increasing isolation of the old
in a changing society.

Homovitch, Maurice B. 1966. Social and Psychological
    Factors in Adjustment in a Retirement Village. In
    The a retirement Process. F. Carp, ed. Pp.
    115-125. Bethesda, Md.: Department of Health,
    Education and Welfare.

A 1964-65 interview study was conducted of 366 older
people before and after they moved into a new private retirement community in the Los Angeles area. Homovitch
discusses their attitudes toward work and retirement, reason for moving, opinions of the community, activities,
relationships, and self-image. As movers into a brand new
setting, their attitudes were rather positive. They would
rather be younger, but for the most part they did not miss
working.

Hoyt, G.C. 1954. The Life of the Retired in a Trailer
Park. **American Journal of Sociology** 59 (4):361-370.

One hundred and ninety-four interviews of retired or
quasi-retired males in Bradenton Trailer Park in Florida
were augmented by observation and park records. Hoyt
found a great range of recreational activities and a premium
placed on sociability. Most retirees, in evaluating the
age-homogeneous community, emphasized its advantages,
such as equal status and possibilities of association.

Jacobs, Jerry. 1974. **Fun City: An Ethnographic Study
of a Retirement Community.** New York: Holt,
Rinehart, and Winston.

Fun City has approximately 6,000 residents, fifty
years of age or older. Jacobs describes the community, its
facilities and government, and then contrasts the life-style
of the active "visible minority" with that of the nonactive
"invisible majority." A political and demographic profile of
community residents is followed by discussion of how the
community is typical or atypical of "Middle American towns."
Verbatim transcriptions from interviews are sprinkled
throughout the text. The conclusion deals with theories of
aging in the light of Jacobs's findings.

Jacobs, Jerry. 1975. **Older Persons and Retirement
Communities: Case Studies in Social Gerontology.**
Springfield, Ill.: Charles C. Thomas.

Sixty pages are devoted to examining High Heaven, a
high-rise apartment building for 420 of the well elderly in a
middle-sized eastern city. Thirty-six pages are devoted to
comparing Fun City (Jacobs 1974) with High Heaven. The
remaining pages compare the two settings to Merill Court
(Hochschild 1973) and discuss their implications for disengagement theory.

Jacobs, Ruth Harriet. 1969. The Friendship Club: A
Case Study of the Segregated Aged. **The
Gerontologist** 9 (4):276-280.

A report on participant observation in Abbott Oakes, a
municipal housing project for fifty senior citizens. The role
of the Housing Authority and the Friendship Club are emphasized. The residents feel a need to assert control and

combat feelings of uselessness engendered by living in a youth-oriented society.

Johnson, Sheila K. 1971. **Idle Haven: Community Building Among the Working Class Retired.** Berkeley, Calif.:   University of California Press.

A 1969, year-long, nonresident participant observation study was supplemented by 146 interviews of about 390 residents in a trailer park near San Francisco.   The community was primarily for retirees.   Johnson provides a general ethnography, including population profile, "the search for community," family and friendship relations, mutual aid, leisure, and social structure.   An appendix lists members of a nationwide club consisting of owners of airstream travel trailers.

Kleemeier, Robert W. 1954. Moosehaven: Congregate Living in a Community of the Retired. **American Journal of Sociology** 9 (4):347-351.

A general description is given of a rural retirement community in Florida for members of the Loyal Order of Moose.   Of the 350 residents, about 30 percent are married, 80 percent are men.   Widows, widowers, and bachelors are included.   Kleemeier discusses their social background, why they came, and what they do.

Lally, Maureen; Eileen Black; Martha Thornock and J. David Hawkins. 1979. Older Women in Single Room Occupancy (SRO) Hotels: A Seattle Profile. **The Gerontologist** 19 (1):66-73.

A few of the misconceptions about the elderly who live in downtown areas are that they are downwardly mobile, emotionally disturbed, and disaffiliated.   This study of twenty SRO elderly women suggests otherwise.   The life histories and daily-routine study showed that these women had professions traditionally held by men, had been very mobile, were extremely individualistic, and needed to be independent.   The style of life they had chosen to live was a natural progression of their earlier life-styles; they were in no way social psychopaths.   The authors suggest that city planners and social workers should develop more services for these independent women that complement their life-styles rather than depreciate them.

Larson, Calvin J. 1974. Alienation and Public Housing for the Elderly. **Aging and Human Development** 5 (3):217-230.

Research using a questionnaire was conducted about those who entered two housing projects for the elderly in northwestern Vermont in 1971. For most categories, thirty or fewer forms were returned. The questionnaire results modestly supported the central hypothesis: "The alienating effects of the move into public housing for the elderly will vary inversely with the tenant's ability to maintain established and acquire new social relationships and group affiliations."

Lawton, Powell M. 1970. Assessment, Integration, and Environments for Older People. **The Gerontologist** 10 (1):38-40.

Assisting the aging adult to relocate in housing appropriate to his functional capacities and his tolerance for variations involves a matching of people and environments. A systematic method for describing levels of personal and social function is described. It is suggested that assessing persons in terms of their ability to function within these levels will allow for a broader range of alternatives in residence selection.

Legesse, Asmarom. 1979. Age Sets and Retirement Communities: Comparison and Comment. **Anthropological Quarterly** 52:61-69.

The author compares the research reported in a symposium (articles in January 1979 **Anthropological Quarterly**) with the corresponding data on the structure and operation of age sets and generation grading systems in traditional societies. He discusses the role of age in human society and the types of social organization that are linked with specific stages of the life course. Topics included are: transition rites; friendship and kinship; age hierarchy and equality of peers; groups in formation; ethnicity and the age homogeneous community; and social integration and resocialization.

Lemon, B.W.; V.L. Bengtson and L.A. Peterson. 1972. An Exploration of the Activity Theory of Aging: Activity Types and Life Satisfaction Among In-Movers

to a Retirement Community. **Gerontology**
27 (4):511-523.

A sample of 411 potential in-movers to a Southern California retirement community was interviewed. The sample
included 31 percent married, 83 percent middle or upper
middle class, 84 percent Protestant, 100 percent white, 39
percent aged fifty-two to sixty-four years, 46 percent aged
sixty-five to seventy-five years. The research assumed
that frequency of activity would be positively correlated
with degree of life satisfaction. The hypotheses were not
confirmed.

Lovald, Keith A.   1962.   The Social Life of the Aged
    Homeless Man on Skid Row.   In **Social and
    Psychological Aspects of Aging.**   C. Tibbitts et al.,
    eds.   Pp. 510-517.   New York: Columbia University
    Press.

A study of the Gateway district of Minneapolis, carried
out between June 1958 and May 1960, is summarized. The
median age of Gateway residents in 1958 was sixty years.
Out of 3,000 inhabitants, all but 27 were men. Lovald discusses income, employment, and assistance; religious rescue
missions and lodging house conditions; leisure time; crime;
and types of drinkers and the role of the tavern in their
lives.

Lynd, Robert S. and Helen Merrell Lynd. 1929.
    Middletown.   New York: Harcourt, Brace, and World.

The Lynds' synchronic study of an American community, done in 1924-25, covers social, economic, religious, and
political institutions. Included are a table of employment by
age and a reference to the aged as a potential social problem in relation to their housing and financial needs.

Lynd, Robert S. and Helen Merrell Lynd. 1937.
    Middletown in Transition.   New York: Harcourt,
    Brace and World.

A continuation of the earlier study of an American
community, this one focuses on change and cultural conflict. Material on changes in housing and welfare is included.

Marshall, Victor W. 1975. Socialization for Impending
Death in a Retirement Village. **American Journal of
Sociology** 80 (5):1124-1144.

The life cycle consists of many roles, and people are
constantly adapting to new roles throughout their lives. In
the later years the new roles could be the
spouse-and-parent shift, growing family and kin in the form
of grandchildren, and eventually preparation for death.
This article primarily deals with the preparation process
and argues that congregate living can provide an optimal
setting for this kind of socialization.

Michelon, L.C. 1954. The New Leisure Class. **American
Journal of Sociology** 59 (4):371-378.

Observation and extended interviews were used to
study types of leisure and successful retirement among a
group of retired and semi-retired people (mostly couples,
ranging in age from fifty-eight to seventy-two) in a trailer
park in Melbourne, Florida. Michelon finds that adjustment
to one's job is inversely correlated with adjustment to retirement, for one has lost the source of self-validation. A
wide range of planned activities might improve one's chances of finding a substitute for work.

Peterson, James A. and Ali E. Larson. 1966.
Social-Psychological Factors in Selected Retirement
Housing. In **Patterns of Living and Housing of
Middle-Aged and Older People.** F. Carp, ed.
Pp. 129-143. Bethesda, Md.: Department of Health,
Education and Welfare.

This is an interview study about older people before
and after moving to Laguna Hills--a large private retirement
community--from Los Angeles and Orange counties. The
authors believe that the population is heterogeneous. In
examining why the people moved, they found that the residents liked the emphasis on leisure and that they were
moving with their friends rather than away from them.

Roberts, Pearl H. 1974. Human Warehouses: A Boarding
House Study. **American Journal of Public Health**
64 (3):277-282.

Roberts offers an expose of structural violations,

overcrowding, lack of medical care, and other problems, in boarding houses in the Pittsburgh area. Teams of investigators evaluated the eighty-one boarding homes known to exist and interviewed as many boarders, managers, and staff members as possible. Forty-one homes were rated as good to excellent, but others had a variety of problems. The author calls for licensing, medical surveillance, and requirements of minimum standards for all boarding houses.

Rosow, Irving. 1962. Retirement Housing and Social Integration. In **Social and Psychological Aspects of Aging.** C. Tibbitts et al., eds. Pp. 327-340. New York: Columbia University Press.

In his review of the literature on the aged, Rosow finds that gerontologists share a "housing ideology": they prefer age-integrated neighborhoods to isolated or segregated ones. In contrast, Rosow finds that age-integrated neighborhoods in modern urban setting are not socially viable for older people. He believes that age-segregated residences can help in the social integration of the aged if they have a homogeneous social composition and the context of segregation is "insulating rather than invidious or stigmatizing."

Rosow, Irving. 1966. Housing and Local Ties of the Aged. In **Patterns of Living and Housing of Middle-Aged and Older People.** F. Carp, ed. Pp. 47-64. Bethesda, Md.: Department of Health, Education and Welfare.

Rosow surveys 1,200 older middle-aged and working-class residents of several hundred Cleveland apartment buildings, including public housing projects and four retirement hotels. Rosow's hypothesis that residential proximity does not stimulate friendships between generations was confirmed. He distinguished four social/personality types: cosmopolitan (32 percent), phlegmatic (4 percent), isolated (19 percent), and unstable (10 percent). He discusses these in terms of the nature of friendships, reference groups, material aid, and the effect of different age densities on morale.

Sheley, Joseph F. 1974. Mutuality and Retirement
    Community Success: An Interactionist Perspective in
    Gerontological Research. **Aging and Human
    Development** 5 (1):71-80.

Forty men from a northern California retirement community of about 1,300 were randomly selected and interviewed. Thirty-eight of the 40 were married and ranged in
age from fifty-eight to eighty-eight. The community was
mostly white and middle-class. Instead of harboring desires
to return to work and being unable to adjust to not working, most of the men liked their retirement. The author
felt this was due to homogeneous social composition and insulation from work-oriented values and attitudes.

Sherman, Susan R. 1975. Mutual Assistance and Support
    in Retirement Housing. **Journal of Gerontology**
    30 (4):479-483.

The study examined whether the elderly in age homogeneous housing gave more mutual assistance to each other
than those living in housing that was not age concentrated.
Six hundred residents in six facilities were interviewed
Retirement housing residents did not differ from those liv
ing in other housing. There was equal interaction and assistance for children regardless of housing type. Residents
in retirement housing did not benefit greatly from their
neighbors.

Stephens, Joyce. 1975. Society of the Alone: Freedom,
    Privacy, and Utilitarianism as Dominant Norms in the
    SRO. **Gerontology** 30 (2):23-235.

Stephens summarizes her research in the Guinevere
Hotel (Stephens 1976). In general, the isolation of the elderly was life-long and voluntary--and not a consequence of
age-related changes. The hotel is described as an atomistic
society, a world of strangers. There was little social solidarity, except for that of the street-peddler segment of the
population.

Stephens, Joyce. 1976. **Loners, Losers and Lovers:
    Elderly Tenants in a Slum Hotel.** Seattle, Wash.:
    University of Washington Press.

A participant-observation study was conducted in an

old hotel in a marginal area of an American city. The 524-room hotel has 108 aged tenants out of 371 occupants (97 men, 11 women). Stephens examined how they coped with poverty and perceived themselves and their environment. A special group in the hotels were carnival workers.

Streib, Gordon F.; W. Edward Folts and Mary Anne Hilker. 1984. **Old Homes-New Families: Shared Living for the Elderly.** New York: Columbia University Press.

Shared living in small homes is explored for those over the age of seventy-five who do not need nursing care. Group homes are examined in the United States and Great Britain. The authors found that most of the homes were locally organized. The topics covered include sponsorship, staffing, costs, selection of residents, and problems associated with shared living arrangements.

Sokolovsky, Jay and Carl Cohen. 1978. The Cultural Meaning of Personal Networks for the Inner City Elderly. **Urban Anthropology** 7 (4):323-342.

In a study done in Manhattan, the authors find conflicting data regarding the degree of isolation of urban elderly, as well as the cultural meaning of their social linkages. Studies in the past, using network analysis as a methodological tool produced heuristic models that had no empirical value. The elderly were portrayed as having very few, if any, networks and as lonely and isolated. The authors suggest that network analysis should be able to produce comparative empirical data as well as qualitative behavioral information on total personal networks. Stronger participant-observation is suggested.

U.S. Senate. Committee on Human Resources. Subcommittee on Aging. 1978. **Special Needs and Problems of Older Americans in Rural and Small Communities: Hearing Before the Subcommittee on Aging, U.S. Senate, 95th Congress, Second Session.** Washington, D.C.: U.S. Government Printing Office.

This booklet addresses concerns of nonurban American elderly.

U.S. Superintendent of Documents. 1978. **Single Room Occupancy: A Need for National Concern.** Washington, D.C.: U.S. Government Printing Office.

This booklet reports on older Americans who live alone in single room occupancy hotels. These are generally located in decaying crime-ridden sections of our cities.

Webber, Irving L. 1954. The Organized Social Life of the Retired: Two Florida Communities. **American Journal of Sociology** 59 (4):340-346.

This paper is an analysis of two Florida communities with a large proportion of older people. The study was based on membership in organizations and on attendance at secular and religious meetings. There was a large proportion of nonparticipation and a preponderance of religious membership and attendance. Formal participation was related to gender, marital status, education, and economic status.

Wright, Nancy. 1972. Golden Age Apartments-- Ethnography of Older People. In **The Cultural Experience, Ethnography in Complex Society.** J. Spradley and D. McCurdy, eds. Pp. 111-136. Chicago: Science Research Associates.

A short research project was based primarily on interviews with an eighty-year-old black woman and a seventy-five-year-old white woman who lived in a large city in an apartment building for senior citizens. The author developed cultural taxonomies of how the residents defined space within the building; she studied social club activities and the physical limitations of being old.

B. THE INSTITUTIONALIZED ELDERLY

Bell, Tony. 1967. The Relationship Between Social Involvement and Feeling Old Among Residents in Homes for the Aged. **Gerontology** 22 (1):17-22.

Fifty-five residents in three California homes for the aged were interviewed. The ten males and forty-five females were all unmarried and ranged in age from sixty-nine to ninety-five. The degree of social involvement (formal, informal, and family) was compared to the idea that "feeling old is part of the total process of disengagement."

Bennett, Ruth and Lucille Nahemow. 1965. Institutional Totality and Criteria for Social Adjustment in Residences for the Aged. **Journal of Social Issues** 21 (4):44-78.

Research findings are based on observations "in a home for the aged, four nursing homes, a supervised apartment residence, two geriatric wards of a mental hospital, and a public housing development with special facilities for the aged." Staff and long time residents were interviewed. The authors were concerned with resident group norms and with how the staff defined a "good resident."

Brody, Elaine M. and Geraldine M. Spark. 1966. Institutionalization of the Aged: A Family Crisis. **Family Process** 5 (1):76-90.

The case histories of five families are given. They were clients of the Home for Jewish Aged of the Philadelphia Geriatric Center. Since the intake process at an institution for the aged is said to add to the stresses already present in any family, the family rather than the aged person is viewed as the client. The prospect of institutionalizing an aged family member exposes the dynamics of family relations.

Gubrium, Jaber F. 1974. On Multiple Realities in a Nursing Home. In: **Late Life: Communities and Environmental Policy.** J. Gubrium, ed. Springfield, Ill.: Charles C. Thomas.

A sociological approach is taken to role definition in Murray Manor, a new, church-related nursing home located in a middle-sized midwestern city. It had about forty residents and ninety patients; the average age was eighty. Gubrium discusses three main role complexes: staff, administration, and patients and how they perceive each other and their roles.

Gubrium, Jaber F. 1975. **Living and Dying at Murray Manor**. New York: St. Martin's Press.

A 1973 participant-observation study was made of a 360-bed nursing home (36 percent occupied at the time of study). Operating part of the time as an unofficial staff member, Gubrium describes how the staff and the clientele define their worlds, how they see themselves and each other, how time is spent, and how activities are defined. Gubrium includes many excerpts from conversations within the home, using ethnomethodological insights into the social organization of care. The layout of the building is carefully diagrammed and described.

Hendel-Sebestyen, Giselle. 1979. Role Diversity: Toward the Development of Community in a Total Institutional Setting. **Anthropological Quarterly** 52 (1):19-28.

This article discusses the processes by which an institution for the elderly becomes a community, and how an institutionalized population can be considered as a basis for ethnographic studies and theories on aging. The subjects were aged people, primarily of Balkan background, living in a Sephardic home.

Henderson, J. Neil. 1981. Nursing Home Housekeepers: Indigenous Aspects of Psychosocial Support. **Human Organization** 40 (4):300-5.

This is a study of Pecan Grove Manor, a privately owned ninety-bed nursing home in rural, southern Oklahoma. Most of the patients are in their eighties, with a female-to-male ratio of 3:1. The author uses the ethnomedical perspective which "allows for the discovery of the design of the functional therapeutic network regardless of the assigned job titles of the actors." The role of housekeeper emerges as significant for the psychosocial support of the patients and includes liaison between patients and other nursing home staff. Questions for further research are raised.

Jacobs, Ruth Harriet. 1969. One-Way Street: An Intimate View of Adjustment to a Home for the Aged. **The Gerontologist** 9 (4):268-275.

A report is made of four years of participant-observation of forty-six women in a section of a Jewish home for the aged. The author examines conflicts of residents with staff and other residents. She concludes that the best of intentions and beautiful surroundings do not make a good home; institutionalization may be a life-denying process.

Kaas, Merrie Jean. 1978. The Sexual Expression of the Elderly in Nursing Homes. **The Gerontologist** 18:372-78.

Eighty-five elderly nursing home residents and 207 nursing home staff participated in this study about differences between the two regarding attitudes about sexual expression among the elderly. The staff were given questionnaires and the residents were interviewed. The staff were found to be less conservative in their attitudes toward sexual expression among the elderly than the residents themselves. The more sexually active among the sample were termed by the residents as "dirty old men" and "dirty old women." Looking attractive was considered the main mode of sexual expression, and most residents felt they did not look attractive. Also most residents felt that the lack of privacy was the main deterrent of sexual expression.

Kastenbaum, Robert. 1965. Wine and Fellowship in Aging: An Exploratory Action Program. **Journal of Human Relations** 13:266-276.

In order to improve the morale of geriatric patients and to increase social interaction within a geriatric ward, small groups of patients were allowed wine in a dayroom setting. Some group meetings took on the character of a social club and there was an improvement in general well-being.

Kayser-Jones, J.S. 1981. **Old, Alone, and Neglected: Care of the Aged in Scotland and the United States.** Berkeley, Calif.: University of California Press.

An institution for the aged in Scotland is compared and contrasted with one in the United States. Kayser-Jones used intensive interviews with patients to elicit their views about what constitutes high- and low-quality care, and their feelings about being institutionalized. The grim, impersonal care and even systematic abuse of the American elderly stands in stark contrast to the generally high-quality, attentive care of the aged in Scotland. The author analyzes the institutions within the contexts of the respective health care systems of the United Kingdom and the United States.

Kayser-Jones, J.S. 1983. Social Exchange and Power in the Care of the Institutionalized Aged. **Human Organization** 42 (1):55-57.

A brief report is offered of serendipitous findings from Kayser-Jones's 1981 study of a geriatric hospital in Scotland and a United States nursing home. The author discusses contrasts in resources that residents can exchange for services from staff, with resources including funds, skills, and charm, along with an example of how a United States resident with no resources was maltreated. Further research is needed to determine a correlation between quality of care and patient resources and to answer other questions.

Koch, Kenneth. 1977. **I Never Told Anybody: Teaching Poetry Writing in a Nursing Home.** New York: Random House.

Koch describes his method of teaching old, ill, and institutionalized people to write poetry. He approaches his students in a manner that allows them to enjoy writing poetry, to take it seriously, and to go on writing while getting better at it. Included are some of the poems of his twenty-five students who are between seventy and ninety-plus years of age.

Rosen, Theodore and Abraham Kostick. 1957. Separation and Adjustment Problems in a Home for the Aged. **Social Work** 2 (1):36-41.

The setting is a Jewish home for the aged in Troy, New York. The modern one-story building houses seventy-six people and serves a twenty-one-county area. Rosen, a case-worker, and Kostick, the executive director of the home, discuss the problems of the aged in leaving their local communities. They believe that a small boarding house is preferable to a total institution.

Tec, Nechama and Ruth Granick. 1958-60. Social Isolation and Difficulties in Social Interaction of Residents of a Home for Aged. **Social Problems** 7 (3):226-232.

This statistical and observational study tests the relation between social isolation prior to admission to a home for Jewish aged and subsequent difficulties in interaction in the home. The fifty former residents who had been transferred to mental institutions between 1943 and 1954 were matched individually with a control group of fifty residents. Results showed that the more isolated a patient had been, the more likely he or she would (1) have difficulty interacting with peers or staff or (2) be transferred to mental institutions.

Townsend, Claire. 1971. **Old Age: The Last Segregation.** New York: Grossman Publishers.

Ralph Nader's study group's report on nursing homes is an exposè of nursing home practices and problems. The government role--past, present, and future--is explored. Appended are letters from citizens, summaries of pertinent laws, a list of questions one should ask when visiting a home, a list of people and agencies to contact (mostly in the Department of Health, Education and Welfare), and a government organization chart related to services for the aging.

Townsend, Peter. 1964. **The Last Refuge: A Survey of Residential Institutions and Homes for the Aged in England and Wales.** London: Routledge and Kegan Paul (abridged edition).

This report is based on statistical information, visits, interviews with welfare officers, questionnaires of 530 pensioners, and 14 diaries. Townsend covers the history of institutional care for the aged, types of present day homes, reasons for admission and the intake process, the nature of life in these institutions, and policy proposals for the future. An appendix provides extracts from case histories of older people applying for admission to homes.

Tuckman, Jacob and Martha Lavell. 1957. Self Classification as Old or Not Old. **Geriatrics** 12 (11):666-671.

Among institutionalized older people, those who consider themselves not old are more intact physically and psychologically than those who considered themselves old. This difference is reflected in their feelings about participation in organized institutional programs, in ways in which they spend their lives, and in their interests.

V. BIBLIOGRAPHIES, INDEXES, AND RESOURCE LISTINGS

AARP. 1985. **A Profile of Older Persons.** Washington, D.C.: American Association of Retired Persons.

This "profile," in brochure form, with statistics, maps, and graphs about older Americans, is produced annually. It includes data about marital status, living arrangements, employment, health, and geographic distribution. Many contrasts are made by gender. Percentages of "Racial and Ethnic Composition" in the sixty-five-years-of-age or over population are provided.

Davis, Lenwood G. 1980. **The Black Aged in the U.S..** Westport, Conn.: Greenwood Press.

This annotated bibliography on the black aged is divided into eight sections. The sections are subdivided by subject and include periodicals, major books, dissertations and theses, government publications and articles. Included are references to such specialized topics as the black aged and slavery and black old folks' homes.

Delgado, Maria and Gordon E. Finley. 1978. The Spanish-Speaking Elderly: A Bibliography. **The Gerontologist** 18 (4):387-394.

This bibliography makes accessible scholarly and professional contributions concerning Spanish-speaking elderly. The items, dated 1960-77, are arranged by broad subjects, and a list of sources searched is cited. The entries are not annotated.

DeLuca, L., et al. 1975. **Aging: An Annotated Guide to Government Documents.** Storrs, Conn.: University of Connecticut.

This work is designed to provide access to documents in the field of gerontology that are in the Government Publications Department of the University of Connecticut Library at Storrs. The bibliography covers the period 1960-74, contains annotated references divided by subject areas with a title index and a series index provided.

Edwards, Willie M. et al. eds. 1982. **Gerontology: A Cross-National Core List of Significant Works.** Ann Arbor, Mich.: Institute of Gerontology, The University of Michigan.

This is a large bibliography covering work on Canada, the United Kingdom, and the United States. A few references to work in other modern countries are included. Historical reviews are offered to put the Canadian, United Kingdom, and United States material in perspective. The bibliography is divided into reference works and subject sources, and is followed by a glossary and author and title index. The subject sources seem most comprehensive in the areas of geriatrics and social services.

Edwards, Willie M. and Frances Flynn. 1978. **Gerontology: A Core List of Significant Works.** Institute of Gerontology, University of Michigan and Wayne State University: Resources in Aging Series.

This bibliography provides information on gerontology divided into subject areas--such as death and dying, nutrition, and psychology. Important journals, abstracts, and conferences are listed. Author and title indexes facilitate the use of this bibliography.

Fadillo, Amado M. 1978. **Hispanic Mental Health
     Bibliography II.** Spanish-Speaking Mental Health
     Research Center. University of California.

This bibliography covers all aspects of Hispanic mental
health problems, and includes articles on gerontology as
well. It is arranged by author, with a good subject index.

The National Center on Black Aged, Inc. 1979. **Topical
     Annotated Bibliography on the Black Elderly.**
     Wahington, D.C.

This bibliography is arranged by broad subjects such
as economics, health, and housing. There are lists of national organizations concerned with aging, congressional
committees on aging, federal programs benefiting the elderly, periodicals on aging, and a selected list of federal government publications of interest to the aged.

National Council on Aging. 1957. **Current Literature on
     Aging.** John Balkema, ed. Washington, D.C.

This is a quarterly subject guide to selected publications in the field of aging and related areas. Book reviews
are included. The items are arranged according to broad
subject areas.

Place, Linna Funk; Linda Parker and Forrest J. Berghorn.
     1980. **Aging and the Aged: An Annotated
     Bibliography and Library Research Guide.** Boulder,
     Colo.: Westview.

Designed specifically as a library research guide to
gerontology for undergraduates, the volume includes sections on physiological and psychological aspects of aging;
social aspects; environment and the elderly; and general
perspectives. This is a companion volume to **The Dynamics
of Aging**, edited by Berghorn and Schafer. It includes author and title indexes.

Sharma, Prakash, C. 1974. **Studies on Aging and Aged in
     America: A Selected Research Bibliography.**
     Monticello, III.: Council of Planning Librarians.

This is a small bibliography covering the research carried out in the field of age and aging through 1974.

Sokolovsky, Jay, ed. 1982. **Teaching the Anthropology of Aging and the Aged: A Curriculum Guide and Topical Bibliography.** Chicago, Ill.: Association for Anthropology and Gerontology.

Specific courses such as Aging in Culture and Society and Biocultural Gerontology are described and outlined, and assignments are suggested. The bibliography includes about 100 mimeographed pages, and it is updated with supplements each year.

Suzuki, Peter T. 1975. **Minority Group Aged in America: A Comprehensive Bibliography of Recent Publications on Blacks, Mexican-Americans, Native Americans, Chinese, and Japanese.** Monticello, Ill.: Council of Planning Librarians.

This bibliography contains an extensive introduction, then an annotated bibliography divided by ethnic group. Coverage includes books, periodical articles, and government publications from about 1960 to the early 1970s.

Torres, Gil F. 1975. Bibliography on the Spanish-Speaking Elderly. In **Proceedings of National Conference on Spanish-Speaking Elderly.** A. Hernandez and J. Mendoza, eds. Kansas City, Mo.: National Chicano (Social) Planning Council.

U.S. Administration on Aging. 1975. **Strategy for the Development of the National Clearinghouse on Aging.** Appendix B. A Handbook of Information Resources in the Field of Aging. Silver Spring, Md.: Applied Management Sciences.

This publication is an alphabetical list of over 100 selected information resource centers that contain materials on the older person.

U.S. Superintendent of Documents. 1978. **Aging.** Washington, D.C.: U.S. Government Printing Office.

This booklet lists government publications on all aspects of aging.

U.S. Superintendent of Documents. 1977. **Research on the Mental Health of the Aging, 1960-1976.** Washington, D.C.: U.S. Government Printing Office.

This collection is of summaries of National Institute of Mental Health research that is relevant to aging persons. The material is summarized by subject areas.

Vesperis, Maria D., 1986. **AAGE Newsletter.** St. Petersburg, Fla.: Association for Anthropology and Gerontology.

The quarterly newsletter contains brief research reports, lists of recent publications, notes about conferences and programs on aging, news briefs, and other information. Members of the Association for Anthropology and Gerontology receive the newsletter.

Wharton, George F., III. 1981. **Sexuality and Aging: An Annotated Bibliography.** Metuchen, N.J.: Scarecrow Press.

The work includes both research studies and popular publications on a wide range of topics about sexuality: psychological aspects, gender roles. problems, counseling, health, homosexuality, and others. Author and title indexes are included.

New Journals on Aging:

The Journal of Aging Studies

This international and Interdisciplinary publication will appear quarterly beginning 1987. Jaber F. Gubrium is the editor. Department of Social and Cultural Sciences, Marquette University, Milwaukee, Wis. 53233.

The Journal of Cross-Cultural Gerontology

This international and interdisciplinary publication is scheduled to appear in 1986. The editors are Cynthia M. Beall, J. Kevin Eckert, and Melvyn C. Goldstein. Department of Anthropology, Case Western Reserve University, Cleveland, Ohio 44106.

Author Index

Subject Index